# POLITICS AND GLOBALIZATION

# RESEARCH IN POLITICAL SOCIOLOGY

Series Editor: Harland Prechel

Recent Volumes:

# POLITICS AND GLOBALIZATION

### EDITED BY

## HARLAND PRECHEL

*Texas A&M University, USA*

**ELSEVIER**
JAI

Amsterdam – Boston – Heidelberg – London – New York – Oxford
Paris – San Diego – San Francisco – Singapore – Sydney – Tokyo

JAI Press is an imprint of Elsevier

JAI Press is an imprint of Elsevier
The Boulevard, Langford Lane, Kidlington, Oxford OX5 1GB, UK
Radarweg 29, PO Box 211, 1000 AE Amsterdam, The Netherlands
525 B Street, Suite 1900, San Diego, CA 92101-4495, USA

First edition 2007

**British Library Cataloguing in Publication Data**
A catalogue record for this book is available from the British Library

ISBN-13:   978-0-7623-1316-7
ISBN-10:   0-7623-1316-1
ISSN:      0895-9935 (Series)

For information on all JAI Press publications
visit our website at books.elsevier.com

Printed and bound in The Netherlands

07 08 09 10 11 10 9 8 7 6 5 4 3 2 1

Working together to grow
libraries in developing countries

www.elsevier.com | www.bookaid.org | www.sabre.org

ELSEVIER   BOOK AID International   Sabre Foundation

# CONTENTS

# LIST OF CONTRIBUTORS

| | |
|---|---|
| *Paul D. Almeida* | Department of Sociology, Texas A&M University, College Station, TX, USA |
| *Robert J. Antonio* | Department of Sociology, University of Kansas, Lawrence, KS, USA |
| *Alessandro Bonanno* | Department of Sociology, Sam Houston State University, Huntsville, TX, USA |
| *Derek Darves* | Department of Sociology, University of Oregon, Eugene, OR, USA |
| *Diane E. Davis* | Massachusetts Institute of Technology, Cambridge, MA, USA |
| *Michael Dreiling* | Department of Sociology, University of Oregon, Eugene, OR, USA |
| *Dana R. Fisher* | Department of Sociology, Columbia University, New York, NY, USA |
| *Leslie C. Gates* | Department of Sociology, State University of New York Binghamton, Binghamton, NY, USA |
| *Theresa Morris* | Department of Sociology, Trinity College, Hartford, CT, USA |
| *David A. Smith* | Department of Sociology, University of California Irvine, Irvine, CA, USA |
| *Tim Woods* | Department of Sociology and Psychology, Manchester Community College, Manchester, CT, USA |

# SPECIAL REVIEWERS

The success of *Research in Political Sociology* depends on the community of scholars in many ways. I am grateful to the advisory editors (see above) who reviewed manuscripts and provided advice on editorial decisions. I also owe a special debt of gratitude to the colleagues listed below who served as referees in the peer review process and reviewed at least one manuscript for *Research in Political Sociology* for Volume 15.

Patrick Akard
*Kansas State University*

Paul D. Almedia
*Texas A&M University*

James Burk
*Texas A&M University*

Leslie C. Gates
*State University of New York Binghamton*

John Harms
*Missouri State University*

David Jaffee
*University of North Florida*

Thomas Janoski
*University of Kentucky*

Robert Kent
*Independent Scholar*

Rob Mackin
*Texas A&M University*

Theresa Morris
*Trinity College*

Steve Valocchi
*Trinity College*

Tim Woods
*Manchester Community College*

# PREFACE

Since its inception, the primary objective of *Research in Political Sociology* (RPS) has been to publish original, high-quality manuscripts to increase our understanding of political structures and processes. *RPS* and the American Sociological Association's Section on Political Sociology share this goal, and the publication cooperates with the section to achieve sociological understanding of political phenomena.

*RPS* is a resource that can be used by political sociologists to strengthen and develop the unique skills and interests they bring to sociology. The articles in *RPS* are directed towards identifying, understanding, and explaining the various interrelations that exist within and between social and political phenomena. This includes exploring the underlying social roots or origins of politics and power; the organization, management, and process of political power structure; and the effects of political decision making and power structures on society. The intent of *RPS* is to facilitate scholarly communication and debate among political sociologists and scholars in other disciplines on the full range of theoretical, methodological, and substantive areas of research in the field. *RPS* is open to all theoretical, methodological, and scholarly points of view, irrespective of political content, so long as they advance our sociological understanding of political dynamics and social structures.

Richard G. Braungart edited Volumes 1–3 and Richard G. Braungart and Margaret M. Braungart co-editing Volume 4. Philo Wasburn edited Volumes 5–8. Betty A. Dobratz with associate editors Timothy Buzzell and Lisa K. Waldner edited Volumes 9–13. They began their editorship with *The Politics of Social Inequality* (No. 9) followed by *Sociological Views on Political Participation* (No. 10), *Theoretical Directions in Political Sociology for the 21st Century* (No. 11), and *Political Sociology for the 21st Century* (No. 12). Volumes 10–12 provide a trilogy on the current state of political sociology at the beginning of the 21st century. Volume 13, edited by Lisa K. Waldner (with Betty A. Dobratz as the series editor and Timothy Buzzell as associate editor), is titled *Politics of Change: Sexuality, Gender, and Aging*. This volume focused on topics that have traditionally received little attention from political sociologists. Volume 14, titled *Politics and the*

*Corporation*, and Volume 15, titled *Politics and Globalization*, were edited by Harland Prechel. These volumes examined how corporations, classes, and other social actors exercise political power to advance their interests in a range of historical and geographic settings. Volume 16 will focus on 'Politics, Neoliberalism, and Market Fundamentalism.'

# POLITICS AND GLOBALIZATION: AN INTRODUCTION

## David A. Smith

"Globalization" is a buzzword, familiar to anyone tuned in to global media, and is rapidly emerging as the favorite mantra of political leaders all around the world. It is clearly one of those faddish neologisms that is frequently invoked but rarely defined (and, in this case, freighted with ideological implications). Mainstream economists generally laud globalization as a major transformations in the global system that occurred in the past two or three decades, that has been overwhelmingly positive (Bhagwati, 2004). But others are much less sanguine about the changes that putative globalization has wrought (Greider, 1997; Rodrik, 1997; Stiglitz, 2003). A third group is composed of outspoken critics of recent economic globalization (Mittelman, 2000; Bello, 2005). While many of the foregoing authors agree that there is something fundamentally different about the current period, some prominent macro-sociologists question this basic premise. World-system scholars like Immanuel Wallerstein (2005) and Giovanni Arrighi (2005) point to the long-term continuity of global capitalism over centuries – and insist that the best way to comprehend the current conjecture is in terms of the *longue duree* (Braudel, 1992).

One of the great lessons of the comparative/historical "turn" in sociology in the 1980s was the importance of placing change in its world-historical context. Much of the discussion of contemporary "globalization" has a distinctly "presentist" favor, so understanding recent dynamics in terms of

Politics and Globalization
Research in Political Sociology, Volume 15, 1–23
Copyright © 2007 by Elsevier Ltd.
ISSN: 0895-9935/doi:10.1016/S0895-9935(06)15001-9

the temporal depth of long-term trends and cycles in global capitalism
can be extremely insightful. Nevertheless, many people are convinced that
there is something new and novel about the past decade or two that suggests
the world has recently been transformed by "globalization." But just what
that means is often surprisingly "slippery" and (conveniently?) ill defined.
Minimalist definitions of "globalization" emphasize increases in "international economic integration" (Rodrik, 1997), sometimes invoking ideas related to "a new international division of labor" (Frobel, Heinrichs, & Kreye,
1981) and the rise of "the global assembly line" (Fuentes & Ehrenreich,
1984).

While all this is useful, there are two particularly insightful arguments in
discussions of contemporary "globalization" to underline:

*First*, is the notion that a basic feature of the current global economy is an
*increasing "time-space compression"* (Harvey, 1989; Arrighi, 1999). This involves a dramatic, asymptotic surge in the sheer velocity of various types of
global exchanges. It becomes especially important (and very frightening!) in
situations like "the East Asian crisis" of the late 1990s when the "global
gambling casino" dynamics of today's international banking and finance
system became obvious (Wade & Veneroso, 1998). Things are not only
happening very fast – the pace is increasing! So even folks as unlikely as
transnational financier George Soros liken the contemporary global economy to a runaway train. Even the "lords" and "high priests" of capitalism
(like Alan Greenspan and his contemporaries at the World Bank or IMF)
may have trouble controlling and breaking this locomotive!

*Second*, and perhaps even more critically, we must understand that
current images of "globalization" are completely saturated with *ideology*.
Epitomized by Maggie Thatcher's proclamation of TINA ("there is no
alternative") to global neoliberalism, this ideology emanates from the capitalist core nations and is relentlessly promoted by western conservative
theorists, large corporations, and wealthy individuals and foundations (the
most popular proponent of this view is probably Thomas Friedman (2000,
2005)). The claim is that forces like deregulation and "marketization"
are "inevitable" and in the long run beneficent. These usages of the term
"globalization" are ideological in the sense that they enshrine the values of
"free market" liberalism and legitimate the global domination of corporate
capitalism (Gill, 1996, p. 211).

Advocates of this "global neoliberalism" believe it is necessary to sub-
ordinate states and politics to the requirements of capital accumulation.
While this view rose to prominence in the early 1980s during the era of
Mrs. Thatcher's and Ronald Reagan's time on the international stage, it has

become one widely shared among political and economic elites around the world. Invocation of the free market mantra is *de rigueur* for western heads of state at G-8 summit meetings, and the ideology is now publically embraced by leaders of many poor underdeveloped countries too (see, e.g., Baer & Maloney, 1997, for a discussion of Latin America).

At the same time that this ideological wind gathered force and swept across the world, real global economic restructuring was underway; these changes fundamentally altered the international division of labor. The late 20th century witnessed a dramatic shift in the location of world manufacturing (Frobel et al., 1981; Ross & Trachte, 1990; Arrighi, Silver, & Brewer, 2003). The accelerating expansion of multinational corporations' production facilities to formerly "nonindustrial" countries encouraged calls for lower tariff barriers in the less developed world. Meanwhile, new financial instruments and technologies allowed finance capital unprecedented freedom to roam the globe (Helleiner, 1999). International agreements on property rights and stable currencies, both overseen by such multilateral agencies as the World Bank and supranational institutions like the World Trade Organization (WTO), furthered this process of economic "denationalization" (Sassen, 1999). These far-reaching changes – engineered by corporate and political elites hidden from the view of most of the world's people – provide the economic underpinning for the striking consensus about "globalization" and its implications, and led to a startling convergence of economic policies around the globe during the 1990s.

The theme of this volume is "politics and globalization": so how does the former come in? The authors of the following essays provide an intriguing range of possibilities, ranging from local popular resistance to the global economic forces, to elite support for pro-business policies, to the potential role of consumers and consumption as a lever for change. But one enduring debate involves the role of "the state": how do states cope with or take advantage of "globalization?" Are we seeing a general "decline of the state" as some prominent analysts suggest?

## STATES AND MARKETS

Clearly, the neoliberal agenda leads to policy changes that have both a domestic and an international component. Within nations they include disengagement of the government from the management of the domestic economy, deregulation, a privatization of state-owned enterprises, and cutbacks in social welfare programs. Globally they entail a reduction of tariff barriers, the opening of capital markets, and a liberalization of restrictions on foreign investment, combined with new incentives to attract it. Overall, there is a generalized increased reliance on market mechanisms and on the private sector, supposedly in the service of upgrading national "competitiveness" (another buzzword that justifies decision making for both nations and corporations, often with deleterious consequences for working people) (Bierstecker, 1992; Cox, 1996).

These recent changes in the global economy tend to advantage strong players in world markets and give transnational corporations more power relative to nation states (Strange, 1996). This promotes a worldwide trend toward privatization and antistatism. International markets for goods and capital are seen as the purveyors of not only healthy economies, but good governance and satisfied citizenries. While various "dislocations" are bound to occur, and there will be clear "winners" and "losers," ultimately, in this vision, the neoliberal process will triumph (Strange, 1996; Rodrik, 1997). Since they are inefficient, distort development and are inherently "rent seeking" and corrupt, states will inexorably decline – and this is all to the good (for "classic" neoliberal arguments (for this see Buchanan, Tollison, & Tullock, 1980)).

While neoliberal globalization rhetoric contains a strong dose of "antistatism," and, at this point, even some nominally left-oriented scholars argue that there is an epochal "decline of the state" in the contemporary world (Strange, 1996), careful examination shows that this view is at least oversimplified (Evans, 1997), if not flat-out wrong (some states – like the United States – are now more powerful than ever!). But as an ideological vision, this antistatism has implications that are troubling if we are concerned about the welfare of the majority of the world's people. States, while not necessarily eager allies of working people and the poor, are, nevertheless, key institutions within which these groups have a chance to have their interests represented. Eroding state sovereignty would have rather obvious negative implications for the lives of working people and their efforts to organize in the core industrial parts of the globe. Efforts to denigrate and diminish states could lead to even more dire consequences elsewhere, particularly in places where IMF "structural adjustment programs" are imposed on countries indebted to international agencies. Here the effective dismantling of states destroys the only institutions that might possibly negotiate with global corporations on the terms of "national development" (or exploitation) – and also makes provision of the population's basic needs like education, health care, infrastructure, etc., very difficult.

However, as some of the elite-driven discussion about whether "globalization has gone too far" acknowledges (cf. Rodrik, 1997), even diehard capitalists are realizing that it is possible to have *too much marketization* and *not enough state power/sovereignty*. To some degree, this is a rediscovery of some verities that Karl Polanyi (1957) pointed to in the early 20th century about the ugly and untenable consequences of increasingly pervasive – and insidious – unfettered markets. Arguably, the current global situation makes some forms of state sovereignty and regulation even more crucial – something needs to control those "runaway trains" mentioned above.

But it also points to a fact that seems, at first, to be paradoxical: *capitalists need states*! States set up the "rules" of the capital accumulation game, facilitate various types of monopoly, and minimize egregious sorts of corporate risk. Furthermore, one of the "beauties" of the contemporary capitalist world economy is the geographic division of nation-states, which offer differential advantages in terms of various factors of interest to big businesses (like amenities for executives in some places, but regulations – or the lack thereof – that makes production inexpensive elsewhere). Currently, with ongoing negotiations over trade rules (see Woods & Morris and Darves & Dreiling, this volume) and the WTO (with the elite meetings, since the "battle in Seattle," now increasingly held in remote locations far from protesters and public scrutiny), we may be seeing a move toward the rise of an overarching "global management system" somewhat akin to a world "state." This makes sense for (nervous?) transnational corporate players worried about keeping things on track. But there might be a danger: one big worldwide capitalist state *could* provide the conditions necessary for international labor solidarity that, taken to its logical conclusion, could lead to something akin to "one big union" worldwide (perhaps finally fulfilling some very old, presumably outdated, Marxist notions). The point is "anti-statism" and neoliberalism may be ideologically appealing to conservatives, but in practice, pushing too far in this direction simply is not compatible with today's "actually existing capitalism."

## ECONOMIC RESTRUCTURING

While the current situation of globalization is best understood as a continuation of the *longue duree* of global capitalism, there has been a real move in the past 20–30 years toward a reorganized "international division of labor." One familiar way to describe the shift is from a regime of "global Fordism" to a new "post-Fordist" reality (Aglietta, 1987; Amin, 1994; and Bonanno & Antonio, this volume). The main idea here is that mid-20th century firms worked out a sort of "deal" with manufacturing labor in core industrial countries – these workers were relatively well paid (but also fairly compliant on the shopfloor). This ended up working well, since Henry Ford's workers also were the primary consumers of his automobiles – thus, "completing the circuit of value realization" (a theme stressed by Bonanno & Antonio, this volume). Even though this economic regime did impose "costly rigidities" on business it "worked" for a long time. Bonanno and Antonio (this volume) point out, one of the keys to this success, particularly during "High Fordism" in the 1950s and 1960s, was the growth of a highly interventionist state that managed various Keynesian strategies whereby government spending promoted aggregate demand.

By the 1970s or so, technological and political–economic changes gave businesses a new set of tools to coordinate and control a different, more geographically dispersed, form of production. There was pressure to create a "new industrial division of labor" using forms of "flexible production" (Scott, 1988). All this oversimplifies greatly, but essentially there was a move by "cutting edge" industries away from standardized mass production toward small batch runs, emphasizing rapid changes in design (often reflecting shifts in consumer tastes or "fashion").

The now familiar macro-pattern that followed involved "deindustrialization" in places like the US, capital flight by manufacturing firms, and the rapid growth of the "global assembly line" in formerly underdeveloped and poor countries such as Mexico and China. Large retailers came to control "buyer-driven commodity chains," particularly in light manufacturing sectors like apparel, shoes, and toys, via outsourcing and international subcontracting (Gereffi, 1994).

This has obvious repercussions for labor and organizing in the wealthier countries, which are rapidly losing their old "industrial base." Capital becomes "footloose"; labor is less so (though recently massive labor migrations are also becoming more commonplace). This economic shift also is not so good for people in the places that optimists and economists label the "developing" countries, either. Whereas previously "industrialization" was seen as tantamount to "development," now a rapidly growing workforce in manufacturing may simply reflect a country's cheap wages (Arrighi et al., 2003). Furthermore, the dispersal of manufacturing jobs – and the pressure to continually seek a "better deal" in terms of wages and other costs – makes labor organizing under this sort of economic regime difficult. This is exacerbated by the increasing prevalence of layers of subcontracting in many industries, where laborers no longer work directly for the controlling firm, but for intermediaries.

Again, like the antistatism/marketization dynamic, this form of economic restructuring hurts labor all around the world and changes the balance of power in favor of capitalists. Nevertheless, there may be a "silver lining": the old Fordist model solved dilemmas of both production and consumption. But when Nike pays Indonesian women the equivalent of $2/day, they are *not* going to be buying any running shoes! The dynamic that promotes continued worker immiseration may lead to short- and even middle-term profits for firms – but might not be sustainable in the longer run, especially as it increasingly "hollows out" the former industrial economies of the West, creating polarization and groups of "new poor" people there. Which leads back to considerations of the wider political dynamics.

## RESPONSES AND RESISTANCE TO THE POLITICS OF GLOBALIZATION

One potentially intriguing byproduct of all the "triumphalist" rhetoric about "globalization" (with its Lexuses and olive trees and such) is the way that this is beginning to stimulate rather active counter-movements (Bhagwati, 2004; Bello, 2005). Again this probably is consistent with Polanyi's claim that excessive reliance on markets and liberal ideology, by its very nature is likely to lead to mobilization from below. In fact, emerging evidence suggests that there is a growing dissatisfaction with neoliberal globalization, both at the "higher levels" of corporate and political leadership, and among the ordinary people who are suffering under "market reforms" and increasingly willing to resist them. I have already alluded to the "elites" who are nervous about excessive global neoliberalism. Prior to September 11, 2001, there was growing evidence, also, of "antiglobalization" mobilizations from below (Fisher, this volume). There were the angry demonstrations that animated "the battle for Seattle," and subsequent mass protests at trade meetings in Quebec and Italy. Commentators remarked on the broad international coalitions of groups that came together for these actions. This movement seems to be in abeyance in the western countries during the recent US "war on terrorism" (but see Fisher's chapter, this volume, and the discussion below). If the worldwide economic difficulties that have characterized the first two years of the 21st century continue, the "antiglobalization" resistance (or, using Fisher's nomenclature "the globalization movement") is bound to make a comeback.

This resurgence of anti-corporate and pro-labor rights activism that we can label "antiglobalization," coupled with the growing realization among more sophisticated economic and political elites that perhaps globalization has gone too far, provides hope that some of the most damaging effects of global neoliberalism are not inevitable – and that there *is* an alternative. It is possible that we might be coming into a new era of resistance to the global economic status quo – and possibly a period of real change and transformation.

This volume begins with a section that examines movements that attempt to mobilize against the repressive excesses of the politics of global capital accumulation. Dana Fisher picks up the question of what happened to the resistance to globalization in the United States after 9/11/01. Conventional wisdom suggests that the "globalization movement" that blossomed in Seattle at the WTO meetings in 1999 subsequently stalled out after the terrorist attacks on the US as the Bush administration used the "War on Terror" to heighten repression and stifle dissent. But Fisher notes that the USA PATRIOT Act and the military campaign in Iraq generated a new wave of protests and demonstrations in this country. While this mobilization was ostensibly quite distinct from the earlier one that targeted globalization and trade liberalization, she shows that, in fact, the two movements are closely intertwined.

Contextualizing her study in the social movements literature and the idea of cycles of protest and movement-to-movement transmission of participants and strategies, Fisher and her research team did interviews (and e-mail follow ups) with participants at five major demonstrations between February 2002 and August 2004. The results show that significant numbers of the people protesting Bush administration policies on the war and civil liberties had been part of globalization protests prior to September 11, 2001. While there is little doubt that the globalization movement ebbed after the terrorists' attacks on that date, there is a significant overlap between participants in the earlier globalization mobilization and more recent anti-Bush demonstrations. Furthermore, the organizers of the "recent protests against the War on Terror consistently employed a global justice frame to mobilize those activists who were involved in the globalization movement." Resistance to corporate globalization in the US has not simply "retreated": some of its energy has been transformed into protest against the imperial pretense of the Bush administration.

This is an intriguing, well-constructed, essay that shows how the recent protest movements are connected and how movements change in response to political repression. It suggests that there has been a "decline in social protest since President Bush was reelected," so perhaps the "cycle of protest" is ending. But, while this might have been true a year or so ago (when the paper was written?), it seems incorrect in mid-2006, a few days after massive antiwar and immigration rallies in major US cities. As Bush's popularity sags and the futility of the war in Iraq becomes more and more obvious, we seem to be in an upswing of protest – and one that may soon lead back to serious questioning of the corporate globalization project.

Paul Almeida's chapter takes the reader back to early 20th century El Salvador and describes a very different sort of mobilization against a vicious authoritarian regime. Salvadorean peasants (foreshadowing events decades later that led to a civil war in the late 1970s and early 1980s) staged a massive uprising against an increasingly repressive state response that eventually led to the bloody *la matanza* massacres, in which up to 30,000 peasants, workers and indigenous people were killed by the military. The conceptual question that Almeida poses still resonates in parts of the world today: "how is a large-scale collective action possible against repressive governments in the global periphery?"

Although the author focuses on events in El Salvador between 1925 and 1932, he actually discusses the historical antecedents of this period in the late 18th century. During this period this small Central American country inserted itself into the world economy as an important coffee exporter, peasant lands were expropriated, major plantations established, and by the 1920s indigenous capitalists had created a local coffee processing industry. At that point, coffee exports accounted for up to 90 percent of total export revenues and the country was governed by an agro-export elite which created an administrative apparatus that included national guard posts at the municipal level.

While this economic situation of exploitation and repression set the stage for popular rebellion and brutal repression, Almeida argues that the proximate explanation of the revolt and violent response was a period of political liberalization in the late 1920s that was then reversed prior to 1932. The economic growth associated with the consolidation of the coffee export regime allowed state managers to loosen political restrictions and respond to popular demands. This involves increasing legal recognition of civic organizations and more competitive elections. But when a phase of prosperity and political liberalization is followed by global economic downturns and reformist challenges from below, ruling elites feel pressure to rollback political liberalization. Facing threats to their very survival, reform-minded organizations may initiate radical collective action. Conceptualizing this as a general model (and one that has been operative at various times and places in Latin America), Almeida draws on historical materials and statistical models to show how it fits the Salvadorean case.

The world market price for coffee began a steep rise in 1921 – and headed into an equally rapid fall in 1928. During the 1927–1930 period, there is a burst

of "civil society" in the country. This was the context for a reformist regime in
El Salvador that took power in 1927 and legalized labor-based associations
and unions, permitted workers to strike, etc. A labor reformist was even elected
in the first competitive presidential election in Salvadorean history – only to be
deposed by military coup in late 1931. Labor organizations were particularly
active in organizing rural workers in western departments. But between 1929
and 1931, wages on coffee plantations plummeted and unemployment grew.
This ignited popular protests, but also set the stage for the military coup.

Much of this story is told via historical narrative and the use of maps and
graphs. But this article also includes a sophisticated quantitative analysis of
the 1932. Data were compiled at the municipality level. Incidents of popular
rebellion during 1932 was much more likely in places where local labor
organization formed during the liberalization phase, and where incidents of
state repression occurred in the preceding two years. This shows that the
initial period of regime liberalization created conditions favorable for later
mobilization and that the renewed repression after 1930 was the match
needed to light the fires of protest and rebellion.

Ultimately, the Salvadorean state and military launched a massive ethnocidal massacre to squash the revolt and this led to almost half a century of
oligarchic authoritarian rule, so the revolt of 1932 was hardly a success. But
Almeida points out that it did provide inspiration for a new generation of
activists who launched the revolutionary movement in the early 1980s.

In terms of wider lessons, this chapter suggests that under conditions of
prior political liberalization it is very hard to "put the genie back in the
bottle": "periods of regime liberalization deposit organizational structures
that can be used to launch much more radical forms of contention when the
political climate becomes more repressive and threatening." When there is
political loosening that includes more electoral competition and labor rights
and organization, later attempts to reassert repressive control may face recurrent collective action and political radicalization. This may be particularly important in places in the global South where contradictory pressures
for political liberalization, while maintaining low-wage labor forces, could
lead to some volatile politics that could, ultimately, challenge the corporate
globalization project.

## THE BUSINESS POLITICS OF GLOBALIZATION

One of the more interesting recent challenges to global neoliberalism has
been the election of several Latin American heads of state from the left who

challenge this economic orthodoxy and have distanced themselves from the current U.S. political leadership. A pivotal event that many see as marking the beginning of this leftward shift was the election of Hugo Chavez as President of Venezuela in 1998. Both media and scholarly accounts of Chavez' victory emphasize a declining confidence in the country's political establishment, coupled with the candidate's populist rhetoric that appealed to the expanding and increasingly politicized poor urban masses; these voters believed Chavez would curb corruption and help their life chances by rejecting globally imposed neoliberal reforms and reviving a more development- and welfare-oriented state.

In her chapter on "the business of antiglobalization politics," Leslie Gates takes a different approach. And points to a paradox. She argues that, while it is generally true that leftist candidates have difficulty succeeding in Latin America because of lack of business support and money – and business people are rarely credited with supporting anti-neoliberal candidates – it is precisely because he received some of this sort of assistance that Hugo Chavez was able to get elected. This help was critical in differentiating him from other populist candidates, particularly in a country and continent where expensive U.S.-style mass media campaigning is becoming predominate and large contributors are playing a growing political role.

One of the key insights of this argument is an appreciation of the contrasting interests within the business community/capitalist class. In particular, some business owners and managers are predisposed to favor protectionist policies (local industrialists) while others are more likely to favor openness to international competition (bankers and those connected to multinational firms). So capitalists in "a fixed-asset non-internationally competitive sector" in a semiperipheral state like Venezuela tend to favor protectionism and might be contributors to a politician like Chavez. One insight of the world-systems perspective is the importance of the state in semiperipheral countries. So a second reason for businesses to support a left-leaning politician might not be because of favoring protectionism, but simply because they "prioritize access to the state." This generic trait of the semiperiphery is expected to be exacerbated in an oil-rich nation like Venezuela, where there are particularly strong incentives to maintain access to the government (so "petro-states" may represent a special case of semiperipheral states).

To understand business support for Hugo Chavez, Gates draws on Venezuelan election records, journalistic reports, and a series of face-to-face interviews for information on financial contributions, logistical support (such as loaning the candidate a private plane), or media access (granting

Chavez free or discounted coverage). Her research yields a list of supporters that included some of the country's wealthiest and most powerful business-people. A variety of information is then used to determine the structural predisposition of each of these Chavez supporters to favor protectionism or trade liberalization, and to prioritize access to the state.

Simple compilation of this data shows that some of Chavez' business supporters probably were predisposed to protectionism, but most were not; many of them did depend on the state for business profits, a few had direct network ties to Chavez, some had particular reasons to distrust one of his close associates who had been involved in a banking crisis under a previous government. While this seems to indicate a diversity of interests without much common pattern, Gates turns to qualitative comparative analysis (QCA) to unravel the common paths that led to support for Chavez. This is a relatively new technique in sociology that relies on Boolean algebra to establish which combinations of factors lead to a particular outcome. The results demonstrate two paths to supporting the candidate. First, a predis-position to prioritize access to the state is a necessary and sufficient con-dition for supporting Chavez (and this was the "path" that the majority of the businessmen in the study take). Gates argues that this indicates the potent influence that Venezuela's oil dependence has on the political interest of business, though some of these supporters were owners or managers of cement and construction companies, were newspaper publishers or bankers, etc. A second path involved protectionist interests in conjunction with net-work ties. Here, the results showed that simply being inclined to be pro-tectionist was not enough: the supportive businesspeople were also linked into personal networks that tied them to Hugo Chavez.

This study has interesting implications. Only a limited number of capitalists supported Chavez because of his trade policy preferences (and then only if they had close network ties to the candidate). On the other hand, this research's strongest finding suggests that leftist can-didates may be able to draw on business support in economies where the private sector has great dependence on the state. This could create op-portunities for the political left because some business people may be willing to bet on a strong electoral candidate, even if they do not share his or her policy convictions. This is particularly true in economies like Venezuela or Bolivia where there is a great dependence on the export of natural re-sources. But a careful examination of sector-based interests may also show divisions within the capitalist classes that can be exploited by the left. It is possible for politicians opposed to globalization to rise to power, with business support.

Mexico City is one of the largest urban agglomerations in the world and a prominent part of the global city system in which various urban areas compete for investment, tourists, etc. In her chapter, Diane Davis points out that various vectors of globalization come together in the politics of downtown development in this rapidly growing city. We can quibble about whether it qualifies as a "global city" or not. But clearly there are powerful groups in Mexico City that are eager to make it into a prominent business hub and tourist destination. Davis' basic storyline pits those who want to develop a swath of downtown into a hotel/office building/convention complex, known as the Alameda project, versus residents of a nearby low income barrio of Tepito, who are against this plan. She shows that the two sides of this political struggle represent "competing 'globalizations'" built on different networks of global actors and investors (of different skill levels, income, status, and employment) that coexist uneasily in a contiguous physical space. The outcome of this politics is far from predetermined: in fact, the forces of corporate globalization may sometimes be stymied – even when it appears that they have carried the day.

Davis makes a compelling case for examining urban politics in this way. Following Saskia Sassen, she not only emphasizes the importance of conceptualizing political struggles in terms of global forces, but also wants to raise issues about how urban residents, even those who are poor and marginalized, can have a political presence and exert some power. Local politics is a largely neglected aspect of recent research on cities and globalization. Frequently, it is assumed that global forces will overwhelm local actors and urban processes will work themselves out in homogenizing ways. Davis wants to problematize this by digging into the details of land use and development politics in Mexico City. She convinces readers it is not so simple.

The contemporary battles over downtown development must be placed in the historical context of the changing nature of planning in Mexico City from the 1930s onward. For most of that period local residents were able to fend off efforts to redevelop the areas and buildings that gave the central city its special cultural and economic flavor (as venue for petty commodity production and trading). But that began to change more recently. The destructive 1985 earthquake, coincident with growing pressures for neoliberal economic reform (part of worldwide economic globalization), was one crucial turning point. Another occurred in 1994 with the approval of the North American Free Trade Agreement (NAFTA) and the emergence of the Zapatista movement. The earthquake, literally, opened up new opportunities for downtown redevelopment, which real estate speculators and business interests were eager to cash in on; the post-NAFTA period brought in a

flood of foreign capital and investors. But in the mid-1990s a strong countervailing force developed as popular sentiment in Mexico City turned
against free trade and there was a groundswell of support for the Zapatista
rebels. The Zapatistas not only promulgated an antiglobalization, anti-
neoliberal rhetoric – they tied this to a critique of the Mexican political
system, and specifically to the failures of democratization for the marginalized and disenfranchised urban poor.

The Alameda project was first proposed in the late 1980s, reintroduced
twice in the early 1990s and finally approved in 2001. It is located in the
city's historic center, with hotels, upscale commercial and residential properties and office buildings designed to lure international visitors, global
corporate headquarters, and foreign investors. The nearby barrio of Tepito
is a middle to lower class residential area, long considered the home to the
city's most vibrant informal sector of hawkers, vendors, and petty traders.
Owing to its battles against official planning efforts like the Alameda
project, this neighborhood earned the nickname "barrio bravo." It is from
Tepito that Davis develops the idea of "competing globalizations." The
barrio's informal sector has a long history of dealing with "illegal goods." In
earlier periods these were mainly "knock off" products. But after NAFTA
the merchants of Tepito began to sell an increasing array of contraband
items (CDs, DVDs, etc.). To procure these increasingly illicit items, local
merchants were increasingly drawn into "dangerous and violent international networks in which drugs and guns were the preferred means of
exchange and/or coercion." Tepito became controlled by politically formidable mafia smuggling rings, stridently opposed to any "clean up" of the
barrio, much less redevelopment of the downtown area.

Finally, a new elected mayor was able to push through a redevelopment
project that included the Alameda project. However, the massive property
development projects that started in 2001 and 2002 have stalled – violence
and crime in the downtown area makes middle and upper income residents
wary of moving in, and many lower income residents have refused to move
out. The main damper is the persistence of illegal and dangerous activities in
Tepito. Thus, the pressure for redevelopment coming from the forces of corporate globalization are in stalemate with forces dominated by an "illegitimate" underworld connected to the global economy in a very different way.

Davis leaves us with a vision of Mexico City at the crossroads, being
transformed by globalization and various licit and illicit business interests,
but also at the edge of an uncertain precipice where major changes are likely
but specific directions are uncertain. It is a fascinating story that reminds us
that the outcomes of globalization are variegated and not predetermined

and that we often have to capture the reality "on the ground" to truly understand where the process leads. Like the previous chapter, this one also reminds us that politics matter a great deal.

## GLOBALIZATION AND THE POLITICS OF TRADE POLICY

The implementation of the NAFTA had important effects on citizens, not just in Mexico City but also in the rest of Mexico, Canada and the United States. Many scholars are interested in the impacts of this treaty. But how was it developed? How is U.S trade policy in general formed? What are the politics that determine these policies and thereby structure the international markets and legal institutions of economic globalization? These questions are addressed in next two chapters.

Tim Wood and Theresa Morris focused specifically on NAFTA and the political process that led to its passage. They claim that previous research on the making of trade policy has tended to adopt either a "state-centered" model (stressing the autonomy of state bureaucrats and managers from direct corporate influence) or a "power structure" model (that emphasizes the role of powerful societal groups, particularly business groups and cap-italist interests, who unify in favor of the neoliberal agenda). Wood and Morris take a middle road in this debate, following Harland Prechel, and employ an "historical contingency" approach that recognizes that neither state autonomy nor capitalist class unity are likely to exist in their "pure" forms, and the "mix" of these influences depends on the historical context. Their chapter is a close-grained historical analysis of the NAFTA case.

In the 1970s and 1980s, as US hegemony in the global system waned, domestic businesses faced increased competition from abroad and could no longer compete, particularly with low-wage manufacturing in the newly in-dustrialized countries. A "nationalist" segment of industry (in sectors like steel and textiles) favored protectionists' policies (this was literally, the US version of the "fixed-asset non-internationally competitive sector" to use the terminology of the Gates chapter, this volume). While the executive branch was nonresponsive to this group's demands, there was sympathy for some forms of trade protection in Congress. Aligned against these interests was an internationalist business segment, anchored by multinational financial and banking capital. This group vigorously promoted free trade. While other agreements to liberalize trade were more contentious, NAFTA garnered support from the nationalist as well as internationalist business segments, since a "regional" trading block offered protection from Asian and European producers while simultaneously expanding consumer markets, particularly in sectors like the automobile industry.

In 1991, the first Bush administration requested "fast-track authority" from Congress for both the NAFTA and the broader General Agreement on Tariffs and Trade (GATT). This would streamline the process of treaty negotiation by granting the executive branch the power to work out the details of the treaty first, then bring the entire agreement to the legislature for an up or down vote, with no amendments permitted (in effect, it transfers congressional authority to the President). Corporate interests quickly coalesced in favor of "fast track," since they felt they could more easily influence the negotiations if they were confined to the executive branch, and it was also believed that this strategy would greatly enhance the prospects of final congressional approval. But there was also significant opposition to granting fast track on the trade agreements from organized labor, environmental groups, and a few business groups (like garment and textile makers). These opponents put a great deal of pressure on congressional Democrats to vote no. In response, the administration issued statements intended to mollify concerns about labor and ecological issues, and managed to persuade some moderate environmental groups to switch sides and back fast track. In the end, this authority was granted by Congress. Woods and Morris argue that congressional approval of fast track came about because of a combination of business pressure, state agendas, and active administration negotiation with environmentalists.

Once fast track was approved, the influence of members of Congress, labor, and environmental groups was greatly restricted, as large business groups exerted enormous influence on the negotiations coordinated by the Office of the US Trade Representative. Various business "advisor committees" were established which made very specific recommendations for provisions that became part of the final agreement. As a result, the negotiated policy included most of the provisions set forth by big business, but very few, if any, recommendations made by environmental or labor organizations.

The stage was set for a final vote to approve NAFTA in 1993, shortly after Bill Clinton became President. But there was significant opposition to the treaty in Congress based on concerns that it would lead to displaced workers in the US, damage the environment in Mexico, and a lack of provision for the infrastructure necessary for increased hemispheric trade. Both the executive branch and capitalists responded. Big business organized a group called USA*NAFTA to lead the charge to build business, media and popular support for passage. The Clinton administration, to assuage wavering Congressional Democrats established a set of (rather toothless) "side agreements" on labor and the environment; it also engaged in a flurry of last minute bargaining with particular congressmen and interests groups to ensure approval in November 1993.

Woods and Morris acknowledge that the passage of NAFTA was the result of a high degree of corporate unity and, alternatively, reflected the declining power of organized labor in the US. But they also emphasize that organizational structure, embodied in the fast-track provision, defined the policy-making process by enhancing the influence of big business and excluding labor and environmental interests. In this case, the state bureaucratic structure wielded great power, but rather than acting "autonomously" it facilitated greater influence for corporate power. While the outcome was not preordained and depended on a degree of historical contingency, this was an instance where US government officials colluded with the capitalist interests to "grease the skids" of global neoliberalism.

While passage of NAFTA was a major victory for corporate interests, it was not the end of their efforts to liberalize world trade. Indeed, under the "fast-track" rules a series of Industrial Sector Advisory Committees (ISACs) are institutionalized to provide advice on trade matters to the executive branch (Department of Commerce, Office of US Trade Representative, and the President). Congress rarely defies the recommendations made by these advisory committees and they are strongly committed to neoliberal trade initiatives, like NAFTA, and generally oppose tariff and nontariff barriers to trade. These non-elected advisory committees play a very active role in the shaping of US regional and global trade policies, and were critical in recent initiatives on a Central American Free Trade Agreement (CAFTA), the establishment of Permanent Normal Trading Relations (PNTR) with China, and various negotiations about the rules and institutions of the WTO.

In their chapter, Derek Darves and Michael Drieling examine corporate participation in these US government trade advisory committees between 1998 and 2003. Developing a new data set on *Fortune* and *Forbes* 500 companies, they attempt to identify the factors that influence business involvement in the ISACs, to explore whether this is driven by converging company rationalities based on firm-specific interests or whether class-wide considerations in intercorporate networks are more important. The key issue, here, is whether a firm's position in larger corporate networks, or its organizational attributes, are the main determinates of its odds of participation in one of the 18 executive branch trade advisory committees. This addresses the relative roles of corporate and state actors in the construction of a new global neoliberal trade order. Darves and Wood suggest that it "is not *whether* business is unified on trade, *but under what conditions* firms from a variety of sectors enter the policy formation process" (italics in the original). They take a "class embedded" perspective on this that class-wide interests trump those of any single firm or industry and these prevail in promoting the project of neoliberal globalization.

To assess this theoretical position, Darves and Drieling collect data on all publicly traded firms in both the *Forbes* and *Fortune* 500 directories. In 2003, 13 percent of these firms (64) participated in one or more ISACs. Information was coded on organizational attributes such as whether or not companies had foreign subsidiaries, were capital intensive, operate in tradeable goods sectors, were large in terms of sales and assets, and had significant Political Action Committee (PAC) contributions. Since network measures are of particular interest, Darves and Drieling also recorded the number of "interlocks" on corporate boards (i.e. people who sit on boards of other companies as well as on a firm's board), firm affiliation to the Business Roundtable, and company participation in temporary trade alliances (like USA*NAFTA, see above).

Darves and Drieling analyze this data using hierarchical non-linear modeling (HNLM), a sophisticated quantitative technique that provides various statistical advantages over alternative methodologies. They find that it is critical to control for industrial sector since much of the variance in ISAC participation is *between* sectors (this suggests that it might be of interest to look at which industries *are* over-represented and most influential on these advisory committees, but that sort of detail is not reported in this chapter). Three factors are critical. There is more participation on the trade advisory boards from (1) the largest firms in certain sectors, (2) firms with high PAC expenditures, and (3) companies with network interlocks, ties to Business Roundtable or membership in temporary alliance networks. This indicates that there is a measure of "class embeddedness" in the government's trade policy formulation apparatus: prominent corporate organizations (like the Business Roundtable) create an institutional framework for the expression of broad capitalist class interests. Business interests have colonized the state's trade policy apparatus and advance the interests of multinational corporations and the larger project of neoliberal globalization. This sort of globalization is not "inevitable" as Ms. Thatcher's famous proclamation that "there is no alternative" implies: it is socially constructed by people acting on behalf of class embedded corporations and the state agencies that they have, in effect, "captured." The global justice movement that seeks more democratized trade institutions is right to assert that "another world is possible," but only if they can muster sufficient political power.

## GLOBALIZATION AND THE CRISIS OF UNDER-CONSUMPTION

By now, it is fairly clear that the form of "globalization" that emerged in the past two or three decades, characterized by a strong dose of global neoliberalism, may benefit some but poses big problems for many other people not only in wealthier countries like the United States, but around the world. The authors of this volume take a critical view of global capitalism, they are concerned with the way that the current world-economy generates inequality and power differentials, and they tend to be sympathetic to those who would respond and resist the worst depredations of corporate globalization. But this raises a very old question of "what is to be done?" And how we answer depends on the way we assess the current state of the global economy.

There is a venerable current in Marxist theory that periodically asserts that capitalism is in "crisis" and that the system's internal contradictions will eventually force some sort of major structural change on it, perhaps even leading to the destruction of capitalism itself. It is fair to say that, over the last century and a half, these predictions of the demise of the system have been premature, one verity about capitalism is that it has proven to be very persistent and resilient. Still there is something very enticing about crisis theory. And even though global capitalism continues to roll along, these approaches *do* provide a number of insights into its structures and weak points.

In the final chapter of the volume, Alessandro Bonanno and Robert Antonio develop a elegant exposition of the argument that current global neoliberalism and economic globalization has created a situation characterized by worldwide social polarization and rampant poverty which, in turn, sets the conditions for a "crisis of realization," as predicted by Marx. This places the focus on the gap between production and consumption: worker's wages are only a fraction of their production (as per the labor theory of value) and only equal the cost of reproduction, so workers cannot consume what they produce – and eventually capitalists have a problem selling the economy's output.

Recounting what is now a fairly familiar story, Bonanno and Antonio tell how this predicament was addressed in the United States in the early

twentieth century by the rise of a form of capitalism that bridged the
gap between production and consumption: Fordism. This involved mass
production via assembly lines, but also mass consumption. Henry Ford
realized that if he paid his factory workers a living wage and produced cars
more efficiently, workers would also be consumers. That coupled with increased state intervention and spending that constituted various forms of
government "deficit spending" on welfare, infrastructure, etc. (what has
been called "state Keynesianism") would "solve" the crisis of under-con-
sumption ("realization"). For decades this system worked well in the US,
based on a "capital–labor accord" and an expanding state.

But in the mid-1960s there was a "crisis of High Fordism" in this country.
The authors tell us of changes in the US – the rise of race riots and campus
disturbances, oil shortages, the Vietnam war, increased taxation and stagflation, etc. – as well as abroad – rising economic challenges to US companies from manufacturers in other parts of the world, emerging challenges
to "Western modernization" in the form of Islamic fundamentalism, etc.
What they are describing, without the historical context of the *longue duree*
of the trends and cycles of historical capitalism, was the beginning of the
decline of US hegemony as the world's leading economic power. In fact, the
"capital–labor accord" that involved paying North American workers a
premium wage was constructed based on inexpensive inputs from the peripheral areas of the world economy, where resource plunder and extreme
labor exploitation were the norm. This "neo-imperial" relationship between
the US and the underdeveloped world (which some Marxists might say
facilitated "primitive accumulation" or what David Harvey (2003) refers to
as "accumulation by dispossession") was a major prop that helped to keep
this US Fordist regime afloat.

While Bonnano and Antonio miss the opportunity to place the US case in this
sort of world historical context, they do a nice job of describing the rise of "post-
Fordism" and its link to economic globalization. With the crisis of US hegemony, corporate interests were eager to free capitalism from "rigidities" imposed
by state intervention, unions, etc. So there was a new push for "flexibility" in
terms of labor and regulation, "privatization" of government functions, and
"liberalization" of trade and markets. Capital mobility and global sourcing
became major business strategies. All of this was designed to boost profitability.

But it also created growing economic inequality, the rich got richer, but
the middle and lower class groups in many parts of the world experienced
declining purchasing power and wages. Which, of course, suggests the
probability of a return to a renewed worldwide crisis of under-consumption/
realization. Global capitalism ends up in another vexing *cul de sac*. One

might think that this would lead to some ugly results (resource wars, global revolution) that would culminate in some sort of radical reorganization of the system, or even the demise of global capitalism itself.

However, Bonanno and Antonio seem to draw quite different conclusions. They see a much gentler solution to the crisis via "new social movement inspired consumption." For instance, the environmental movement, they claim, despite its political fragmentation and foibles, has created widespread consciousness in society for more democratic and sustainable consumption. The authors believe that this new awareness will counter the corporate capitalist agenda, creating new "reflexive consumption" (epitomized by a "food movement" that challenges the neoliberal ethos). This will create "democratic spaces" from which the logic of capitalist production itself can be challenged. Of course, there are such consumers and social movements, particularly in various US college towns in the so-called "blue states." But what about the immiserated masses in the poor countries of Africa, Latin American, or Asia? This is an attractive scenario, but as a way to transform the global economy it demands skepticism.

The authors end their chapter on a less sanguine note. They point to the worldwide condition of poverty and inequality and the crisis it produced for global production overcapacity and a crisis of realization. And, if, as Friedman (2000) tells us the "Lexus trumps the olive tree" and the world follows the US path of high consumption (the Chinese with their over-developed cities and clogged highways seem to be headed in that direction), then how can even demand for resources like oil be met? Bonanno and Antonio leave us with two useful lessons: First, states *do* still matter. They have helped form the current contours of globalization. Ultimately, state regulation might be the only way to stop the out-of-control impulses set loose by global neoliberalism. Second, the level of consumption currently practiced in the US is not sustainable – trying to export the high levels of consumption that characterized High Fordism to the rest of the world will not work, because of environmental and resource limits. "Genuine democratic reconstruction requires a radical rethinking of environmental priorities and the very idea of a 'consumer society.'"

## CONCLUSION

Globalization, in the form of worldwide neoliberal economic restructuring, is a pervasive force in the lives of us all – and not necessarily for the better. Its macro-dynamics will affect us, our children, and the generations that follow (or may even contribute to human extinction). But it is very poorly understood by most of us, including many social scientists. And the first step toward changing the world for the better is to have some "analysis" of its underlying structures and processes. To formulate an efficacious "politics" we need to begin with some understanding of global processes.

Sociology has not been particularly attentive to globalization. Often scholars who specialize in various subfields of our discipline attempt to apply general "models" of economic, or cultural or political organization to contemporary processes without understanding that these operate in an increasingly globalized world. The articles in this volume make a material contribution to our understanding of globalization, the way it is politically constructed, and the manner in which it can be challenged. They are a welcome contribution which, literally, broaden the sociological imagination. We need this sort of understanding not only to build better theories, but also to formulate a more meaningful political response to the various dangers of the contemporary world condition. And to attempt to put the brakes on the train of global neoliberalism.

# REFERENCES

Aglietta, M. (1987). *A theory of capitalist regulation: The U.S. experience*. London, UK: New Left Books.

Amin, A. (Ed.) (1994). *Post-Fordism: A reader*. Cambridge, MA: Blackwell.

Arrighi, G. (1999). Globalization, state sovereignty, and the endless accumulation of capital. In: D. Smith, D. Solinger & S. Topik (Eds), *States and sovereignty in the global economy* (pp. 53–73). London, UK: Routledge.

Arrighi, G. (2005). Globalization in world-systems perspective. In: R. Appelbaum & W. Robinson (Eds), *Critical globalization studies* (pp. 33–44). New York, NY: Routledge.

Arrighi, G., Silver, B., & Brewer, B. (2003). Industrial convergence, globalization and the persistence of the north–south divide. *Studies in Comparative International Development, 38*(1), 3–31.

Baer, W., & Maloney, W. (1997). Neoliberalism and income distribution in Latin America. *World Development, 25*(3), 311–327.

Bello, W. (2005). The crisis of the globalist project and the new economics of George W. Bush. In: R. Appelbaum & W. Robinson (Eds), *Critical globalization studies* (pp. 101–109). New York, NY: Routledge.

Bhagwati, J. (2004). *In defense of globalization*. New York, NY: Oxford University Press.

Bierstecker, T. (1992). The "triumph" of neoclassical economics in the developing world: Policy convergence and the bases of governance in the international order. In: J. Rosenau & E.-O. Czempiel (Eds), *Governance without government: Order and change in world politics* (pp. 102–131). Cambridge, MA: Cambridge University Press.

Braudel, F. (1992). *Civilization and capitalism, 15th–18th century*. Berkeley: University of California Press.

Buchanan, J., Tollison, R., & Tullock, G. (Eds) (1980). *Toward a theory of rent-seeking society.* College Station: Texas A&M University Press.

Cox, R. (1996). A perspective on globalization. In: J. Mittelman (Ed.), *Globalization: Critical reflections* (pp. 21–30). Boulder, CO: Lynne Reinner Publishers.

Evans, P. (1997). The eclipse of the state? Reflections on stateness in an era of globalization. *World Politics, 50*(1), 62–87.

Friedman, T. (2000). *The Lexus and the olive tree.* New York: Farrar, Straus and Giroux.

Friedman, T. (2005). *The world is flat: A brief history of the 21st century.* New York: Farrar, Straus and Giroux.

Frobel, F., Heinrichs, J., & Kreye, O. (1981). *The new international division of labor.* London: Cambridge University Press.

Fuentes, A., & Ehrenreich, B. (1984). *Women in the global factory.* Boston, MA: South End Press.

Gereffi, G. (1994). The organization of buyer-driven global commodity chains: How U.S. retailers shape overseas production. In: G. Gereffi & M. Korzeniewicz (Eds), *Commodity chains and global capitalism* (pp. 95–122). Westport, CT: Greenwood.

Gill, S. (1996). Globalization, democratization, and the politics of indifference. In: J. Mittelman (Ed.), *Globalization: Critical reflections* (pp. 205–228). Boulder, CO: Lynne Reinner Publishers.

Greider, W. (1997). *One world, ready or not: The manic logic of global capitalism.* New York: Simon & Schuster.

Harvey, D. (1989). *The condition of postmodernity: An enquiry into the origins of cultural change.* New York, NY: Blackwell.

Harvey, D. (2003). *The new imperialism.* New York, NY: Oxford University Press.

Helleiner, E. (1999). Sovereignty, territoriality, and the globalization of finance. In: D. Smith, D. Solinger & S. Topik (Eds), *States and sovereignty in the global economy* (pp. 138–157). London, UK: Routledge.

Mittelman, J. (2000). *The globalization syndrome: Transformation and resistance.* Princeton, NJ: Princeton University Press.

Polanyi, K. (1957). *The great transformation.* Boston, MA: Beacon Press.

Rodrik, D. (1997). *Has globalization gone too far?* Washington, DC: Institute for International Economics.

Ross, R., & Trachte, K. (1990). *Global capitalism: The new Leviathan.* Albany: State University of New York Press.

Sassen, S. (1999). Embedding the global in the national: Implications for the role of the state. In: D. Smith, D. Solinger & S. Topik (Eds), *States and sovereignty in the global economy* (pp. 158–171). London, UK: Routledge.

Scott, A. (1988). Flexible production systems and regional development. *International Journal of Urban and Regional Research, 12,* 171–186.

Stiglitz, J. (2003). *Globalization and its discontents.* New York, NY: W. W. Norton & Company.

Strange, S. (1996). *The retreat of the state: The diffusion of power in the world economy.* New York, NY: Cambridge University Press.

Wade, R., & Veneroso, F. (1998). The gathering world slump and the battle over capital controls. *New Left Review, 231*(September/October), 13–42.

Wallerstein, I. (2005). After developmentalism and globalization, what? *Social Forces, 83*(3), 1263–1278.

# PART I:
# POLITICAL MOBILIZATION AND GLOBALIZATION

# TAKING COVER BENEATH THE ANTI-BUSH UMBRELLA: CYCLES OF PROTEST AND MOVEMENT-TO-MOVEMENT TRANSMISSIONS IN AN ERA OF REPRESSIVE POLITICS

Dana R. Fisher

## ABSTRACT

*What happened to the globalization movement in the United States? Since September 11, 2001, large-scale protest in the U.S. has predominantly targeted aspects of the so-called "War on Terror" and the Bush administration's policies more broadly, rather than on issues related to economic globalization and trade liberalization. Although from the outside, these protest events seem to be unrelated instances of citizens mobilizing to express their dissatisfaction, this paper argues that they are related. Building off of the research on cycles of protest and those who have theorized about movement-to-movement transmission within a cycle of protest, this paper explores what happens to social movements within the context of increasing political repression. Using data collected through two stages of surveys with protesters who were randomly sampled at*

Politics and Globalization
Research in Political Sociology, Volume 15, 27–55
Copyright © 2007 by Elsevier Ltd.
ISSN: 0895-9935/doi:10.1016/S0895-9935(06)15002-0

*large-scale protest events in the United States from 2002 to 2004, this paper provides data to show how recent protest movements are connected and how movements change in response to political repression.*

# INTRODUCTION

With the 1999 protests against the World Trade Organization in Seattle, social scientists have increasingly studied the globalization movement.[1] Significant attention has been devoted to understanding the ways in which this movement represents a new form of transnational contention and how this movement is different from earlier movements (e.g. Ancelovici, 2002; Ayres, 2001; Bandy & Smith, 2004; della Porta & Tarrow, 2004; Fisher, Stanley, Berman, & Neff, 2005; Guidry, Kennedy, & Zald, 2001; Meyer & Tarrow, 1998; O'Brien, Goetz, Scholte, & Williams, 2000; Risse-Kappen, 1995; Rothman & Oliver, 1999; Smith & Johnston, 2002; Smith, Chatfield, & Pagnucco, 1997; Tarrow, 2001, 2005; Tilly, 2004, Chapter 5; but see Atwood, 1997; Boli & Thomas, 1999; Cortright & Pagnucco, 1997; Korey, 1998). As has been noted by Ayres and Tarrow (2002), in the wake of the terrorist attacks on the United States on September 11, 2001, political repression has escalated "both in the United States and elsewhere" (p. 1). Concurrent with this heightened repression, protest in the United States has shifted away from issues related to globalization – such as trade liberalization and the polices of international financial institutions – to focus on the so-called "War on Terror"[2] and the policies of the Bush Administration more broadly. This paper explores the relationship between these presumably unrelated protest movements and studies them as components of one specific cycle of protest.

In particular, I build off of the work by scholars who have explored the relationship between movements within a cycle of protest to understand how collective action changes in the wake of political repression. In this paper, I focus particularly on how the globalization movement in the United States was redirected to protest the War on Terror and the policies of the Bush Administration since September 2001. Presenting data collected from five large-scale protests in the United States between 2002 and 2004, I show that there are significant similarities among these protesting populations. Moreover, I contend that these movements are all part of one specific cycle of protest within which collective action shifted in the wake of increased political repression. This paper is separated into three sections. First, I review the literature on cycles of protest and the research that looks at social movement transmission within cycles of protest. Second, I present data collected through two stages of surveys with protest participants at five large-scale protest events in the United States. Third, I discuss the implications of these findings to our understanding of contemporary cycles of protest and the ways that social movements respond to political repression.

## STUDYING THE RELATIONSHIP BETWEEN SOCIAL MOVEMENTS AS CYCLES OF PROTEST

Scholars have studied the connections between social movements for years (e.g. Buechler, 1990; Evans, 1980; McCarthy & Zald, 1977; Morris, 1984; Zald & McCarthy, 1980). Nonetheless, as McAdam (1995) points out, much of the research tends to provide a "highly static view of collective action that privileges structure over process and single movements over cycles of protest" (p. 218). Although there has been a recent increase in research on the relationship between social movements, the scholarship is constrained by differing terms that refer to similar aspects of collective action. In addition there is yet to be consensus regarding which perspective best explains how collective action changes in response to political repression. Scholars exploring the dynamics of movement-to-movement transmission have studied social movement spillover (Meyer & Whittier, 1994), the relationship between initiator and spin-off movements (McAdam, 1995), and the sequencing of social movements (Minkoff, 1997). Although all these studies focus on different aspects of the connections between movements, there has been some level of agreement by their authors that movements can be better understood by looking at them within what Tarrow has called a "cycle of protest."[3] In the pages that follow, I review the scholarship that has presented details on the relationship between social movements, paying particular attention to the ways each theory conceptualizes political repression's role in the process through which activism breeds activism.

### *Cycles of Protest*

Building off of Tilly's (1978, 1986) work on repertoires of contention (see also the volume edited by Traugott, 1995), the notion of the cycle of protest was conceived by Tarrow (1993) to explain the broad process of the mobilization through which innovations in collective action are diffused. In his more recent work, Tarrow (1998) defines a cycle of contention as "a phase of heightened conflict across the social system: with a rapid diffusion of collective action frames; a combination of organized and unorganized participation; and sequences of intensified information flow and interaction between challengers and authorities" (p. 142; see also Tarrow, 1991, 1993, 1994; the volume edited by Traugott, 1995). Within this work, the author states that cycles begin with what he calls "early risers" who mobilize when they perceive that there is a political opportunity. The collective action then diffuses to include "latecomers." Implicit to the cycle of protest is the recognition that many forms of collective action can take place during a period of time and that they are related as part of a distinct cycle. After conflict widens, protest becomes routinized with "more conventional protests with more instrumental goals" becoming common (Tarrow, 1991, p. 53). Although Tarrow (1998) points out that the end of such cycles of protest are "diverse," he states that "as the cycle winds down ... polarization spread[s] and the initiative shifts to elites and parties" (p. 160).

Tarrow (1993) also discusses the role of political repression in his work on cycles of protest. He states that collective action will not "cease just because a particular group has been satisfied, repressed, or becomes tired of life in the streets" (pp. 285–286). Instead, in the face of repression, collective action changes. More recently, Tarrow (1998) has suggested that radicals push for "more violent forms of action" when the state becomes repressive (p. 150). This radicalization is likely to lead to the defection of more moderate participants. In his own words, "the spiral of tactical innovation [in the form of disruptive collective action] contributes to a decline in mass participation" (Tarrow, 1991, p. 55). Thus, the author sees political repression leading to increased violence, which tends to turn-off more mainstream movement participants.[4]

By looking at *cycles* of protest, we can see the ways that multiple forms of contention against various targets during a specific period of time are interrelated and build off of the initial sense of political opportunity. Within his discussion of the "elements of cyclicity," Tarrow discusses the role of new frames of meaning. He states: "Protest cycles characteristically produce new or transformed symbols, frames of meaning and ideologies that justify and dignify collective action and around which a following can be mobilized" (p. 286). Here, the author builds off of the work on framing and frame alignment (e.g. Snow, Rochford, Worden, & Benford, 1986; Snow & Benford, 1992; see also Gamson, 1992). In fact, Snow and Benford (1992) themselves highlight the importance of framing on movement-to-movement transmission within cycles of protest: "movements that surface early in a cycle of protest are likely to function as progenitors of master frames that provide the ideational and interpretive anchoring for subsequent movements within the cycle" (p. 144). In other words, a particular frame of meaning can be seen as one of the central themes within a cycle of protest.

Even with the utility of the notion of cycles of protest, however, research on the subject remains limited. Tarrow (1998) himself recognizes the lack of research on such cycles and periods of contention, acknowledging that "they occupy no clearly demarcated space with respect to institutional politics" (p. 143). There are, however, three particularly relevant perspectives that do, to some degree, build off of the notion of cycles of protest to present more specificity to understanding the ways that movement-to-movement transmission takes place. In the sections that follow, I will review each perspective paying particular attention to the role that they see for frame alignment and political repression in their understanding of movement-to-movement transmission.

## Social Movement Spillover

Perhaps one of the earliest clear articulations of movement-to-movement transmission within a cycle of protest was put forward by Meyer and Whittier (1994) in their work on "social movement spillover." The authors conceptualize social movement spillover to explain the ways that "ideas, tactics, style, participants, and organizations of one movement often *spill over* its boundaries to affect other social movements" (Meyer & Whittier, 1994, p. 277, emphasis in original). The authors acknowledge that protests in the United States frequently involve a diversity of organizations "that address a 'laundry list' of demands ... A bellwether issue, generally representing what activists view as either the most threatening and urgent problem or the most promising vehicle for action, comes to unify a broad spectrum of groups that share similar or related concerns" (Meyer & Whittier, 1994, p. 290). Owing to the diversity of interests of the organizations and participants involved in the movement, spillover becomes possible.

Looking specifically at the connections between the women's movement and the U.S. Peace Movement in the 1980s, Meyer and Whittier (1994) find that participants of social movements change their focus to issues that they consider more critical: "as a movement shifts into abeyance on one set of issues, its personnel and organizations may switch the grounds of the challenge to another set of issues" (p. 279; for an application of social movement spillover to the connections between the political left and gay liberation movements, see Valocchi, 2001). In other words, the shifting of targets is the product of differing perceptions about the most urgent issue

and impressions of changing political opportunities. One of the major connections that the authors identify between these movements is their frame
alignment. The authors conclude that the peace movement combined frames
about peace and feminism, which was successful in recruiting "both feminist
and non-feminist women as activists for the [nuclear] freeze" (Meyer &
Whittier, 1994, p. 287).

Although the authors do not explicitly discuss the role that political repression may play in social movement spillover, they find in their case that,
when there was hostility to political challenge from the Left, there was more
"impetus for movement–movement linkages as beleaguered activists and
organizations pool their strength against powerful opponents" (Meyer &
Whittier, 1994, p. 293). In other words, the authors conclude that a hostile
political environment leads to a broader coalition of activists and organizations involved in social movements. Such a broader field leads to a cas-
cading effect within which activism gives way to activism.

## Initiator and Spin-Off Movements

Another perspective on movement-to-movement transmission is presented
in McAdam's work on initiator and spin-off movements. Written as a
chapter in an edited volume on *Repertoires and Cycles of Collective Action*
(Traugott, 1995), McAdam addresses the ways that movements are connected within a cycle of protest. He distinguishes between "two broad
classes of movements whose origins reflect very different social processes":
initiator movements, which "signal or otherwise set in motion an identi-
fiable protest cycle"; and spin-off movements, which "in varying degrees,
draw their impetus and inspiration from the original initiator movement"
(McAdam, 1995, p. 219).

By separating these two related types of movements, McAdam adds
specificity to movement-to-movement transmission within a cycle of protest.
In particular, he explores the differences in the ways early rising initiator
movements and spin-off movements, or what Tarrow would call "latecomers," engage in collective action. The author finds that spin-off movements
"develop within the formal organizations or associational networks of an
earlier movement, while also appropriating and adapting elements of its
collective action frame" (McAdam, 1995, p. 231). In other words, the initiator movement develops the frame and the spin-off movement adapts it.

McAdam finds that this adaptation takes place in a different political
context than that of the initiator movement. Although they are borne of the

organizations and connections among participants within the initiator movement, McAdam posits that spin-off movements tend to emerge in the "context of *contracting* political opportunities" such as political repression (McAdam, 1995, p. 225, emphasis in original). As a result, spin-off movements are not expected to be particularly politically successful. Instead, they respond to what he calls "cultural processes" that include common tactics and collective action frames. While the initiator movement emerges to respond to political opportunity, the spin-off movement responds to a broadening acceptance of the repertoire of contention, be it sit-ins or more recent marches and demonstrations involving puppets. Thus, when there is a repressive political environment, a spin-off movement can emerge in response to cultural opportunity when the public perceives there to be political *inopportunity*.

## The Sequencing of Social Movements

Minkoff also explores the relationship between social movements within a cycle of protest in her work on the organizational behavior and connections between the civil rights and feminist protest movements (1997). Going beyond what she considers to be "predominantly cognitive" conceptualizations of cycles of protest that include cultural elements such as frame alignment (Minkoff, 1997, p. 780), she finds protest cycles to be "the visible manifestation of the interaction between organization trajectories and protest-event trajectories" (p. 779). Adopting Tarrow's terminology, she notes that early risers help to facilitate the expansion of the cycle of protest by mobilizing organizational growth and what she calls "organizational density."

Although Minkoff also does not look specifically at political repression and the role that it might play in social movement sequencing, she does explore the role that political allies and political opponents (in the form of democratic and republican dominance in the U.S. Congress) plays in the diffusion of protest. She finds that "Republican dominance [or what some might consider a repressive political environment] limited the diffusion of protest from the civil rights movement to the feminist movement" (Minkoff, 1997, p. 795). In other words, protest does not tend to spread as quickly in such a repressive political environment.

In short, these three theories – of social movement spillover, initiator and spin-off movements, and the sequencing of social movements – provide some insight into understanding the relationship between social movements within a distinct cycle of protest. Table 1 presents a summary of the

**Table 1.** Expectations of the Literature.

| Theory | First Wave | Later Wave | Role of Repression |
|---|---|---|---|
| Cycle of protest (Tarrow, 1991, 1993, 1994, 1998) | Early-risers | Latecomers | Repression causes movement radicalization and increases in violent tactics, which then discourages broader participation |
| Social movement spillover (Meyer & Whittier, 1994) | Movement | Subsequent movement (no temporal terminology) | Repression leads activists and organizations to work more closely together |
| Initiator and spin-off movements (McAdam, 1995) | Initiator | Spin-off | Narrowing political opportunities lead to spin-off movements, which respond to cultural opportunities and are less politically successful |
| Sequencing of social movements (Minkoff, 1997) | Early-risers and initiators | Later-entrants | Repression in the form of political opposition limits the diffusion of protest |

expectations of these theories with regard to the timing of social movements in a cycle of protest and the role that repression plays.

Although these perspectives on movement-to-movement transmission are a good starting point, they provide limited assistance in understanding the actual effects that political repression has on social movements within a cycle of protest. Accordingly, this paper traces the ways that protest changes during a particular cycle of protest as the political opportunities constrict. In the pages that follow, I present the case of the globalization movement in the United States since September 11, 2001.

*Political Context and Shifting Political Opportunity since September 11th*

After the September 11th attacks on the United States in 2001, politics and political opportunity for collective action in the United States changed significantly. On October 7, 2001, the United States began military strikes in Afghanistan. On the following day, President Bush signed an executive order to establish the Office of Homeland Security. The office was created to "develop and coordinate the implementation of a comprehensive national strategy to secure the United States from terrorist threats or attacks" (Bush, 2001). Later that month, on October 26th, the Patriot Act was signed into law. In an overview provided by the American Civil Liberties Union, it reported: "many sections of this sweeping law need proper checks and balances to protect our constitutional freedoms."[5] The Center for Constitutional Rights (2002) summarized the effects of this Act on everyday people living in the United States: "From the USA PATRIOT Act's over-broad definition of domestic terrorism, to the FBI's new powers of search and surveillance, to the indefinite detention of both citizens and non-citizens without formal charges, the principles of free speech, due process, and equal protection under the law have been seriously undermined" (p. 1). In other words, the new powers awarded to the government through the Act have affected how Americans can legally criticize the government and protest its practices.

Of particular consequence to collective action in the United States, the Act broadly defines "domestic terrorism" so that it includes many activities that have been used by activists to protest. In addition, through the Act, the American government has expansive powers to investigate anyone who is engaging in what it defines as domestic terrorism.[6] Thus, the rights afforded those criticizing the American government have become limited while the potential risks to protesters have increased.

Data for this paper were collected from protests that took place since the implementation of the Patriot Act and before and after the United States began its military campaign in Iraq.[7] By looking at participation in large-scale protests over time since September 11th, we are able to explore the role that the shifting political climate in the United States played on social movements within this cycle of protest. As such, we can observe the changes in the cycle of protest as social movements in the United States respond to the increasingly repressive government that provides narrowing political opportunities. In particular, my analysis will focus on the priorities of the protesting populations at these events and how they are similar and different. The remainder of the paper is separated into three parts: first, I outline how and where the data were collected; second, I present the analyses of the data; and third, I discuss the implications of my findings to understanding cycles of protest and the relationship between social movements in America today.

# DATA AND METHODS

Data were collected through a two-stage process: random surveying of protest participants at five large-scale protest events in the United States since
September 11, 2001, and an Internet follow-up survey with those in the
original sample who were willing to participate. Initially, data were collected
by randomly surveying participants at five large-scale protests held from
February 2002 to August 2004. All five protests were legally permitted rallies
in outdoor public places and were large gatherings of broad coalitions of
organizations as well as unaffiliated activists and others who joined the protest. All the demonstrations took place on weekend days to maximize citizen
participation.[8] Three of the protests were chosen because they were seen as
the most important globalization protests in the United States during this
time period according to the globalization movement itself.[9] The other two
protests included one of the most important antiwar protests in the United
States, which was part of an internationally coordinated day of protest
against the War in Iraq,[10] and one of the largest protests against the policies
of the Bush Administration, which was scheduled to coincide with the Republican National Convention (RNC) in summer 2004.[11] By including data
from these five protest events, we are able to explore the shifting focus of
social movements within this cycle of protest and examine the commonalities
among the protesting populations and their grievances over time. While
surveying protesters at each of these protest events, subjects were asked if
they would be willing to participate in a follow-up Internet survey. Data
from both stages of this project are included in the analysis. Each stage will
be discussed in detail below.

*Random Survey of Protest Participants at Large-Scale Protest Events*

First, protesters were randomly surveyed at five large-scale protests held in
the United States since the September 11th attacks on the United States.
Survey participants were chosen using a field approximation of random
selection at the demonstrations. Starting from different points across the
field site, field surveyors "counted off" protesters standing in a formal or
informal line, selecting every fifth protester to participate. Because field
situations varied, random selection was achieved at some events by choosing
every fifth person standing in a line to enter a rally area and, at others, by
choosing every fifth person in a line or row as determined by the researcher
working in a particular area.

The survey was designed to be short and noninvasive, so as to facilitate data collection in the field and encourage the widest possible participation among the demonstrators. It includes six short questions that are designed to elicit responses that can easily be coded into categories regarding how the respondent came to be participating in the protest. Beyond survey data collected from protesters, data on the protest events were collected through pamphlets, fliers, and other materials that were distributed by the organizers of each protest. In addition, media coverage of each protest was monitored, along with the websites of the coordinating coalitions of each protest, and the movement news websites (such as Indymedia.org).

### Protests Surveyed

Data from five large-scale protests that took place in the United States from February 2002 to August 2004 are included in this paper: (1) the Another World is Possible March at the 2002 World Economic Forum, New York City; (2) the A20 Stop the War at Home and Abroad/Mobilization for Global Justice at the spring 2002 meetings of the World Bank/IMF, Washington, DC; (3) the Mobilization for Global Justice at the fall 2002 meetings of the World Bank/IMF, Washington, DC; (4) the International ANSWER Antiwar protest in Washington, DC in April 2003; and (5) the World Says No to the Bush Agenda March on the Eve of the RNC in New York City in August 2004.

Overall, 2,230 demonstrators were sampled. Of the sample, 2,036 – or 91.3% – agreed to participate in the survey. In total, 194 people refused to take the survey, representing an overall refusal rate of approximately 9%. Using data collected from field notes, media accounts, and protest materials provided by organizations that were involved with the protests studied, each of the five protests will be briefly summarized in turn.

*The Another World is Possible March at the World Economic Forum, New York City.* The World Economic Form (WEF) is a meeting of invited global elites ranging from heads of state to heads of the world's largest corporations. As described by Ben Wright (2002) of the BBC, "the Forum is meant to be a sort of town hall meeting for the world's movers and shakers, a place where Colin Powell can mingle with German trade unionists and Archbishop Desmond Tutu can swap ideas with the president of Coca-Cola." Held annually in Davos, Switzerland, the WEF was moved to New York for the 2002 meeting as a gesture of support for the City after the attack on the World Trade Center. Similar to the meetings of the World

Trade Organization, World Bank, and the IMF, the WEF has become an annual opportunity for globalization protesters to voice grievances against corporate globalization as well as other global concerns such as labor conditions, AIDS, and environmental degradation. According to Another World is Possible (AWIP), a coalition of more than 100 social movement organizations that organized the protest, the purpose of the 2002 WEF protest was to "tell the 'Masters of the Universe' that they don't have the answers to our problems. Join us in the streets as we visualize solutions that build a better world where the people are in control."[12]

On Saturday, February 2, 2002, approximately 7,000 people gathered for a rally at the southeastern corner of Central Park to protest the WEF and to march to the Waldorf-Astoria hotel where the meeting was being held (Sanger, 2002, p. A1). All interested organizations and individuals were invited to participate. Although groups that practiced varying action forms were invited to join the protest, the organizers asked that participants honor their request that the protest be completely nonviolent and exclude direct action, or in the parlance of globalization demonstrations, they asked for a "green" demonstration. In the words of a flyer that was handed out at the demonstration: "many local activists would prefer not to alienate our local heroes (i.e. police and fire fighters) right now, especially since so many of them are feeling screwed by the same system we are protesting" (AWIP flyer, 2002). Because the protests that had been scheduled to take place during the 2001 fall meetings of the World Bank/IMF had been canceled in response to the September 11th attacks on the United States,[13] this demonstration, which aimed to protest the practices of the World Economic Forum, was the first large-scale organized protest to take place in the United States after September 11. Even with the plea for a nonviolent demonstration from the protest organizers, 38 people were arrested during the Saturday protest (Sanger, 2002, p. A1).

Protesters were surveyed at the rally prior to the march. Surveyors entered the rally site from the four corners of Grand Army Plaza, on Fifth Avenue between 59th and 60th Streets, where the rally was taking place. Researchers completed 316 surveys with participants from four countries. Twenty-seven people refused to answer questions and one person did not complete the full survey.

*The A20 Stop the War at Home and Abroad/Mobilization for Global Justice at the Spring Meetings of the World Bank/IMF, Washington, DC.* Since the 1999 protests against the World Trade Organization in Seattle, the spring joint meetings of the World Bank/IMF in Washington, DC had also become an annual gathering of globalization protesters. During the spring meetings in April 2002, globalization protesters were joined by activists calling for peace in Palestine as well as by activists calling for peace "at home and abroad."

On Saturday, April 20, 2002, protesters who were part of the A20 coalition to "Stop the War at Home and Abroad," gathered at the Sylvan Theater, an outdoor stage in the shadow of the Washington Monument.[14] A20 protesters clustered in groups preparing for the march while listening to lectures and musicians who were performing on the stage. When the march began, the A20 protest participants were joined by other demonstrators, who had been organized by International ANSWER (Act Now to Stop War and Racism). The march was described as a blend of "teenage anti-capitalists with black bandannas over their faces marching alongside Muslim mothers wrapped in traditional headdress and pushing baby strollers alongside campus peace activists" (Fernandez, 2002; see also Kaplan, 2003). From researchers' observations and media reports, it appeared that participants in the Palestine rally/antiwar component of the protest far outnumbered the globalization protesters. Perhaps as a result, this protest lacked the direct action component seen at the Another World is Possible March and was generally uneventful with respect to arrests and vandalism. The mainstream media reported local police estimates of the crowd at 50,000–70,000 (Fernandez, 2002).

Surveys were conducted at the Sylvan Theater prior to the march, and alongside the A20 and Mobilization for Global Justice feeder marches. Researchers surveyed 177 participants, none of whom reported traveling from outside the United States to participate in the protest. Twenty-four people refused to participate in the survey.

*Mobilization for Global Justice at the Fall Meetings of the World Bank/ IMF, Washington, DC.* Like the spring meetings of World Bank/IMF, the fall meetings have also become an annual gathering of globalization protesters. The locations of the fall meetings rotate and the 2002 meetings were held in Washington, DC on September 28 and 29. Many of the same characteristics, messages, and organizing principles of that spring's A20 protest were used during the fall protest. On Saturday, September 28, 2003, participants in the Mobilization for Global Justice rally gathered at the Sylvan Theatre and then marched to the World Bank/IMF headquarters where the meetings were being held. Protesters voiced concern on a number of issues including reducing third world debt, corporate power, AIDS, environmental degradation as well as the war with Iraq.

Attendance for the protest fell far short of the 20,000 expected with crowds estimated from 3,000 to 5,000 people (Reel & Fernandez, 2002). As a result of direct action taking place on the Friday prior to the protest, which involved the breaking of windows at a Citibank building and the arrest of 649 people (Fernandez & Fahrenthold, 2002), there was a very large and highly publicized police presence. In the words of Reel and Fernandez (2002, p. C4), "swarms of police may have kept some protesters away" (see also Andrews, 2002). In fact, rumors spread throughout the rally prior to the march that busses of protesters were being held outside the city. Despite the reduced attendance and the earlier unrest, the protest was generally festive with speakers and musicians performing on the Sylvan stage prior to the march.

As with the A20 protest, demonstration participants were surveyed at the Sylvan Theatre prior to the march. The research team surveyed 730 participants from 11 countries, with 83 people refusing the survey. It is important to note that the number of people who were surveyed at this event is much higher than for any of the other demonstrations included in this paper. In fact, protest participants from this event represent about a third (36%) of the total number of protesters surveyed. This high number is the result of a large research team attending the protest and not attributable to the size of the overall protesting population at this event. In order to ensure that the data from this protest do not bias the paper's overall findings, the majority of data analyses are presented by protest event.

*International ANSWER March on Washington in Spring 2003*. On Saturday, April 12, 2003, protesters came to Washington, DC to participate in a day of protest against the war in Iraq. The protest was coordinated with events taking place in San Francisco, Los Angeles, Seattle, and cities around the world (Fernandez & Perlstein, 2003). It was the third to take place in the four weeks since the war in Iraq had begun on March 19, 2003. The protest was organized by International ANSWER to coincide with the spring meetings of the World Bank/IMF. In so doing, the organizers expected members of the globalization movement to come to Washington and participate in the antiwar event scheduled on Saturday, as well as the globalization-focused event that was scheduled for Sunday. The protest began with a rally in Freedom Plaza at 14th Street and Pennsylvania Avenue, NW and ended with a march to the Justice Department. With the media reporting the fall of Baghdad during the week prior to the protest and television stations broadcasting images of the Iraqi people tearing down a statue of Saddam Hussein in the middle of Baghdad (Dobbs, 2003), turn-out at the event was lower than expected and the protesters adjusted their focus to be the U.S. *occupation* of Iraq.

During the march, protesters also stopped outside the FBI to express their dissatisfaction with policies included in the Patriot Act. They chanted: "tapping our phones, reading our mail – the FBI should go to jail" (Fernandez & Perlstein, 2003). The *Washington Post* reported that the protest was relatively peaceful, with no protesters being arrested and local police estimates of the crowd at 30,000 (Fernandez, 2003). Surveys were conducted on Freedom Plaza prior to the march and while protesters were lining up to begin marching. Researchers entered the Plaza from its four corners and surveyed 424 participants, one of whom was from Canada. Twenty-five people refused to participate in the survey.

*The World Says No to the Bush Agenda March on the Eve of the Republican National Convention.* On Sunday, August 29, 2004, United for Peace and Justice coordinated what they called an "impassioned, peaceful, and legal march" in protest of the Bush Administration's policies.[15] This legal march was the cornerstone of a week of protest organized by a coalition of organizations that mobilized activists to protest the Bush Administration and its policies.[16] Prior to the event, the protest received national attention when the New York Mayor's office denied the organizers their request to rally in Central Park. This refusal to permit access to a common site of protest in New York City, ostensibly to protect the grass on the Great Lawn, was perceived by many activists as "free speech and not the grass being trampled" (McFadden, 2004).

The march was endorsed by groups that focused on a diversity of issues, including peace and globalization as well as Iraq Veterans Against the War, Military Families Speak Out, and the group September 11th Families. It also included participation from antiwar, civil rights, labor, feminist, and environmental groups.[17] While critics of the protest tried to link it with the Democratic Party, many organizations involved in the protest had also protested the Democratic National Convention in Boston. In addition, the Kerry campaign "distanced itself from the protests" that were organized during the Republican Convention (Mishra & Robertson, 2003).

On the United for Peace and Justice's Website, they explained that the purpose of the march was to protest political repression. In the words of its website: "Democracy begins with an absolute commitment to the rights and civil liberties of all ... we march for peace, we march for justice .... Another world is possible!"[18] Beyond clearly stating that the march was intended to protest the repressive political environment, the organizers also invoked one of the main slogans of the global justice/globalization movement.

Even though the New York State Supreme Court ruled against United for Peace and Justice's bid to rally in Central Park, people came out in droves. Attendance at the march was very high, with United for Peace and Justice estimating the crowd at 500,000 people (McFadden, 2004). Although a papier maché dragon was ignited as it passed in front of Madison Square Garden, the march was relatively peaceful. Even though there were widespread expectations that the protest would turn violent, the police reported that only about 200 people were arrested during the march (McFadden, 2004).

Surveys were conducted with participants as they queued up to march on the cross streets between 5th and 9th Avenues from 14th to 21st Streets in Manhattan. Researchers entered the holding area and began surveying protesters at its four corners.[19] During the march, surveys were also conducted with participants as they marched up 7th Avenue to Madison Square Garden. In all, 454 participants were surveyed, with seven people reporting that they had come from outside the United States to participate. Forty-one people refused to participate in the survey.

### Internet Follow-Up Survey of Protest Participants

All protesters who participated in the first stage of the study and agreed to be contacted via e-mail about the follow-up Internet survey were contacted. The follow-up web-based survey included questions about the protesters' involvement in multiple social movements, which large-scale protest events and days of protest that they had attended, and what particular issues motivated them to participate in social protest. Overall, approximately three-quarters of those protesters initially surveyed at the five-protest events agreed to provide an e-mail address and expressed interest in participating the follow-up component of the study. Of those people who provided e-mail addresses, 334 people – or 22.3% – participated in the follow-up survey. The follow-up response rate varies from 16.7 to 31.7%.[20] Although the overall response rate is not as high as some studies that employ Internet surveys (for a full discussion see Porter & Whitcomb, 2003; see also Cho & LaRose, 1999 for a full discussion of the role of trust in Internet survey response rates), it is consistent with the limited number of studies that have used this method to understand participation in social movements (e.g. Allen, 2000; Park, 2003). The sample of respondents to such a Web-based Internet survey are likely to be biased somewhat toward the more affluent and well-educated protest participants (e.g. Hewson, Laurent, & Vogel, 1996). Even with this limitation, however, as participants in social protest have become increasingly tentative about being studied, the technology of the Internet provides a unique opportunity to gain additional information from the protest participants who were randomly surveyed at demonstrations. Because the Internet

***Table 2.*** Summary of Protest Participants Surveyed.

| | Another World is Possible | A20 | Mobilization for Global Justice | International ANSWER | The World Says "No" to the Bush Agenda |
|---|---|---|---|---|---|
| | New York, February 2002 | Washington, April 2002 | Washington, September 2002 | Washington, April 2003 | New York, August 2004 |
| Reported attendance | 7,000 | 50,000–70,000 | 3,000–5,000 | 30,000 | 500,000 |
| Participants initially surveyed | 317 | 177 | 730 | 399 | 413 |
| Refusal rate (%) | 9.8 | 7.8 | 11.4 | 5.9 | 9.0 |
| Percentage providing e-mail addresses (%) | 72.2 | 87.0 | 64.0 | 75.1 | 76.5 |
| Participants in follow-up survey | 38 | 26 | 85 | 84 | 101 |
| Follow-up response rate (%)[a] | 16.7 | 16.9 | 18.2 | 28 | 31.7 |

[a]Percentage is calculated based on those participants who provided their e-mail addresses to participate in the follow-up Internet survey.

allows a person to be contacted without his or her identity being known,[21] it is likely that participants at these protest events were more comfortable providing an e-mail address, rather than a phone number or mailing address. Table 2 presents an overview of the protests included in this paper, along with the numbers of people originally surveyed at each protest event and the response rate for the follow-up survey.

# RESULTS

As has been previously discussed, these five protest events provide a sample of protests that took place during the period after September 11 when the

U.S. government was implementing repressive policies that limited the ability of its citizens to express their dissatisfaction with the government. In fact, prior to the RNC protest, the *New York Times* reported police officials plans to use an army of "police officers to deter violence" during the protest and had identified "about 60 people as militants, some of whom were arrested for violent acts in past protests," whom they were investigating prior to the event at the end of August (Archibold, 2004). As can be seen by the overview of the protest events studied, the targets of the protests had moved away from global justice to the practices of the Bush Administration, focusing on different aspects of its "War on Terror."

Even with this shift in target, however, the organizers of the protests continued to employ the global justice frame to mobilize participants. At every event, protesters could be heard chanting slogans made popular by the globalization movement, such as "Another World is Possible." Also, all of these protests continued to employ the repertoire made popular during the earlier protests of the globalization movement: at all of these events, some participants dressed in costumes, carried puppets, and the protests created an atmosphere that included festive street theater (for a discussion see Wood, 2004).[22] During the RNC protest, this technique was innovated, with the so-called "Billionaires for Bush" joining the March, as well as protesters dressed as pallbearers carrying "a thousand mock coffins of cardboard draped in black or in American flags" (McFadden, 2004).

The consistency of the collective action frame employed and the tactics used suggests that these movements are, indeed, related and part of the same cycle of protest. The question that remains, however, is: what happened to those people who were participants in the globalization movement and, to what degree, did they spillover into the movement to protest the Bush Administration in post 9/11 America? In the analysis that follows, I will present data collected from the protest participants at these five large-scale protest events since September 11 to answer questions and discuss how these findings help us to understand movement-to-movement transmission during a period of heightened political repression in the United States.

*How Engaged are these Protesters Overall*

Overall, most protesters who participated in the follow-up survey were very engaged, with the average protester reporting having attended an average of about ten protests in last two years. Table 3 presents the numbers of protests attended by participants at each protest event. Although participants at all

***Table 3.*** Number of Protests Attended in the Past Two Years.

| | Another World is Possible | A20 | Mobilization for Global Justice | International ANSWER | The World says "No" to the Bush Agenda |
|---|---|---|---|---|---|
| | New York, February 2002 | Washington, April 2002 | Washington, September 2002 | Washington, April 2003 | New York, August 2004 |
| Minimum | 1 | 1 | 1 | 1 | 1 |
| Maximum | 150 | 50 | 101 | 100 | 50 |
| Mean | 22 | 12 | 12 | 13 | 5 |

of these protest events were very engaged and had participated in numerous protests in the past two years, those who were originally surveyed at the RNC protest had participated in significantly fewer protest events. In fact, they were half as engaged, averaging only about five protests in the past two years. Although the maximum protests attendance reported by RNC protest participants was the same as that for the A20 March in 2002, the mean for those at the RNC protest was much lower. In other words, the protesting population at this event was less engaged in protesting overall. This finding suggests that participants at the RNC protest were less radical in terms of their being protest "regulars," attending multiple protests over time.

## What did they Protest?

These protesters were very engaged in protesting multiple social issues. In fact, participants at these events came out to protest what Meyer and Whittier (1994) call a "'laundry list' of demands. Broad issues ... have pulled together groups from diverse movements including the peace, women's, anti-intervention, gay and lesbian, and AIDS movements" (p. 290). In other words, participants in these large-scale protest events were not single-issue protesters; they were active in many different political issues and reported protesting multiple social causes. The top-four issues that the protest participants reported protesting in the past two years were peace, globalization, civil rights, and the environment.

Peace was a priority for protesters at all of the events since September 11, 2001: overall, 92% of the protest participants reported participating in protests that were about peace.[23] Even though the cycle of protest began

with the globalization movement, fewer and fewer protest participants reported attending protests that were about globalization. At the A20 March
in spring 2002, where the focus was on globalization *and* stopping the war at
home and abroad, only about three-quarters of the protesters reported attending protests about globalization. By spring 2003, after the war in Iraq
had begun, less than 40% of the protest participants at the International
ANSWER March reported attending protests about globalization, despite
the fact that the march was scheduled to take place on the same weekend as
the protests at the spring meetings of the World Bank-IMF. More recently,
at the RNC protest in summer 2004, less than 20% of the protesters reported attending protests about globalization. It is also worth noting that,
with the increasingly repressive political environment in America during this
period of time, about a third of the protesters at each event reported attending protests about civil rights, which would certainly include protests
about civil liberties and components of the Patriot Act. Table 4 summarizes
these responses.

### Participation in the Globalization Movement

Even though the globalization movement seemed to retreat after September
11, 2001, in terms of protest participants who reported protesting globalization in the past two years, many of the participants in these protest events
had been relatively active in the globalization movement. Table 5 lists the
percentages of respondents from each protest event who had participated in
some of the most well-known protests of the globalization movement *prior*
to September 11, 2001. Because most respondents were originally surveyed
at protests taking place on the East Coast of the United States, it is
not surprising that the respondents reported the highest levels of protest

*Table 4.*   What Subjects were the Foci of Protesters' Protest?.

|  | Peace | Globalization | Civil Rights | Environment |
| --- | --- | --- | --- | --- |
| Another World is Possible (%) | 92.1 | 97.4 | 42.1 | 50 |
| A20 (%) | 100 | 76.9 | 42.2 | 38.5 |
| Mobilization for Global Justice (%) | 94.1 | 92.9 | 30.6 | 31.8 |
| International ANSWER (%) | 92.9 | 36.9 | 25.0 | 15.5 |
| The World Says "No" to Bush (%) | 88.1 | 18.8 | 33.7 | 28.7 |
| All Five Protests (%) | 92.2 | 55.7 | 32.3 | 29.3 |

***Table 5.***   Attendance at Major Globalization Protests.

|  | Another World is Possible (%) | A20 (%) | Mobilization for Global Justice (%) | International ANSWER (%) | The World Says "No" to the Bush Agenda (%) |
|---|---|---|---|---|---|
| Seattle, November 1999, WTO | 2.6 | 3.8 | 4.7 | 0 | 4.7 |
| Washington, DC, April 2000, World Bank-IMF | 26.3 | 15.4 | 23.5 | 11.9 | 1.0 |
| Washington, DC, January 2001, Presidential inauguration | 36.8 | 11.5 | 16.5 | 16.7 | 5.9 |
| Quebec, Canada, April 2001, Summit of the Americas | 15.8 | 3.8 | 5.9 | 2.4 | 2.0 |
| Washington, DC, April 2001, World Bank-IMF | 23.7 | 38.5 | 24.7 | 10.7 | 4.0 |
| Washington, DC, September 2001, Anti Capitalist Convergence/March against War and Racism | 21.1 | 46.2 | 32.9 | 21.4 | 2.0 |

attendance at events in that region. Also not surprising is the fact that participants at the first three protests, which directly targeted aspects of globalization, were more active in the globalization movement overall. Participants at the International ANSWER protest in April 2003 were less involved in earlier globalization protests, but still had attended a number of these well-known events. In fact, about a fifth of the participants at this event reported participating in the march associated with the Anti-Capitalist Convergence in Washington, DC in fall 2001, right after the September 11 attacks on the United States. Participants at the RNC protest in August 2004 reported even lower attendance at these large-scale globalization protests, with less than 10% reporting having attended any of these major globalization events.

These data suggest that participants at the protests that specifically targeted the Bush Administration's policies had dwindling interest and involvement in the globalization movement. However, to get a better sense of the proportion of the participants at these protests who *had* been involved in the globalization movement at some time, we must look at those who reported protesting globalization *together with* those who reported attending a major globalization protest prior to September 11, 2001. Combining the results of these two questions will provide clearer evidence of the degree to which the globalization movement spilled over to the movement against the War on Terror. Table 6 summarizes the comparison of responses to these

**Table 6.**   International ANSWER Protest Participants' Involvement in the Globalization Movement.

| Reported Protesting the Issue of Globalization | Reported Being at a *Major* Globalization Protests | |
|---|---|---|
| | No | Yes |
| No | 40 | 13 |
| | 47.6% | 15.5% |
| Yes | 13 | 18 |
| | 15.5% | 21.4% |

**Table 7.**   RNC Protest Participants' Involvement in the Globalization Movement.

| Reported Protesting the Issue of Globalization | Reported Being at *Major* Globalization Protests | |
|---|---|---|
| | No | Yes |
| No | 70 | 12 |
| | 69.3% | 11.9% |
| Yes | 11 | 8 |
| | 10.9% | 7.9% |

questions for participants in the International ANSWER protest in April 2003. Although only about a fifth of the participants at this protest reported attending at least one of the most well-known globalization protests before September 11 *and* reported attending protests that were mainly about globalization, when I also include those participants who attended any of the biggest globalization protests *or* who reported attending protests that were mainly about globalization, the percentage of the protest participants who had been involved in the globalization movement increases to over half (52.4%). In other words, these data suggest that there was significant spillover from the globalization movement to this stage in the anti-Bush movement.

Table 7 summarizes the same comparison of responses to these questions for participants in the RNC protest in August 2004. Here, only about 8% of the protest participants had reported attending any of the most well-known globalization protests prior to September 11 *and* reported attending protests that were mainly about globalization. When I incorporate those respondents who attended at least one of the biggest globalization protests *or* and those who reported attending protests that were mainly about globalization in the past two years, the percentage of participants at this event who had been involved, to some degree, with the globalization movement increases to about a third (30.7%). Although the participants in the RNC protest remain less involved in the globalization movement, these results suggest that about a third of them had changed the target of their protesting from globalization to the policies of the Bush Administration.

## DISCUSSION AND CONCLUSION: ENDING THE CYCLE OF PROTEST?

In sum, the results from this paper support the notion that, in the wake of increasing political repression after September 11, 2001, the globalization movement retracted and a movement emerged to target the Bush Administration's War on Terror. Although initially these movements seem to be relatively disconnected, data collected from protest participants at five large-scale protest events after September 11 show that there was significant overlap in the participants at these protests events. Thus, these findings support the claim that there was movement-to-movement transmission from the globalization movement to the anti-Bush movement.

Upon first glance, this shift in movements seems to support Meyer and Whittier's (1994) statement that "as a movement [such as the globalization movement] shifts into abeyance on one set of issues, its personnel and organizations may switch the grounds of the challenge to another set of issues" [such as targeting the Bush Administration's policies] (p. 279). But, based on my analysis of the protest events after 9/11, the globalization movement does not seem to have shifted into abeyance. Rather, activists involved in this movement shifted their targets based on their perceptions of narrowing political opportunity.

In addition, although the relationship between these movements provide an example of what Meyer and Whittier (1994) would call the ways that the "ideas, tactics, style, participants, and organizations" spilled over from one movement to another (p. 277), these data do not support the authors' expectation that these movements were "allied, but separate, challenges" (p. 278). In fact, the organizers of the more recent protests against the War on Terror consistently employed the global justice frame to mobilize those activists who were involved in the globalization movement and get them involved in the movement to protest the Bush Administration's policies. United for Peace and Justice, the organizer of the RNC protest, even lists global justice as one of its six major campaigns. The organization produced a statement paper on "How Globalization Promotes War" to appeal to members of the globalization movement and mobilize them to participate in protests against the war on terror.[24]

Upon closer consideration, these findings are actually more consistent with McAdam's (1995) work, which finds that, as political opportunities narrow, spin-off movements emerge that respond to the political inopportunity. In this case, as the political climate changed after September 11, a movement emerged to protest the policies of the Bush Administration and the initiator movement – the globalization movement – became less active. Even though it became *less* active, however, these data show that many members of the initiator movement were involved in the spin-off movement. In addition, it is clear that the movement against the Bush Administration's War on Terror adapted the tactics and collective action frames that were originally designed within the context of the globalization movement.

Although these data do support the notion that these movements were all part of a single cycle of protest, they do not support Tarrow's expectation that cycles of protest will radicalize over time (e.g. Tarrow, 1991, 1998). In fact, the RNC protest experienced neither more radicalized protest forms, nor was there increased violence,[25] many protest participants reported coming out for such mainstream reasons as to support the Left and the Democratic Party. The lack of violence at the largest of these large-scale protests is particularly interesting given the "fears of explosive clashes with the biggest security force ever assembled in New York" (McFadden, 2004). In addition, data collected from these protest events do not support Minkoff's (1997) prediction that repression in the form of political opposition will limit the diffusion of protest, at least not in the short term. Nonetheless, given the decline in social protest since President Bush was reelected and the Republican majorities were upheld in both houses of the US Congress in 2004, Minkoff's claim may still be correct. Even with the on-going War on Terror, which involves American soldiers being killed on a regular basis, protest has significantly decreased. In fact, this more recent decline in protest activity may suggest that on-going political opposition in the form of a reelected Republican Administration and Congress can halt the sequencing of social movements and, perhaps more important, it can end a cycle of protest.

The findings of this study of movement-to-movement transmission in the face of political repression suggest the need for future research to focus on three main areas. First, future research must examine the conclusions of cycles of protest and test the claim that the cycle of protest that began with the globalization movement has ended. Second, future research should study how political repression of other types and in other cultural contexts affects movement-to-movement transmission. Third and finally, in order to understand movement-to-movement transmission more clearly, future research must look at the specific connections between initiator and spin-off movements. Without understanding more specifics of cycles of protest and the movements therein, we will never be able to understand how repression affects collective action.

# NOTES

1. The globalization movement is often termed the "antiglobalization movement," particularly by the popular media. As Graeber (2001, p. 12) has observed, the expressions "globalization movement" and "antiglobalization movement" are often used interchangeably despite the fact that the movement has benefited from globalization per se, that many within the movement call for "globalization with a human face," "globalization from below" (Brecher, Tim, & Brendan, 2002) and the "globalization of people and ideas" (Hardt & Negri, 2000) and that the term "antiglobalization" is one many within the movement have "never felt comfortable with" (Graeber, 2001, p. 12). I will use the term "globalization movement" in favor of the alternatives.

2. This term includes the wars in Afghanistan and Iraq as well as the perceived war against civil liberties in the United States.

3. More recently, Tarrow (1998) has renamed "cycles of protest" to be "cycles of contention." Because I am focusing particularly on social protest and in order to maintain consistency within this paper, I will refer to work mainly as "cycles of protest."

4. In some cases, however, Tarrow notes that increased violence can lead to terrorism and/or revolution (Tarrow, 1998, p. 150; see also Tarrow, 1991; Tilly, 1993; Goldstone, Gurr, & Moshiri, 1991; for a case of extreme repression, see Almieda's (2003) work on protest waves under authoritarian regimes).

5. See action.aclu.org/reformthepatriotact/primer.html (accessed on November 11, 2005).

6. For more information see www.aclu.org/NationalSecurity/NationalSecurity. cfm?ID = 11437&c = 111 (accessed on November 11, 2005).

7. The official beginning of the campaign was March 19, 2003.

8. All of the protest events took place on a Saturday except the World Says No to the Bush Agenda Protest before the Republican National Convention, which took place on Sunday, August 29, 2004.

9. Protest.net and Indymedia.org list protests at international economic summits, such as the World Economic Forum and the annual World Bank/IMF meetings, as among the most important international demonstrations.

10. International ANSWER, which coordinated this protest, reported concurrent demonstrations taking place in 60 countries on this day (for an archive of the call for the event and its endorsements, see iacenter.org/archive2003/a12_endor4.htm (accessed on November 11, 2005)).

11. In fact, this protest was said to be the largest in New York City since the 1982 antinuclear rally in Central Park (McFadden, 2004).

12. See www.artistsnetwork.org/news2/news98.html (accessed on October 4, 2004).

13. Although the larger protest was canceled, as were the meetings of the World Bank/IMF, the simultaneously scheduled Anti-Capitalist Convergence was not canceled and an estimated 2000 people attended the Convergence in Washington and participated in the March Against War & Racism that weekend.

14. For the remainder of this paper, I will refer to this protest in the same manner as its organizers, as the "A20," which was so named because it took place on the 20th of April.

15. www.unitedforpeace.org/article.php?id = 1810 (accessed on November 11, 2005).

16. Because it was organized to coincide with the beginning of the RNC and is best known as the largest protest during the Convention, for the remainder of this paper, I will refer to this protest at the "RNC Protest."

17. For a list of "member groups," see www.unitedforpeace.org/article.php?list = type&type = 27 (accessed on November 14, 2005).

18. www.unitedforpeace.org/article.php?id = 1810 (accessed on November 8, 2005).

19. Researchers began surveying at 5th Avenue and 9th Avenue on 14th Street and 5th Avenue and 9th Avenue on 22nd Street.

20. The variance in follow-up response rates can be explained, to some degree, by the difference in time between when protest participants were originally surveyed and when they received e-mails asking them to participate in the follow-up survey. Protesters at the International ANSWER protest and the United for Peace and Justice March, which had higher follow-up response rates, received e-mails the week following the protest to participate in the follow-up survey. Owing to constraints in acquiring Human Subjects approval for the follow-up component of the study, participants in the earlier follow-up surveys were not contacted as quickly.

21. Many protest participants provided e-mail addresses that were not traceable to their names and/or places of work.

22. To see a call for such street theater at the 1999 WTO protest in Seattle, see www.infoshop.org/octo/wto99_1.html (accessed on November 15, 2005).

23. Most of these protests, however, were framed as being "antiwar" instead of pro-peace.

24. www.unitedforpeace.org/downloads/Globalization_and_War.pdf (accessed on June 15, 2004).

25. Although 200 people were reported arrested during the RNC protest, they represent less than 0.04% of the estimated protest participants.

# ACKNOWLEDGMENTS

I would like to thank all of the sociology students who helped collect data at the multiple protest events. Also, I would like to thank the Contentious Politics Workshop at Columbia University and three anonymous reviewers for comments on earlier drafts of this paper. Research for this project was supported, in part, by the United Nations University Institute of Advanced Studies.

# REFERENCES

Allen, L. D., II (2000). Promise keepers and racism: Frame resonance as an indicator of organizational vitality. *Sociology of Religion, 61*(1), 55–72.

Almeida, P. D. (2003). Opportunity organizations and threat-induced contention: Protest waves in authoritarian settings. *American Journal of Sociology, 109*(2), 345–400.

Ancelovici, M. (2002). Organizing against globalization: The case of ATTAC in France. *Politics & Society, 30*(3), 427–463.

Andrews, E. L. (2002). World financial officials back new debt framework. *The New York Times*, September 28, p. A6.

Archibold, R. C. (2004). Anarchists emerge as the convention's wild card. *The New York Times*, August 20, p. A1.

Atwood, D. C. (1997). Mobilizing around the United Nations special sessions on disarmament. In: J. Smith, C. Chatfield & R. Pagnucco (Eds), *Transnational social movements and global politics* (pp. 141–158). Syracuse, NY: Syracuse University Press.

Ayres, J. M. (2001). Transnational political processes and contention against the global economy. *Mobilization, 6*(1), 55–68.

Ayres, J., & Tarrow, S. (2002). The shifting grounds for transnational civic activity. Retrieved 28 January 2002, from www.ssrc.org/sept11/essays/ayres.html

Bandy, J., & Smith, J. (Eds) (2004). *Coalitions across borders: Transnational protest and the neoliberal order*. Lanham, MD: Rowman & Littlefield Publishing Group.

Boli, J., & Thomas, G. M. (1999). *Constructing world culture: International nongovernmental organizations since 1875*. Stanford, CA: Stanford University Press.

Brecher, J., Tim, C., & Brendan, S. (2002). *Globalization from below: The power of solidarity* (2nd ed.). Cambridge, MA: South End Press.

Buechler, S. M. (1990). *Women's movements in the United States: Woman suffrage, equal rights, and beyond*. New Brunswick, NJ: Rutgers University Press.

Bush, G. W. (2001). Executive order establishing office of homeland security. Retrieved 11 November 2005, from www.whitehouse.gov/news/releases/2001/10/print/20011008-2.html

Center for Constitutional Rights (2002). The state of civil liberties: One year later. Retrieved 11 November 2005, from www.ccr-ny.org/v2/reports/docs/Civil_Liberities.pdf

Cho, H., & LaRose, R. (1999). Privacy issues in Internet surveys. *Social Science Computer Review, 17*(4), 421–434.

Cortright, D., & Pagnucco, R. (1997). Limits to transnationalism: The 1980s freeze campaign. In: J. Smith, C. Chatfield & R. Pagnucco (Eds), *Transnational social movements and global politics* (pp. 159–174). Syracuse, NY: Syracuse University Press.

della Porta, D., & Tarrow, S. (Eds) (2004). *Trananational protest & global activism*. Lanham, MD: Rowman & Littlefield Publishers, Inc.

Dobbs, M. (2003). After the fall of a Tyrant, An uneasy climb out of chaos. *The Washington Post*, April 10, p. C1.

Evans, S. M. (1980). *Personal politics: The roots of women's liberation in the civil rights movement and the new left*. New York: Vintage Books.

Fernandez, M. (2002). Demonstrators rally to Palestinian cause; Arab Americans, supporters drown out other issues. *The Washington Post*, April 21, p. A1.

Fernandez, M. (2003). D.C. Braces for weekend of rallies. *The Washington Post*, April 11, p. B1.

Fernandez, M., & Fahrenthold, D. A. (2002). Protests oroduce very few problems; hundreds arrested in rally's 1st day. *The Washington Post*, September 29, p. C1.

Fernandez, M., & Perlstein, L. (2003). Marchers bring new signs, same passion; war protesters, Bush supporters rally in Washington. *The Washington Post*, April 13, p. A25.

Fisher, D. R., Stanley, K., Berman, D., & Neff, G. (2005). How do organizations matter? Mobilization and support for participants at five globalization protests. *Social Problems*, *52*(1), 102–121.

Gamson, W. A. (1992). *Talking politics*. New York: Cambridge University Press.

Goldstone, J. A., Gurr, T. R., & Moshiri, F. (1991). *Revolutions of the late twentieth century*. Boulder: Westview Press.

Graeber, D. (2001). The globalization movement: Some points of clarification. *Items*, *2*(3–4), 12–14.

Guidry, J. A., Kennedy, M. D., & Zald, M. (2001). *Globalizations and social movements: Culture, power, and the transnational public sphere*. Ann Arbor: University of Michigan Press.

Hardt, M., & Negri, A. (2000). *Empire*. Cambridge, MA: Harvard University Press.

Hewson, C., Laurent, D., & Vogel, C. M. (1996). Proper methodologies for psychological and sociological studies conducted via the Internet. *Behavioral Research Methods, Instruments, and Computers*, *28*, 186–191.

Kaplan, E. (2003). A hundred peace movements bloom. *The Nation*, January 3, pp. 11–16.

Korey, W. (1998). *NGOs and the universal declaration of human rights: A curious grapevine* (1st ed.). New York: St. Martin's Press.

McAdam, D. (1995). Initiator' and 'spin-off' movements: Diffusion processes in protest cycles. In: M. Traugott (Ed.), *Repertoires and cycles of collective action* (pp. 217–239). Durham, NC: Duke University Press.

McCarthy, J. D., & Zald, M. (1977). Resource mobilization and social-movements – partial theory. *American Journal of Sociology*, *82*(6), 1212–1241.

McFadden, R. D. (2004). Vast anti-Bush rally greets republicans in New York. *The New York Times*, August 30, p. A1.

Meyer, D. S., & Tarrow, S. G. (1998). *The social movement society: Contentious politics for a new century*. Lanham: Rowman & Littlefield Publishers.

Meyer, D. S., & Whittier, N. (1994). Social movement spillover. *Social Problems*, *41*, 277–298.

Minkoff, D. C. (1997). The sequencing of social movements. *American Sociological Review*, *62*(5), 779–799.

Mishra, R., & Robertson, T. (2003). Crowd protest as GOP gathers hundreds of thousands march against Bush, war. *The Boston Globe*, August 30, p. A1.

Morris, A. D. (1984). *The origins of the civil rights movement: Black communities organizing for change*. New York: Free Press.

O'Brien, R., Goetz, A. M., Scholte, J. A., & Williams, M. (2000). *Contesting global governance: Multilateral economic institutions and global social movements*. Cambridge, UK: Cambridge University Press.

Park, E. (2003). *'Net' profit of the nonprofits: The effect of the Internet on social movement mobilization and participation*. Dissertation thesis, Cornell University, Ithaca.

Porter, S. R., & Whitcomb, M. E. (2003). The impact of contact type on web survey response rates. *Public Opinion Quarterly*, *67*(4), 579–588.

Reel, M., & Fernandez, M. (2002). Protesters' momentum weakens. *The Washington Post*, September 29, p. C1.

Risse-Kappen, T. (1995). *Bringing transnational relations back in: Non-state actors, domestic structures, and international institutions*. New York: Cambridge University Press.

Rothman, F. D., & Oliver, P. E. (1999). From local to global: The anti-dam movement in Southern Brazil, 1979–1992. *Mobilization: An International Journal, 4*(1), 41–57.

Sanger, D. E. (2002). Economic forum shifts its focus to new dangers. *The New York Times*, February 3, p. A1.

Smith, J., Chatfield, C., & Pagnucco, R. (Eds) (1997). *Transnational social movements and global politics: Solidarity beyond the state*. Syracuse: Syracuse University Press.

Smith, J. G., & Johnston, H. (2002). *Globalization and resistance: Transnational dimensions of social movements*. Lanham, MD: Rowman & Littlefield.

Snow, D., & Benford, R. (1992). Master frames and cycles of protest. In: A. D. Morris & C. M. Mueller (Eds), *Frontiers in social movement theory* (pp. 133–155). New Haven: Yale University Press.

Snow, D., Rochford, E. B., Jr., Worden, S. K., & Benford, R. D. (1986). Frame alignment processes. *American Sociological Review, 51*, 464–481.

Tarrow, S. (1993). Cycles of collective action: Between moments of madness and the repertoire of contention. *Social Science History, 17*(2), 281–309.

Tarrow, S. (1998). *Power in movement: Social movements and contentious politics* (also section from 1994 edition). Cambridge: Cambridge University Press.

Tarrow, S. (2001). Transnational politics: Contention and institutions in international politics. *Annual Review of Political Science, 4*, 1–20.

Tarrow, S. G. (1991). *Struggle, politics, and reform: Collective action, social movements and cycles of protest*. Ithaca, NY: Center for International Studies Cornell University.

Tarrow, S. G. (1994). *Power in movement: Social movements, collective action, and politics*. Cambridge, England: Cambridge University Press.

Tarrow, S. G. (2005). *The new transnational activism*. New York: Cambridge University Press.

Tilly, C. (1978). *From mobilization to revolution*. MA: Addison-Wesley.

Tilly, C. (1986). *The contentious French*. Cambridge, MA: Belknap Press.

Tilly, C. (1993). *European revolutions, 1492–1992*. Oxford, UK and Cambridge, MA: Blackwell.

Tilly, C. (2004). *Social movements, 1768–2004*. Boulder, CO: Paradigm Publishers.

Traugott, M. (1995). *Repertoires and cycles of collective action*. Durham: Duke University Press.

Valocchi, S. (2001). Individual identities, collective identities, and organizational structure: The relationship of the political left and gay liberation in the United States. *Sociological Perspectives, 44*(4), 445–467.

Wood, L. (2004). *The diffusion of direct action tactics: From Seattle to Toronto and New York*. Unpublished Ph.D. dissertation, Columbia University, New York.

Wright, B. (2002). WEF: New York's big deal. *BBC News*, February 1. Retrieved October 4, 2004, from news.bbc.co.uk/1/hi/business/1795521.stm

Zald, M. N., & McCarthy, J. (1980). Social movement industries: Conflict and cooperation among movement organizations. In: *Research in social movements, conflicts and change* (Vol. 3, pp. 1–20). Greenwich, CT: JAI.

# ORGANIZATIONAL EXPANSION, LIBERALIZATION REVERSALS AND RADICALIZED COLLECTIVE ACTION

Paul D. Almeida

## ABSTRACT

*The paper addresses a core question in the literature on states and political challenges from excluded social classes: how is large-scale collective action possible against repressive governments in the global periphery? Using the case of El Salvador's 1932 peasant-worker uprising, the paper contributes to theories of organizational expansion and radicalization in nondemocratic settings. The case study suggests that periods of regime liberalization deposit organizations in civil society that persist beyond the political opening in the system. Combining historical materials with logistic regression and hierarchical linear modeling (HLM), it is found that the political threats constituting liberalization reversals provide negative incentives for surviving reform-minded organizations to attempt revolutionary forms of collective action in more hostile political environments.*

Politics and Globalization
Research in Political Sociology, Volume 15, 57–97
Copyright © 2007 by Elsevier Ltd.
ISSN: 0895-9935/doi:10.1016/S0895-9935(06)15003-2

# INTRODUCTION

The paper elaborates a sequential framework of collective action suitable to authoritarian contexts and addresses the conditions associated with El Salvador's January 1932 rebellion. The 1932 peasant-worker insurgency and subsequent state-sponsored massacre serve as major events in Central American history as well as defined the future of modern state-civil society relations in El Salvador. The mass uprising still stands as one of the largest in scale in Latin America during the global depression of the 1930s. The rebellion involved thousands of peasant and worker participants who attempted to occupy several towns in western El Salvador and take over key army barracks and National Guard posts. The state-sponsored massacre that followed (known as "la matanza") was also one of the greatest single acts of human rights violations witnessed in the Western Hemisphere in the past century (Monteforte Toledo, 1972, p. 124) – killing over 1 percent of the national population. Fifty years later, the insurgent rebels and death squads in El Salvador's civil war of the 1980s named themselves after key protagonists of the events of 1932 (e.g., the insurgents' western front "Frente Francisco Sánchez" and the para-military's "Maximiliano Hernández Martínez anti-communist brigade") (Ching, 1998). Moreover, the largest oppositional political party in contemporary El Salvador (Farabundo Martí Front for National Liberation (FMLN)) takes it title from one of the alleged plotters of the 1932 rebellion – Agustín Farabundo Martí.

This article analyzes the period in El Salvador between 1925 and 1932. The episodes of popular unrest in this era provide a chain of events found in other nondemocratic contexts, but underdeveloped in prevailing political sociology and social movement theories – an authoritarian regime attempts to liberalize the political system and then abruptly reverses these efforts. Hence, the objective of this study is to contribute to explanations of the emergence of radicalized collective action under the unlikely conditions of a regime moving onto a more authoritarian trajectory. I employ both historical and quantitative analysis to examine the relationship between regime change and forms of popular contention.

# STATE-MOVEMENT DYNAMICS IN NONDEMOCRATIC POLITICAL SETTINGS

Nondemocratic governments in most times and places decrease the potential for social movement activity because of restricted access of the citizenry to state institutions, the lack of political and associational freedoms, and the heavy penalties incurred for trying to obtain such rights (Johnston & Mueller, 2001; Schock, 2005). In fact, most authoritarian states are constructed in such a fashion as to prevent independent collective action by civil society (Osa, 2003; Johnston, 2005). Nonetheless, excluded social groups have at times overcome these obstacles and launched successful mobilization campaigns in an effort to alter the prevailing structure of power, push for new advantages, or defend existing benefits. Below, I examine the case of popular rebellion in El Salvador in the late 1920s and early 1930s to better specify the conditions that increase the likelihood of mass mobilization materializing and the form it takes in nondemocratic political settings.

## REGIME LIBERALIZATION AND ORGANIZATIONAL EXPANSION

For states in the capitalist periphery, ruling elites may decide to liberalize the polity under conditions of sustained economic growth, especially before the current wave of global democracy promotion (Robinson, 1996). During much of the twentieth century, economic growth in Third World nations was directly tied to global market prices for the few primary commodities they exported (Paige, 1975). Favorable international economic conditions grant state managers in the capitalist periphery a slightly greater sense of autonomy by loosening political restrictions and responding more to popular grievances. In such circumstances, the state retains more resources to address pressing social and economic issues as well as use the opportunity to gain a greater level of mass legitimacy.

Political liberalization periods in authoritarian regimes are analogous to the widening of political opportunities as described in democratic regimes (Tarrow, 1998). The expansion of political opportunities in nondemocratic polities creates more favorable conditions for the founding and expansion of secondary associations and civic organizations (i.e., trade unions, professional associations, and cooperatives) via a diminution in governmental repression, formal certification, and state promotion of competitive elections. These three specific opportunities roughly match the core components of opportunity structure in the synthetic reviews of McAdam (1996) and Tarrow (1998) in terms of their discussions of declining repression, institutional access, and electoral realignments. When these liberalizing conditions appear at the same time and reinforce each other in nondemocratic regimes, they act as "system wide" opportunities (Meyer & Minkoff, 2004) with the potential to produce a wave of collective action by several groups. First, however, students of collective action should think sequentially about the process of widening opportunities and its specific contribution to organizational expansion in civil society for mass dissent to even materialize in authoritarian settings.

A relaxation in state repression signals to organizational entrepreneurs outside of the polity that their efforts in establishing new collectivities have a better chance of survival (Markoff, 1996; Tilly, 2004). Lifting martial law, freeing political prisoners, and enacting new social welfare policies are all indicators that the state is easing its authoritarian grip on civil society. Formal state certification of emergent civic organizations provides a key incentive for civil society activists to continue organization-building efforts. With formal recognition or registration, the government acknowledges the civic organization as a legitimate entity to operate and mobilize within its territorial jurisdiction and reduces the probability that it will be repressed or liquidated. With their newly acquired legal status, civic organizations increase the likelihood of gaining new benefits and advantages in subsequent rounds of collective action (Goldstone & Tilly, 2001; Amenta & Caren, 2004). Hence, a relaxation in state coercion and institutional access "facilitate" the emergence of organization building and joint action (Kriesi, Koopmans, Duyvendak, & Giugni, 1995, pp. 38–39).

Another condition associated with regime liberalization and an expansion of political opportunity in authoritarian settings is a move toward more competitive elections (Markoff, 1996). Tilly (1978) contends that by convoking a series of multi-party elections national governments generate a shielding umbrella for a variety of civic groups to organize themselves beyond strictly electoral concerns. Even holding successive local elections sends a strong message to civil society that the regime tolerates reform efforts and it may be a propitious time to establish and expand civic organizations. Moreover, in regions with a recently consolidated nation-state, local elections may be more meaningful to the citizenry than national elections, with the struggle for municipal control, power, and authority as a greater motivator for civic action and grievance adjudication. Hence, a nondemocratic regime that begins to liberalize via competitive elections on a national scale will likely positively influence civic organization expansion within civil society.

The formation of a field of civic organizations encouraged by these regime liberalization practices greatly expands the scale of potential political mobilization. Gould's (1995) work on nineteenth century Parisian popular insurgencies contributed to resource mobilization perspectives by noting that one of the most important functions of formal organizations (e.g., associations, social clubs, labor unions, cooperatives, educational institutions, etc.) in relation to collective action is to greatly extend the range of collective identity formation – well beyond what would be possible for groups limited by informal organizational ties (e.g., single neighborhood, village, workplace, etc.). This scale expansion is made possible by the greater level of mutual awareness and shared recognition that organizations supply by connecting previously isolated groups to one another that are experiencing similar circumstances. The ability of civic groups to make successful mobilization appeals across regions and sectors hinges largely on the degree of organizational connectedness between the units of the identity in question. In Oberschall's (1973, p. 119) resource mobilization model, sustained resistance by challengers, as opposed to short-term outbursts or momentary riots, requires the erection of such an organizational base along either communal or associational lines – especially for instrumental and politically oriented movements (Kriesi, 1995). Once collective actors develop organizational assets, they retain access to a fungible resource infrastructure that may be appropriated for a variety of purposes (Edwards & McCarthy, 2004).

In brief, periods of regime liberalization may include three system wide political opportunities: (1) a relaxation in repression (e.g., freeing political prisoners, lifting martial law, etc.); (2) increasing legal recognition of civic organizations; and (3) a growing competitiveness in the electoral arena. These nationally based state gestures act as mutually reinforcing conditions for groups in civil society to expand organizational capacities in specific localities and establish a field of interacting civic associations (Minkoff & McCarthy, 2005). In stable democratic political settings, there is likely more of a direct relationship between political openings and upsurges in collective action (Soule, McAdam, McCarthy, & Su, 1999). In authoritarian and transitioning regimes in the global periphery, civil society must first develop an organizational base before popular movement activity can be sustained.

Liberalization periods more likely eventuate in nonviolent forms of contention led by newly founded or greatly expanded civic organizations that make claims for new advantages and/or to deepen democratic reforms (Kriesi et al., 1995, p. 39). This was the pattern of civil society opposition reported for the final years of Perestroika in the former Soviet Union and Eastern Europe (Fish, 1995; Bunce, 1999; Mueller, 1999) as well as for democratic transitions in Brazil and Chile in the 1980s (Hipsher, 1998). As common as these sequential episodes of regime liberalization, civil society formation, and democratic transition may be, social movement scholarship is less informed about the process of *liberalization reversals* whereby the state rolls back political freedoms and attempts to repress the newly created civic organizations (Tilly, 2003).

## LIBERALIZATION REVERSALS: THE THREATENING AUTHORITARIAN POLITICAL ENVIRONMENT

When states reverse liberalization policies by taking away basic rights and suppressing the political opposition, they potentially risk radicalizing civic organizations and their memberships leftover from the preceding liberalization period. These new negative conditions encroaching into the political environment act as threats to organized civic groups. *Threats* are defined as conditions or incentives that will make groups worse off if they fail to mobilize (Tilly, 1978; Goldstone & Tilly, 2001).[1] The multi-dimensional concept of threat is the underdeveloped corollary to political opportunity (McAdam, Tarrow, & Tilly, 2001, pp. 42–43). Instead of the probability of gaining new advantages driving collective action via expanding political opportunities, it is the perception of current benefits being taken away that acts as the incentive for new rounds of mobilization (Goldstone & Tilly, 2001; Van Dyke & Soule, 2002; Almeida, 2003; Van Dyke, 2003; Jenkins & Form, 2005). These negative incentives may occur during downturns in the world economy – such as when international commodity prices fall for poor countries that depend on favorable prices for foreign exchange and to meet their balance of payments obligations (Fearon, 1979). Two important forms of threat that seem most important in catalyzing mass mobilization include economic threats and political threats, which can arise when regimes reverse earlier liberalization reforms.

*State-attributed economic threats*: When organized groups convincingly attribute responsibility to specific agents for a decline in their economic conditions they may initiate campaigns to resist unwanted changes (Klandermans, 1997, pp. 17–18; Van Dyke & Soule, 2002; Javeline, 2003; Snow, Soule, & Cress, 2005). The expansion of the nation-state as the chief regulator of economic life and vital resources makes it a common target for redress of deteriorating economic conditions – even globally induced ones. Specific state-attributed economic problems in the global periphery include land access (Wickham-Crowley, 1992), basic price increases (Goldstone, 1986; Goldstone, 2001; Osa, 2003), and mass unemployment (Iñigo, Carrera, &

Cotarelo, 2001).[2] These economic grievances may increasingly become politicized under authoritarian regimes when the state itself is viewed as incapable or unwilling to ameliorate the issue (Goodwin, 2001).

In the developing world, when state-sponsored agro-export policies fail to institute substantive agrarian reform or alleviate mass unemployment problems during global economic slumps, incentives increase for organized groups to mobilize defensive campaigns. For example, in Argentina between 1997 and 2002, state-initiated structural adjustment programs combined with economic recession to unleash a nation-wide movement of unemployed workers (*los piqueteros*). Organized by pre-existing neighborhood groups, oppositional political parties, and church parishes, the principal actions of the *piqueteros* include highway roadblocks until the government agrees to provide short-term job programs (*los planes trabajar*) in the affected communities (Oviedo, 2001). By the late 1990s and early 2000s, more *piquetero* roadblocks than labor strikes were registered in the country. In a related case, Almeida (2002) documented that state-initiated fiscal austerity policies fueled a wave of mass action throughout Latin America between the late 1990s and early 2000s. In sum, state-attributed economic problems experienced directly in the immediate lives of well-networked groups may be a threat incentive to join in resistant collective action. Even though state-attributed economic problems increase the probability of heightened protest among organized actors, the form of contention will likely only become more radicalized and violent when combined with the political threats of an erosion of basic rights and escalating state repression.

*Erosion of rights and state repression*: After a period of extending civil rights and regime liberalization, taking away voting and the freedom to assemble obstruct the conventional avenues of political participation.[3] Alternative nonconventional political strategies and organizations appear much more attractive under these circumstances (Amenta & Young, 1999). When competitive elections are canceled or special states of emergency decreed, the government announces the shutting down of the polity on a national scale and calls into question its institutional credibility. This conveys a strong message to civic organizations that the state as an audience and adjudicator to reform-type demands is greatly restricted (if not outright hostile). State managers maintain greater incentives to shut down political openings during economic recessions and depressions in order to cut off channels for redistributive demands from excluded social groups. Such authoritarian state behavior would also likely be reinforced and supported by agro-export elites and capitalist class factions connected to the international economy that view popular demands from below as a zero-sum game (Paige, 1975).

Over time, challengers will likely use their in-place organizational infra-structure to form revolutionary-type organizations and radicalize surviving civic organizations in order to seek political influence.[4] Unaccountable state managers who are popularly perceived as no longer even making pretenses of acting under the rule of law encourage more militant forms of popular demands and protest, while petitioning authorities through routine conflict resolution channels appears ineffective (Jenkins & Bond, 2001). Such sce-narios create a widespread crisis in normative political behavior, opening the way to mass disruption and collective political violence as alternate strat-egies to exercise political power for challenging groups.

Research on the impacts of state repression on mobilization finds evidence for both deterring and escalating effects (Lichbach, 1987). These contra-dictory findings divide into three general predictions for the effect of re-pression on collective action: (1) deterrence; (2) escalation to some threshold point and then declining; and (3) a positive "backlash" result. Political opportunity versions of the political process model generally view repression as a deterrent to collective action (Rule, 1988, p. 176). The deterrent view is consistent with a relaxation in state repression acting as a core opportunity motivating collective action in a liberalizing political environment. Another literature on the relationship between governmental coercion and mass dis-sent predicts a curvilinear effect (an inverted U-curve or parabola), with moderate levels of state repression increasing protest and high levels deter-ring it (Gurr, 1970; Brockett, 1993; Opp, 1994). Other studies predict a "backlash" effect (Francisco, 1995; Beissinger, 2001) with high levels of repression increasing protest behavior (Olivier, 1991; Khawaja, 1993; Rasler, 1996), including government massacres of civilians (Francisco, 2005). A number of empirical studies outside of advanced industrialized democracies have demonstrated *positive* effects of state repression on the level of popular contention (Goodwin, 2001; Jenkins & Schock, 2004; Almeida, 2005; Francisco, 2005; Schock, 2005). The incentives for such an effect include moral outrage (Wood, 2003) and regime delegitimation. Coercive state behavior also breaks publicly held beliefs of expected state–civil society relations in obvious and powerful ways – especially when the repressive acts are way out of proportion to the type of demands and claims protesters pursue (Goldstone, 1998).

Activists can use state repressive acts as empirical verifications of the unworthiness of state managers to rule as well as for motivational appeals within organizations to participate in future protest actions. These organ-izational settings provide solidary incentives, shared activist identities, and normative pressures to engage in high-risk protest (Gould, 1995; Kim &

Bearman, 1997). In both curvilinear and backlash models, state repression, as erosion of rights, also pushes well-networked challengers into more radical forms of organization and dissent as repeated outrageous acts of state violence convince challengers that a fundamental reorganization of the state and society are desirable goals (Goldstone, 1998). That is, state-sponsored violence and fundamental rights violations against regime challengers changes the character of mass dissent toward more disruptive or coercive tactics and revolutionary-oriented goals. In sum, the radicalization of civic organizations conditioned by an erosion of rights and state repression will create the potential for revolutionary-type collective action.

## THEORETICAL SUMMARY

The framework outlined above addresses a gap in social movements research: how mass collective action takes place in oppressive settings in the global South where political opportunities are in short supply or frozen by renewed authoritarian state practices. Liberalization efforts (including incomplete efforts) initiated by state managers and political elites leave civil society organizations intact in particular localities that may persist into the post-liberalization era. In other words, periods of regime liberalization and widening political opportunity produce a "glacier effect" by depositing organizational sediment on the political landscape and then receding. State-attributed economic threats and the political threats associated with liberalization reversals (erosion of rights and state repression) act as incentives for the communities organized during the political opening to launch new rounds of collective action in a much more hostile political environment. Organized localities will attempt to hold back the rising tide of renewed dictatorial rule. State-initiated repressive measures increasingly radicalize the goals and forms of collective action of erstwhile reformist groups, increasing the potential for mass insurgency in organized regions. In the following analysis, I show that organizations were crucial to the emergence of radicalized collective action under an increasingly repressive regime in El Salvador in the early 1930s.

## METHODS

The study employs both qualitative and quantitative analysis of the sequencing of mass mobilization and its forms to analyze the case of popular revolt in El Salvador during the global depression. I draw on primarily historical materials to first examine the rise of regime liberalization, the formation of a civil society organizational infrastructure and a reformist wave of contention, followed by the reversal of regime liberalization. I then use quantitative methods (logistic regression and hierarchical generalized linear models) to explain the geographical variation in radical revolt during El Salvador's January 1932 mass uprising. Social movement scholars have repeatedly noted that theory is especially underdeveloped in explaining mobilization dynamics in lesser-developed countries (McAdam, McCarthy, & Zald 1996, pp. xii–xiii; Meyer, 2002, p. 17; McAdam et al., 2001). The case study approach is a useful method to identify conceptually important issues not accounted for in prevailing theories (Prechel, 2000, p. 9). In particular, I use a sequential analysis of opportunity (i.e., regime liberalization) and threat to demonstrate how popular mobilization occurs under conditions of a regime reversing liberalization practices in the global capitalist periphery. Using this particular case should contribute to the "refining or extending movement-related theoretical arguments or conceptualizations" (Snow & Trom, 2002, p. 161).

## ANTECEDENTS TO POLITICAL LIBERALIZATION (1885–1927)

For five decades (1885–1927), interlocking elite family clans with large landholdings politically dominated Salvadoran politics (including control of the legislature) (Lindo-Fuentes, 1990; Paige, 1997). However, this governing structure changed in the mid-1920s with the ascendancy of Don Pío Romero Bosque to the presidency. Romero Bosque was a political insider or institutional activist (a brother-in-law of the former President) that decided to break with the dynastic clan system of the Meléndez-Quiñónez families and liberalize the polity. He was appointed president in early 1927 and took power on March 1st. Immediately, Romero Bosque implemented a number of unprecedented political reforms. The most important were: (1) removal of martial law; (2) legalization of labor organizations; (3) labor reforms and institution of labor arbitration courts; (4) university autonomy and legalization of university-based organizations; (5) reducing corruption in local elections in El Salvador's 258 municipalities; and (6) organization and convocation of the first competitive presidential elections (Ching, 1997; Guidos Véjar, 1982). The result of these political reforms included a tremendous growth in the organizational infrastructure of civil society, which witnessed the spread of labor union formation, organizations of urban renters and students, establishment of autonomous political parties, and the organization of peasants.

At the same time, El Salvador had undergone a rapid economic and political shift in the period between 1880 and 1930. This was the epoch when El Salvador securely inserted itself in the world economy as a coffee-exporter (Lauria-Santiago, 1999). Indigenous farming lands in the western departments were privatized by a series of central government decrees in the 1880s and 1890s (Menjívar, 1995, pp. 103–104; Pérez Brignoli, 1995). In the typical fashion of primitive accumulation practices (such as those described by Polanyi (1944) for the case of the English peasantry), many rural communities lost their means of livelihood in subsistence farming (Zamosc, 1989). Particular indigenous villages in western El Salvador launched local rebellions to slow down the pace of the land usurpations (Menjívar, 1995, p. 90). In the end, however, the central state and landed interests clearly gained the upper hand in setting aside the most fertile regions on the western pacific slope for coffee cultivation.[5] The expropriated lands were soon transformed into coffee plantations by elite ladino families. By the 1920s, local capitalists had also created a domestic coffee processing industry. Thus local landed elites, via vertical economic integration, controlled both cultivation and processing for export. The most successful agro-capitalists "controlled the processing, marketing, and export of coffee" (Lauria-Santiago, 1999, p. 228). The newly displaced peasantry, especially indigenous communities, filled the ranks of the rural labor force on the western coffee farms. Coffee exports rose rapidly accounting for up to 90 percent of total export revenues by the 1920s (Wilson, 1970).

Besides this colossal economic shift, the state complemented economic concentration and expansion of coffee by centralizing its administrative apparatus. This was partially accomplished by setting up national guard posts at the municipal level beginning in 1912 (Williams & Walter, 1997). In addition, the central government began to use its official political party – *El Partido Nacional Democrático* (PND) – by the end of the 1910s to control local municipal elections and impede regionally based rebellions, which frequently erupted in the late nineteenth and early twentieth centuries (Ching, 1997). Spanish troops trained the newly created National Guard force. The combined Salvadoran security forces (army, National Guard, and national police) were reportedly the best instructed in the region (Wilson, 1970). This precedent of governmental bureaucratic expansion clearly positioned the Salvadoran state to retain a monopoly of coercive capacity and administrative authority over all other organizations within its territory (Tilly, 1990).

## REGIME LIBERALIZATION: 1927–1930

In 1927, Pío Romero Bosque ascended to the presidency ushering in a period of sustained political liberalization. The broad liberalization mechanisms that Romero Bosque focused on during his presidential tenure included government recognition of civic organizations and local competitive elections. The early years of his presidency also were characterized by a reduction in state repression. Government recognition could be seen in the right to form and legalize labor associations, the subsidizing of labor federations, the formation of labor courts, and university autonomy. In addition, Romero Bosque also lifted a state of siege in April 1927 that had been in place since 1920 (Menjívar, 1982). This particular action allowed much more freedom of movement and association for urban and rural groups until the second half of 1930. This unprecedented political liberalization occurred with a peak in world coffee prices, El Salvador's number one export commodity (see Fig. 1) (Williams, 1994).

In 1928, Romero Bosque established an Office of Labor that allowed urban groups to form and expand labor-based associations and unions as well as strike. Labor unions officially registered with governmental bodies permitting them greater organizational legitimacy in the eyes of state managers. The Romero Bosque government reportedly provided a monthly subsidy to the largest labor organization – the *Federación Regional de Trabajadores* (FRT) – of up to $1,000 and annually sent the Federation salutatory "Happy New Year's" greeting cards until 1930 (Ching, 1997; Ching, 1998). Don Pío Romero Bosque also permitted the first competitive elections at the municipal and executive levels of government.

Romero Bosque worked most arduously in changing the structure of local and presidential elections. Competitive municipal elections took place during the month of December in 1927, 1929, and 1930 (Ching, 1997). In January 1931, Arturo Araujo, a labor reformist, won the first competitive presidential elections in the history of El Salvador. However, Araujo's presidency lasted less than a year, when military officers overthrew his elected government in early December of 1931. In the short period from 1927 through mid-1930, the liberalization program created a marked growth in labor, civic, and educational organizations.

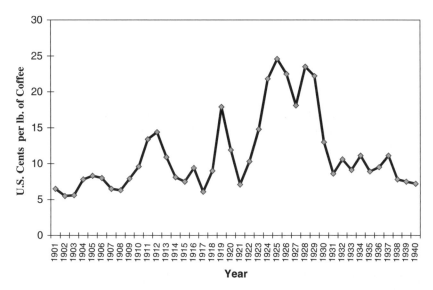

*Fig. 1.* World Market Price for Coffee, 1901–1940. *Source:* Williams, 1994.

## ORGANIZATIONAL INFRASTRUCTURE 1927–1930

The dynastic governance system of Meléndez-Quiñónez (1913–1927) did allow the formation of state-connected organizations before Romero Bosque's reforms, such as the *Ligas Rojas* ("Red Leagues") (Alvarenga, 1996) and mutual aid associations of urban workers based on trade or craft between 1918 and 1927. However, these groups organized along clientilist lines and mobilized largely for staged election campaigns. The *Ligas Rojas* formed from existing craft associations and indigenous-based Catholic fraternal orders (*las cofradías*). The government feared autonomous labor organizing so much that they placed guards outside the first labor union federation conference in Armenia, Sonsonate in 1918. The labor congress, nonetheless, established the *Confederación de Obreros de El Salvador* (COES) ("Workers Confederation of El Salvador").

By the early 1920s, more union organizations emerged as opposed to mutual aid associations. In 1922, the labor federation *Unión Oberera Salvadoreña* (UOS) ("Salvadoran Workers Union") was established with 35 affiliated labor organizations. In 1924, COES and UOS briefly fused together.

Most importantly, In that same year the *Federación Regional de Trabajadores* (FRT) ("Regional Federation of Workers") formed on September 21st. The FRT would become the single most important organizational unit connecting various groups to push for political and economic reforms in the late 1920s. The FRT linked labor-based organizations throughout western El Salvador stretching from Lake Ilopango to Ahuachapán and Santa Ana, which border neighboring Guatemala (see Fig. 2). By the end of the 1920s, the liberalizing regime tolerated (if not actively encouraged) a wave of organizational activity by FRT militants.

Guidos Véjar (1982, p. 143) maintains that the 1927–1930 period created an unprecedented "civil society" in El Salvador. In 1929, for example, the FRT registered 42 organizations in 5 of El Salvador's 14 departments. Fig. 2 displays the municipalities with FRT labor organizations reported in December of 1929. By the end of 1931, a high-estimate reports that the FRT had 75,000 members, which would have represented 10.6 percent of the economically active population at the time (Menjívar, 1985, p. 74). Salvadoran organized labor would not reach this level of union density again until the 1970s (Montes, 1984). The real organizational take off point appears to be in the 1927–1930 period, which coincided with Romero Bosque's liberalization program. The FRT used its newly acquired legal protection to begin organizing rural workers in the western departments between 1927 and 1931 (Elam, 1968; Alvarenga, 1996; Gould & Lauria-Santiago, 2004).

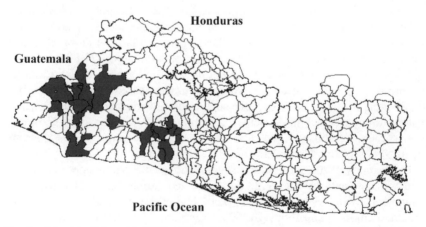

*Fig. 2.*   Municipalities with FRT Affiliated Organizations, December 1929 (Shaded).

Already, between 1924 and 1927, the FRT reportedly held seven strikes (Ching, 1997). Between 1927 and 1930, activists coordinated several orderly and nonviolent protest campaigns (see Fig. 3). These included urban strikes, petitions, street marches, and boycotts against exorbitant electricity prices, bus fares, and housing rents (Guidos Véjar, 1982). Also, another organizational unit affiliated with the FRT that appeared in these years – the *Universidad Popular* – provided educational and cultural seminars by sympathetic university students and intellectuals to workers and peasants throughout western El Salvador. An organization of urban renters (*Liga de Inquilinos*) was formed in 1929 that grew nearly to the size of FRT (*Ibid.*).[6] The FRT created a communicative structure through its newspaper – *El Martillo* – and the use of pamphlets for popular education, especially allegorical drawings in the rural sector given the high illiteracy rates among the peasantry (Larín, 1971, p. 139; Martínez, 1987; Ching, 1995).

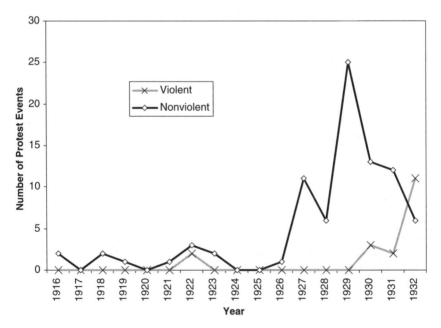

*Fig. 3.* Nonviolent and Violent Protest Events, 1916–1932. *Source:* La Prensa (1916–1932). Protests were defined as three or more people in civil society making claims on the government or economic elites. Violent protests were coded as actions that damaged property or harmed people.

The early FRT chapters organized themselves as largely craft-based associations (e.g., bakers, shoe makers, construction workers, barbers, public transport workers, carpenters, tailors, etc.). FRT affiliates outside of the larger western towns of Ahuachapán, Santa Tecla, San Salvador, Santa Ana, and Sonsonate recruited largely rural workers and maintained regular interaction with peasant groups (Kincaid, 1987; Alvarenga, 1996; Gould & Lauria-Santiago, 2004). Using pre-existing organizational ties in the *cofradías* (Catholic-based brotherhoods in indigenous communities), the FRT was able to quickly wield organizational influence in some of the most densely populated indigenous towns and villages of Sonsonate Department in western El Salvador (Kincaid, 1987). The forms of protest from the period 1927–1930 appear largely to be reformist. Indeed, there is a clear upsurge in nonviolent protest during the years of political liberalization (see Fig. 3). Urban renters demanded cheaper rents and electricity prices, workers in towns demanded the implementation of the eight-hour work day and overtime for working at night. This all began to change in late 1930 with the onset of increasing economic and political threats linked directly and indirectly to the global economic depression. By 1931, the Salvadoran state played the role of "switch operator" (Wickham Crowley, 1989, p. 139) shifting the political environment onto a more threatening trajectory.

## LIBERALIZATION REVERSAL: THE THREATENING POLITICAL ENVIRONMENT, 1930–1932

*State-attributed economic problems*: Already by 1930 in El Salvador, there was a rapid economic decline as the worldwide depression caused a plunge in international coffee prices (see Fig. 1). Coffee served as El Salvador's number one export accounting for between 85 and 95 percent of all export earnings in the late 1920s (Wilson, 1970). By 1931, a growing number of small landholders were becoming dispossessed (up to 28 percent). The presidential election campaign covered most of the second half of 1930, and the leading candidate, Arturo Araujo, elevated land redistribution as a major campaign issue (Marroquín, 1977; Alvarenga, 1996; Gould, 2001). This increasingly made land access a state-attributed economic problem for the land-starved peasantry (Castellanos, 2001). Indeed, within days of taking office in March 1931, Araujo's new residence, the presidential palace in San Salvador, was swarmed by workers and peasants demanding land reform (Anderson, 1971).

In addition, between 1929 and 1931, the wages on coffee plantations plummeted between 50 and 70 percent (Castellanos, 2001; Gould, 2001) and unemployment grew in rural areas throughout the region (Alvarenga, 1996; Ching, 1998) leading to several FRT-sponsored demonstrations headed by jobless workers by mid-1930. For example, on June 25, 1930, a leading daily newspaper reported that a mass mobilization of unemployed workers marched through San Salvador with mini-rallies held at the *Casa Presidencial*, the mayor's office, and the *Palacio Nacional* – hence attributing blame for the unemployment crisis to three levels of government in a single rally. One of the demonstrator's placards stated, "Los Padres de la Patria con medio sueldo en receso y nosotros sin pan" (roughly translated as: "The parliamentary deputies during legislative recess receive half of their salary and we don't even have bread to eat" see *El Día* June 26, 1930, p. 1).[7] By April and May of 1931, even peasants initiated rural strikes and occupations of coffee plantations demanding owed back wages and the end of payments in the form of company store vouchers (Guidos Véjar, 1982).

*Political threats – erosion of rights and state repression*: Between 1927 and 1930, rights were expanding with the legalization of civic associations and labor unions and the unprecedented convocation of competitive municipal elections. There was a rapid retreat in this opening by the end of 1930 with a series of declarations by Romero Bosque prohibiting union assemblies and a state of siege implemented by newly elected president Araujo in 1931. Orderly street protests and other types of public gatherings were now banned (see Table 1). Then, after the military coup in December 1931 that toppled Araujo's civilian presidency, the newly installed General Hernández Martínez's dictatorship cancelled the municipal election results in the first week of January 1932. The new dictator nullified local elections in the municipalities where the newly formed Communist Party had won or was perceived to have won (e.g., Ahuachapán, Turín, Tacuba, Santa Tecla, Sonsonate) (Cuenca, 1962; Anderson, 1971). This act was especially a powerful signal of the end of the last remaining vestiges of the political reforms initiated by Romero Bosque in that it was precisely the municipal elections that acted as the most democratic part of regime liberalization between 1927 and 1930.

The Salvadoran state demonstrated less repressive behavior between 1927 and the first half of 1930. There was comparatively more legal space for civil society groups to organize (e.g., the lifting of the state of siege that had been in place in the previous years). However, by the end of 1930, the intermittent arrest campaigns against labor-based groups and massacres of civilians (e.g., in Santa Ana in 1930) marked a clear increase in state authoritarianism. The

***Table 1.***   Reported Major Acts of Rights Violations and State
Repression against Organized Workers Movement, 1930–1931.

| Date | Location | # Killed | # Injured | # Arrested |
|---|---|---|---|---|
| 8/02/30 | Antiguo Cuscatlán | | | 90 |
| 8/12/30 | Executive decree prohibiting workers' rallies and subversive propaganda | | | 600 |
| 10/30/30 | Executive decree prohibiting all demonstrations by worker or peasant organizations | | | |
| 11/27/30 | Police repress demonstration in Santa Ana | | | |
| 12/21/30 | Police massacre in Santa Ana | 8 | | |
| 2/31 | Police repression in Santa Tecla | 8 | 15 | 80 |
| 5/17/31 | Sonsonate (government massacre of Pacific street march) | 3 | 25 | 65 |
| 5/21/31 | National (law against communist meetings and associations) | | | |
| 8/11/31 | Entire nation (state of siege) | | | |
| 9/22/31 | Asuchillo, Zaragoza, La Libertad (government massacre of rural workers) | 15 | 20 | 14 |

*Source:* Schlesinger (1946); Anderson (1971).

state security forces increasingly persecuted the FRT. Several organizational
meetings, street demonstrations, and coffee plantation strikes were brutally
repressed by the National Guard between mid-1930 and early January 1932
(Alvarenga, 1996). Gould and Lauria-Santiago (2004, p. 229) report that in
August of 1930 alone the National Guard suppressed labor demonstrations
in at least 10 towns in western El Salvador resulting in hundreds of arrests.
Table 1 lists major acts of state repression against the organized workers
movement reported between mid-1930 and 1931.[8]

The growing repressive threats in the early 1930s radicalized the previously reformist FRT. In March of 1930, leaders within the labor movement
and FRT founded a small communist party (El Partido Comunista Salvadoreño (PCS)) with a clandestine ceremony on the shores of Lake Ilopango. The PCS appropriated part of the existing FRT structure to wield
organizational influence (Menjívar, 1985; Ching, 1998). The PCS also created other organizations to assist the politically persecuted, such as the

*Socorro Rojo Internacional* ("International Red Aid") (SRI) and the *Liga Pro-Luchadores de Perseguidos* ("League in Defense of the Persecuted") (LPLP) that mobilized in the 1930–1931 period. These new organizations clearly reacted to the increasingly threatening environment. In early 1930, the FRT convoked a special meeting strongly encouraging each individual affiliate organization to form a separate local branch of the LPLP in their respective municipalities (Schlesinger, 1946). Though there existed internal divisions within the FRT, the PCS faction appears to have become hegemonic in its rivalry with labor reformists and anarcho-syndicalists. As Fig. 2 demonstrates, the FRT organized local chapters in the western municipalities and this is precisely where the PCS and its affiliated organizations, such as the SRI would have growing political influence between 1930 and early 1932 (Schlesinger, 1946; Alvarenga, 1996).

Guidos Véjar (1982, p. 169) reports how these gathering state-attributed threats in the late 1930–1931 period converted reformist contention into more threat-induced episodes of collective action. Demonstrations for new advantages and specific policy changes were increasingly replaced by protests demanding the end of political persecution and the state of siege. For example, on July 4, 1931, posters appeared in the FRT-organized municipalities of Santiago Texacuangos, Ahuachapán, and Sonsonate demanding that the government rescind its recently enacted law prohibiting meetings and public gatherings.[9]

The newly formed communist party of El Salvador was calling for more radical changes and was denied municipal electoral victories in early January 1932. Security forces repressed a number of labor strikes on coffee plantations during this time. These repressive threats against organized workers and peasants culminated in the legendary peasant-worker uprising and massacre of January 1932. During the revolt, workers and peasants attempted to occupy several towns in western El Salvador (see Fig. 4). In general, protest did not become overwhelmingly violent until after the military overthrew the elected government in December 1931 and the nullification of municipal elections in January 1932 (see Fig. 3). Insurgent activities began in early January as rolling strikes on coffee plantations (Gould, 2001) and sporadic protests against the cancellation of the municipal elections (McClintock, 1985). The uprising included an estimated 16,000–30,000 peasants and workers with rudimentary weapons (mostly agricultural instruments and a few small arms) attempting to occupy local municipal governments and attack army and national guard posts (López Vallecillos, 1964). Rebel activity was reported as early as January 10 (when the PCS gave its support for the rebellion (Ching, 1998)) peaking around

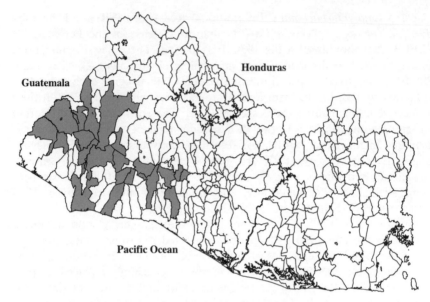

*Fig. 4.* Municipalities Reporting Rebellious Events or Contributing Rebel
Participants, January 10–28, 1932.


January 22, and continued until around January 28 when overwhelming
state repression set in.[10] The popular revolt was brutally crushed by early
February.

Following the uprising of January 1932, a wave of government-backed
violence struck rural and urban El Salvador. The security forces killed between 8,000 and 30,000 people in the weeks following the rebellion. This
makes it one of the largest acts of state-sponsored repression (and human
rights violations) in the twentieth century in the Western Hemisphere
against non-European peoples. The overwhelming majority of massacre
victims were indigenous peasants in the western departments (descendants
of the Nahuatl-speaking Pipil Indians) (making the mass slaughter a
veritable ethnocide). In four municipalities at the center of the rebellion
(Tacuba, Juayúa, Nahuizalco, and Izalco), Montes (1979) estimates that state
security forces and government-armed vigilantes exterminated 28.5 percent
of the total population in the repression that followed the uprising. It was
reportedly the first time that the national guard, police, army, and airforce
used rapid-fire machine gun weaponry and aerial bombardment. Vigilante
squads and government forces dumped hundreds of bodies in hastily dug

collective graves throughout the western towns and villages. During this reign of state-sponsored terror, security forces completely dismantled the organizational infrastructure of the FRT.

## QUANTITATIVE ANALYSIS OF THE 1932 REBELLION

As stated above, the 1932 uprising and massacre served both as one of the largest single acts of popular insurgency and of state repression witnessed in Latin America during the worldwide Great Depression of the 1930s. What is even more perplexing is how the insurgents mobilized and coordinated such a widespread rebellion with relatively few resources and under close surveillance by estate owners and security forces. For example, in the years prior to the uprising, the Salvadoran government organized the National Guard nationwide along bureaucratic lines to prevent the outbreak of rebellions. The following section presents a discussion of the data, methods, and results of a quantitative analysis of the organizational role of the reformist FRT labor groups and acts of state repression in contributing to the 1932 uprising. While the interpretive historical analysis in the previous section demonstrated the sequence of events of regime liberalization, organizational expansion, liberalization reversal, and movement radicalization, it did not explain the precise geographical variation of the 1932 revolt. The analysis of municipal data shows that the organized regions benefiting from regime liberalization and most affected by its subsequent reversal (i.e., via state repression) were the ones most likely to rise up in revolutionary-type revolt in January 1932.

Historical materials are limited for political events in Central America in the 1920s and 1930s. Relevant data were gathered from Salvadoran historiography, the geo-spatial mapping of El Salvador's municipalities, and 1930 census records to model the relationship between pre-existing FRT organizations, state repression, and the January 1932 uprising. The units of analysis are the 258 municipalities, which are equivalent to US counties, embedded in El Salvador's 14 departments at the time of the revolt. A multilevel model predicting the incidence of a municipality-based rebellion in 1932 is also estimated using independent variables at both the municipality and departmental levels.

*Rebellion variable*: The dependent variable is the occurrence of a rebellion in 1932, which is denoted below as R_1932. This is measured as a dummy variable scored 1 if the municipality reported a rebellious event or contributed participants to a rebellion in another municipality between January 10 and 28, 1932, and coded 0 if not. Rebellious events ranged from theft and small-armed attacks to the sustained occupation of towns for several days by hundreds of insurgents. Data on rebellious events were collected and coded from Anderson's (1971)[11] seminal monograph on the revolt and from López Vallecillos (1964).

The independent variables are the following: *FRT labor organization* (FRTPRES) is a level-1 municipality dummy variable scored 1 if the municipality reported the presence of an FRT labor organization in December 1929, and 0 if otherwise. December 1929 was the high point of regime liberalization and the FRT was the major civil society group to expand its organizational reach during this political opening. A second level-1 organizational variable is whether the FRT was in an adjacent municipality (DUFRTBOR); this dummy variable is scored 1 if the municipality was geographically contiguous to a municipality reporting an FRT organization in December 1929, and 0 if not. These data were obtained from Schlesinger's (1946) list of FRT organizations, a source used repeatedly by prominent Salvadoran social scientists and historians (see Larín, 1971; Guidos Véjar, 1982; Menjívar, 1982, 1985; Lungo, 1987). In addition, Schlesinger's list appears to be similar to an independent directory of FRT organizations uncovered by Ching (1998) in an archive on the Salvadoran Communist Party uncovered in a Moscow library in the early 1990s.

Another level-1 independent variable is state repression defined as arrests, injuries, or deaths caused by government security forces on civil society groups between January 1, 1930 and January 4, 1932, as reported by Anderson (1971).[12] These are all observable coercive events initiated by the state (Earl, 2003). Repression was measured as a dummy variable (REPRESS) scored 1 if the municipality experienced at least one act of state repression, and 0 if otherwise. A second state repression dummy variable was constructed for municipalities bordering others that experienced an act of state repression (BOREPRE). Often, state acts of coercion took place during demonstrations or meetings where participants came from neighboring municipalities.

Several other variables were included as controls (population size, concentration of indigenous peoples, and coffee cultivation). Population size (LOGPOP) was measured at the level of the municipality using data from the 1930 census. Owing to outliers, the natural log of population size was used. The percentage of land cultivated in coffee in the 1929–1930 harvesting season (PER_CAFE) was measured at the departmental level[13] and taken from Iraheta Rosales, López Alas, and Escobar Cornejo (1971).[14] Coffee production is an important variable because a large number of participants in the 1932 rebellion are reported to have been laborers on coffee estates. Therefore, regions of relatively higher coffee cultivation should have a greater likelihood of rebellion.

Information on the size of the indigenous population (INDIG) was based on data from the 1930 census. This variable was measured at the departmental level as a percentage of the department's total population. The historiography of the 1932 revolt clearly demonstrates that indigenous groups were key actors in the rebellion, and the epicenter of the revolt, in Sonsonate department, comprised the highest density of indigenous peoples in the country at the time (Montes, 1979; Pérez Brignoli, 1995; Ching, 1998). Since information on coffee production and the indigenous population are only available at the departmental level, their effects on the likelihood of a municipal rebellion are estimated using hierarchical generalized linear modeling (HGLM) techniques (presented in Table 3). Recent reviews of collective action research suggest that scholars apply hierarchical modeling where "societal processes refer to different levels of aggregation" in order to "capture embedded processes" (Jenkins & Form, 2005, p. 348). In this case, municipal-level data on rebellion, labor organizations and state repression are embedded within departmental-level data on indigenous population size and coffee production. The descriptive statistics for all variables used in the quantitative analyses are listed in Table A1 in the appendix.

# RESULTS

In December of 1929, the FRT registered 42 organizations with at least one labor organization in 19 of El Salvador's 258 municipalities (7.4 percent). Between January 10 and 28, 1932, an anti-government disturbance occurred (or contributed rebels) in 24 of the 258 municipalities (9.3 percent). In 14 out of the 24 (58 percent) rebelling municipalities in 1932, an FRT organization was present at the end of 1929. Moreover, 20 of the 24 municipalities participating in the insurgency (83 percent) were geographically adjacent to a municipality with an FRT labor organization. To estimate with statistical precision the contribution of FRT organizations and state repression in predicting the occurrence of rebellion in 1932, two types of multiple regression models are estimated. The first is a logistic regression of a municipal rebellion using only municipality-level independent variables (Table 2). The second is a multi-level (HGLM) logistic regression of a municipal rebellion using both municipal-level and departmental-level independent variables (Table 3).

***Table 2.*** Logistic Regression Model Predicting the Likelihood of a
Municipality Rebelling in 1932.

| Independent Variable | Logit Coefficient | Odds Ratio |
|---|---|---|
| *Regime liberalization organizations* | | |
| FRT labor organization established in municipality (1929) | 2.68** (0.926) | 14.65 |
| FRT labor organization adjacent to municipality (1929) | 0.327 (1.34) | 1.39 |
| *Political threats* | | |
| State repression in municipality (January 1, 1930 to January 4, 1932) | 4.33** (1.44) | 76.12 |
| Municipality adjacent to state repressive event (January 1, 1930 to January 4, 1932) | 2.75* (1.27) | 15.63 |
| *Size* | | |
| Municipality population size | 0.793 (0.487) | 2.21 |
| LR $X^2$ | 102.60*** | |
| Log likelihood | −28.54 | |
| Pseudo $R^2$ | 0.64 | |
| N | 258 | |

*Note:* Standard errors are in parentheses.
*$p \leq 0.05$
**$p \leq 0.01$
***$p \leq 0.001$ (two-tailed tests).

Table 2 reports the results of a logistic regression predicting the likelihood of a municipality experiencing a rebellious event in January 1932 using organizational, state repression, and population size explanatory variables, all measured at the level of the municipality (level 1). To facilitate the interpretation of these effects, the logit coefficients shown in the first column were exponentiated and their odds ratios are reported in the second column. The odds of a municipality experiencing a rebellious event in January of 1932 are almost 15 times greater for those where an FRT labor organization was established at the end of 1929. If an act of state repression occurred in the municipality between 1930 and the first week of January 1932, the odds that an insurgent event connected to the January 1932 uprising occurred in the municipality were 76 times greater than in a municipality without such state repression. In addition, municipalities contiguous to those witnessing state repression had odds of experiencing an insurgent event in 1932 that

**Table 3.** HGLM Logistic Regression Predicting Rebellion Occurrence in January, 1932.

| Independent Variables | HGLM Logit Coefficient | Odds Ratio |
|---|---|---|
| Intercept | $-3.186^{****}$ (0.610) | |
| **Level-1 predictors** | | |
| *Regime liberalization organizations* | | |
| FRT labor organization established in municipality (1929) | $2.651^{***}$ (0.973) | 14.174 |
| FRT labor organization adjacent to municipality (1929) | $-0.763$ (0.963) | 0.466 |
| *Political threats* | | |
| State repression in municipality (January 1, 1930 to January 4, 1932) | $2.887^{***}$ (0.989) | 17.945 |
| Municipality adjacent to state repressive event (January 1, 1930 to January 4, 1932) | 1.342 (1.096) | 3.828 |
| *Size* | | |
| Municipality population size | $0.558^{*}$ (0.305) | 1.748 |
| **Level-2 predictors** | | |
| Percent indigenous in department (1930) | $0.094^{*}$ (0.045) | 1.099 |
| Coffee cultivated in hectares in department (1929–1930) | $0.218^{*}$ (0.109) | 1.244 |

*Note:* Standard errors are in parentheses.
$^{*}p \leq 0.10$
$^{***}p \leq 0.01$
$^{****}p \leq 0.001$ (two-tailed tests).

were 15 times greater than those not contiguous. Thus, Table 2 provides evidence that enduring labor organizations and repressive state behavior contributed significantly to the outbreak of local mass rebellions. These effects were estimated controlling for the population size of the municipalities.

Because there was substantial variation in the level of intensity of rebellions across municipalities, an additional test was conducted predicting the potency of the local uprisings. In this model only the 81 municipalities within the 5 western departments that experienced a rebellious event (Ahuachapán, La Libertad, Santa Ana, Sonsonate, and San Salvador) were included as the units of analysis. Ordered logistic regression was used to predict the level of rebellion intensity using the municipality-level independent variables shown in Table 2. Intensity of the 1932 rebellion was measured with an ordinal coding scheme ranging from 0 to 2. Municipalities reporting no rebellious activity were scored 0. Those reporting small-armed attacks, sabotage, arson, and robbery were scored 1. Those reporting larger armed attacks on National Guard and army posts and/or sustained occupations of towns by rebels were coded 2. The results were very similar to those shown in Table 3 with FRT labor organization and state repression positively associated with the intensity of municipal rebellions at less than the .05 level of significance.[15]

In order to examine the role of organizational perseverance and state repression in explaining the 1932 uprising in more contextual detail, two important control variables were added in Table 3, namely, indigenous concentration and coffee production, both measured at the departmental level. In order to incorporate the departmental-level covariates into a single multi-variate estimation with municipality-level variables an HGLM model is employed (see Raundenbush & Bryk, 2002). Such an estimation technique improves on earlier statistical options for incorporating multi-level data. One of the earlier strategies was to collapse the departmental-level variables down to the municipality level, however, all municipalities in the same department would automatically have the same values on the collapsed variables, thus violating the assumption of independence of observations (Poston & Duan, 2000). Another traditional strategy would have been to group the municipality-level data up to the contextual (departmental) level. One could sum or average the municipality-level data at the departmental level. The weakness with this option is that it would be discarding of all of the municipality-level variation. Indeed, in the case of El Salvador, there is substantial variation at the level of the municipality. Aggregating to the departmental level would completely miss this more fine-grained variation in rebellion.

Hence, in this study a multi-level HGLM model is also utilized to determine the likelihood of a municipality taking part in El Salvador's 1932 mass rebellion. To estimate this type of multi-level model, several structural equations are shown below. The level-1 independent variables are measured at the municipality level and centered at the group mean. The level-2 independent variables, percentage of departmental population that is indigenous (INDIG), and percentage of total land in the department dedicated to coffee cultivation (PER_CAFE), are measured at the departmental level and are centered at the grand mean. The level-1 and level-2 structural equations are as follow:

*Level 1 Equation*

$$\text{Log}[\varphi/(1 - \varphi)] = \eta$$
$$\eta = \beta_0 + \beta_1(\text{FRTPRES}) + \beta_2(\text{DUFRTBOR})$$
$$+ \beta_3(\text{REPRESS}) + \beta_4(\text{BOREPRE}) + \beta_5(\text{LOGPOP})$$

*Level 2 Equations*

$$\beta_0 = \gamma_{00} + \gamma_{01}(\text{INDIG}) + \gamma_{02}(\text{PER\_CAFE}) + \mu_0$$
$$\beta_1 = \gamma_{10}$$
$$\beta_2 = \gamma_{20}$$
$$\beta_3 = \gamma_{30}$$
$$\beta_4 = \gamma_{40}$$
$$\beta_5 = \gamma_{50}$$

The level 2 equations are integrated into the level 1 equation, resulting in the following multi-level logistic regression equation:

$$\eta = \gamma_{00} + \gamma_{01} \times \text{INDIG} + \gamma_{02} \times \text{PER\_CAFE} + \gamma_{10} \times \text{FRTPRES}$$
$$+ \gamma_{20} \times \text{DUFRTBOR} + \gamma_{30} \times \text{REPRESS}$$
$$+ \gamma_{40} \times \text{BOREPRE} + \gamma_{50} \times \text{LOGPOP} + \mu_0$$

In the level one model $\eta$ is the predicted log odds of a municipality experiencing a rebellious event between January 10 and 28, 1932. In Table 3 (as in Table 2) the logit is converted into an odds ratio by exponentiating its coefficient (see column 2 of Table 3). The odds of an outbreak of rebellion in a municipality is predicted by the presence of an FRT labor organization in the locality (FRTPRES), FRT labor organization in adjacent municipality (DUFRTBOR), acts of state repression in the municipality preceding the rebellion (REPRESS), municipalities bordering acts of state repression (BOREPRE), municipality population size (LOGPOP), the percentage of the departmental population that is indigenous (INDIG), and the percentage of the department's total land under coffee cultivation (PER_CAFE). Table 3 presents the results of the HGLM multi-level model predicting an insurgent rebellion in each of El Salvador's 258 municipalities embedded in 14 departments.

The presence of a local FRT labor organization remains a strong predictor of a 1932 rebellious event occurring within a municipality even after controlling for the effects of the level of coffee production and indigenous population at the departmental level. Additionally, the odds of a municipality rebelling are 18 times greater where acts of state repression took place preceding the rebellion. Repressive threats occurring in the municipality in the years and months immediately before the rebellion made the municipality much more likely to experience radicalized revolt in 1932 even when controlling for important departmental characteristics of indigenous population size and percent of land used to cultivate coffee.[16]

Size of the indigenous population, municipality population size, and area of coffee production were found to be statistically related to the outbreak of rebellious events. A one percent increase in the departmental indigenous population increases the odds of a municipality rebelling by almost 10 percent (i.e., the odds ratio $- 1 \times 100$). A one percent increase in land cultivated in coffee (in $km^2$) at the departmental level increases the odds of a municipality rebelling by 24 percent. These findings give cautious support to historiographical research pointing to the key role of the indigenous population (Pérez Brignoli, 1995) and agricultural wage laborers proximate to coffee estates in the rebellion (Paige, 1997).

Nonetheless, large portions of the national territory where coffee is cultivated (e.g., in the Department of Usulután) and where indigenous communities reside (e.g., in the Departments of La Paz and Morazán) remained calm during the revolt. Even in the western departments where the insurgency took place, there existed indigenous majority municipalities that the FRT failed to penetrate (Gould & Lauria Santiago, 2004) and subsequently neglected to participate in the uprising. At the same time, some of the rebelling municipalities, such as Tacuba, were primarily *mestizo*, not indigenous. The FRT and PCS benefited enormously, though, by capturing the support of the largest communally organized indigenous *cofradías* in Sonsonate Department – especially through winning the support of the cacique (traditional leader of the *cofradía*) that acted as a broker that could bring in hundreds if not thousands of followers into the movement via bloc recruitment.[17] Indeed, some of the largest and most intense local rebellions occurred in municipalities with large indigenous populations in which the FRT and PCS maintained influence (i.e., Juayúa, Izalco, Sonzocate, and Nahuizalco).

## SUMMARY OF QUANTITATIVE ANALYSIS

The above quantitative analyses suggest that in January of 1932 regime challengers partially appropriated the pre-existing labor organizations created in the liberalization period (i.e., "liberalization holdovers") to launch a much more radical uprising against a repressive regime. This finding fits Menjívar's (1985) interpretation that the more radical Communist Party of El Salvador (PCS) "captured" many of the FRT local chapters by 1930. Municipalities that were *already* organized by reformist labor associations in the late 1920s were more likely to experience more radical insurgent activity in January 1932. Solidarities, information flows, relationships of trust, and organizational know-how were already well established in the western municipalities by 1930 (Gould & Lauria-Santiago, 2004) following nearly 3 years of political liberalization. Those municipalities that were rich in labor organizing activity were much more likely to resist the encroaching authoritarian regime than those regions that suffered from labor organizing deficits during regime liberalization. This finding supports the core notion in resource mobilization perspectives that collective action much more likely occurs in areas with relatively more organizational assets (Edwards & McCarthy, 2004). In addition, municipalities that recently experienced state-sponsored repressive actions were also more likely to witness revolutionary-type rebellion. Such repressive threats made radicalized collective action (i.e., participation in the 1932 rebellion) much more likely in the municipalities in which they took place.

FRT propaganda, well-seasoned foreign and domestic organizers, and educational seminars by the FRT-sponsored *Universidad Popular* all found their way into the western municipalities between 1927 and 1931. These organizational elements taught workers and peasants (many already structured in the indigenous *cofradías*) important organizing skills as well as the basic rights of working people. This impressive organizing drive was carried out under the protection of the Romero Bosque political reforms. When the regime closed back down by late 1930 and 1931, labor organizations persisted and radicalized. Acts of governmental repression signaled to the recently organized challengers that the state was no longer receptive to popular demands (if not completely antagonistic). Acts of state violence were much more likely to be carried out in the municipalities organized or influenced by the FRT, in effect radicalizing or speeding up the pace of radicalization of the geographical regions that were previously organized.[18]

In a special workers' congress in 1930, the FRT appealed to its affiliates to strengthen rural organizing in the western departments. Already by 1931, workers in rural regions were holding demonstrations against the increasing state repression. For example, in mid-May 1931 an anti-state repression demonstration (i.e., threat-induced) was held in the western municipality of Sonsonate. Participants reportedly came from the nearby municipalities of

Izalco, Caluco, Nahuizalco, and Juayúa. Three out of these five municipalities (including Sonsonate) maintained a local FRT chapter at the end of 1929. At least 800 people marched down the streets of the town. One of the demonstrator's signs read, "Abajo los decretos fascistas del 12 de Agosto y 30 de Octubre" (Down with the fascist decrees of August 12 and October 30!) in reference to the two states of emergency declared by the national government in the second half of 1930.[19] Local security forces fired on the street march to disperse it – resulting in three deaths and several more injuries. The demonstration may have portended that even more dramatic actions were to come. Four out of the five municipalities that attracted protest participants to this particular protest event in mid-1931 also experienced high-intensity rebellion in January 1932, and one of the municipalities, Juayúa, was reportedly the strategic headquarters for the entire revolt (Méndez, 1932).

The above quantitative findings suggest that periods of regime liberalization deposit organizations that coordinate the mobilization of excluded social classes, such as agrarian and urban wage laborers, and make possible much more radical forms of contention when the political climate becomes more repressive and threatening. It is the state itself that shapes and "incubates" these changing forms of contention (Goodwin, 2001) by literally revolutionizing the groups it initially invited to participate in political society as reform-minded citizens' associations and labor-based organizations.

## DISMEMBERMENT OF CIVIL SOCIETY ORGANIZATIONS: 1932–1962

The rise of the General Hernández Martínez presidency, a patrimonial dictator (Wickham Crowley, 1992) marked a new era in Salvadoran history. The period from 1932 to 1962 was one in which the ascendant military rulers effectively checked the growing expansion of the organizational infrastructure of Salvadoran civil society. In 1932, the Martínez regime reportedly used the voting lists from the municipal elections to hunt down sympathizers of the Salvadoran Communist Party (Marroquín, 1977; Montes, 1979; McClintock, 1985). After the January 1932 massacre, unions were declared illegal, and labor-based organizations did not re-emerge until the late 1930s and early 1940s as "societies" and mutual aid associations. For example, in 1940 a national survey of all civic organizations conducted by a governmental commission found that almost none existed with the exception of local chapters of the Martínez dictatorship's *Pro-Patria* Party (Ching, 2004).

In sum, the massive repression following the 1932 uprising totally destroyed the organizational infrastructure set up in the late 1920s and early 1930s around the FRT and other civic groups. Moreover, El Salvador was under nearly an uninterrupted 13-year state of siege from 1932 to 1944 following the January bloodbath.[20] The growing organization of civil society had been impeded by the state and would experience a 30-year hiatus (even though important short-term protest campaigns emerged) until it would expand and surpass the levels achieved in the late 1920s and early 1930s. The 1932 massacre also marked the beginning of Latin America's longest enduring military government (Williams & Walter, 1997).

## FINDINGS

For social movements emerging in nondemocratic contexts, the current case may offer a few salient processes that operate in other authoritarian political settings. More specifically, this study finds that periods of regime liberalization create the kinds of conditions favorable to the establishment and growth of civic organizations capable of launching a wave of reformist and nonviolent protest as political opportunity perspectives would suggest (Kriesi et al., 1995; Tarrow, 1998). When state actors rollback these liberalization efforts and close down political opportunities, they might radicalize the newly created civil society organizations, which vary in their geographical distribution. If regimes continue to steer themselves on a more authoritarian trajectory, they may induce episodes of militant collective action in the pre-organized communities, such as witnessed in the January 1932 rebellion. Extremely high levels of state coercion, such as the ethnocidal massacre squashing the revolt, will wipe out opposition all together as curvilinear models of state repression on collective action have long predicted (see Boswell & Dixon, 1990; Muller & Weede, 1994).

By employing a historical sequencing framework scholars may be able to better predict when state repression will deter, escalate, and/or radicalize collective action. El Salvador was under a state of siege from 1920 to 1927. Under these restrictive conditions the level of civil society mobilization was relatively low (as reported in Fig. 3). Thus, repressive state policies acted as an effective deterrent to collective action when rulers applied coercion before a civil society infrastructure had been created. When the state relaxed its repressive apparatus during the first three years of the Romero Bosque presidency (1927–1930) civil society associations proliferated and provided collective vehicles to organize reform-minded protests.

The reversal in regime liberalization from mid-1930 to 1932 both radicalized and escalated collective action because civil society activists effectively formed and/or expanded several civic and labor organizations during the short-lived political opening, and they increasingly perceived their interests threatened with a loss of employment, rights, and safety. The main regions of the radical 1932 uprising involved municipalities where labor organizations established themselves during regime liberalization and the localities most victimized by mounting state-sponsored violence with the resumption of dictatorial governance. Periods of attempted polity liberalization, even incomplete and partial attempts, appear to plant organizations that persist in the political environment and carry on collective action under the unlikely conditions of a government reasserting its authoritarian rule over civil society. The present case informs scholars interested in the escalating effects of state repression on mobilization, either curvilinear or backlash proponents, that they should give closer analytical attention to the level of organizational buildup and associational life in civil society immediately before the state launches a repressive campaign. The 1932 uprising instructs us that state coercion on the heels of a rapid expansion of civic organizations may radicalize and accelerate mass defiance until the government employs overwhelming violence to quell the movement. In short, the density of civil society's organizational field conditions the various impacts state repression may have on popular mobilization.

While the Salvadoran regime and the landed agrarian classes restored relative political order for several decades via the genocidal massacre and bloodbath, there remained long-term backlash effects, at least in the sphere of political culture. New generations of activists in the 1970s drew on the events of 1932 as a political identity and a conceptual map to arrange contemporary class conflicts (Paige, 1997). One of the largest street marches in Salvadoran history – of an estimated 200,000 people – took place on January 22, 1980 to commemorate the 48th anniversary of the 1932 uprising and massacre. Ten months later, the opposition united against the military government under the name of the "Farabundo Martí Front for National Liberation" (FMLN) (a title in memory of a key organizer of the 1932 rebellion who was sentenced to death and executed by a firing squad) and launched a protracted guerrilla war for nearly 12 years until signing a peace agreement with the government in early 1992. This former revolutionary organization continues today as the largest electoral opposition political party in the country and maintains the Farabundo Martí label.

# CONCLUSION

A case study largely contributes to social science by expanding and refining existing theoretical concepts. The current case informs political process models by highlighting that the particular political opportunities of competitive elections and institutional access may be the most important features of political liberalization in relation to initiating collective action in authoritarian and semi-authoritarian regimes. These two opportunities not only encourage the launching of reformist social movement campaigns, but the establishment of enduring organizations. The founding of organizations provides a fungible resource infrastructure that can be appropriated for a variety of purposes – including the launching of more radical episodes of defensive collective action if a regime moves to a more threatening and repressive posture. In addition, this case found that the political threats of rights violations and state repression against organized challengers as most responsible for the radicalization in collective action.

Future studies of nondemocratic and transitioning regimes in other times and places may want to examine the kinds of sequences explored here to better understand the likelihood of the emergence of collective action and the forms it takes (i.e., reformist or revolutionary). El Salvador also experienced a similar sequencing of political changes in the late 1960s and 1970s. In the mid-1960s, during a period of rapid economic growth, the ruling military regime permitted competitive elections for the first time since the late 1920s and early 1930s as well as recognized the legality of a variety of civic organizations. The liberalization of the late 1960s gave birth to a vast field of civil society organizations (e.g., rural cooperatives, education-based organizations, and labor unions) that initiated a series of nonviolent protest campaigns. By the mid-1970s, military state managers closed down the electoral system and regime liberalization policies. Several of the organizational leaders of the reformist labor, cooperative, teacher, and student movements would become leaders of the emerging revolutionary organizations that launched the FMLN guerrilla insurgency in the early 1980s against a more repressive regime (Almeida, 2003).

This study suggests that the practices of regime liberalization, organizational formation under liberalization, and the particular threats associated with liberalization reversals (especially the erosion of rights and state repression) may be recurrent processes driving collective action and its radicalization in a variety of political environments in the global South. More investigations are needed in authoritarian and semi-authoritarian political settings to determine the generalizabilty of these observed patterns. Particularly insightful would be comparative research whereby the sequences and trajectories vary, such as regimes that maintain their liberalization pathways (e.g., Portugal and Spain in the 1970s; Latin America and Eastern Europe in the 1980s and 1990s) in contrast to regimes that reverse or shutdown democratic transitions (e.g., Guatemala in the 1950s and 1960s; Brazil in the 1960s; Chile in the 1970s; Algeria in the 1990s[21]; and Nepal in the 2000s). In such comparative studies, the pace and duration of both the liberalization and the reversal periods should inform scholarship on the likelihood of the emergence of large-scale collective action and the shapes it manifests.

# NOTES

1. The concept of threat shares some similarities with Smelser's (1962) concept of "structural strains." I use the multi-dimensional concept of threat in this study in the more narrow meaning of Tilly (1978) whereby a specific negative economic and/or political threat impacts on the interests of challengers – that are perceived to make the group worse off in the event of inaction – motivates new rounds of collective action. Smelser's much more general definition and discussion of structural strain was conceived to explain all types of collective behavior from fads, natural disasters, workplace conflicts, to revolution. In this study, I use threat to explain the likelihood of collective action for only state-oriented social movements in nondemocratic regimes.

2. There are a number of potential state-attributed economic problems that may activate challengers into defensive collective action in *both* liberalizing and repressive contexts (e.g., roll-back of work-related social-welfare benefits, wage arrears, new taxes, mass unemployment, etc.). The core of the concept centers on convincingly attributing to the state threats to material well-being that will make ordinary people worse off if they are not attended to and alleviated by the appropriate jurisdictional authorities.

3. Useem (1985) observed an analogous process in a New Mexico prison riot, which exploded after a period of extending rights was taken away from inmates.

4. Erosion of rights in democratic societies also induces episodes of defensive collective action. The current analysis focuses on the loss of fundamental rights that change the entire nature of political competition in a society, such as the loss of citizenship rights and the freedom to publicly assemble.

5. However, it should be noted that several indigenous communities did receive land titles in western El Salvador (Ching, 1997).

6. Some accounts suggest that the FRT also organized urban renters in addition to craft workers and peasants (see Larín, 1971, p. 7).

7. See, "Los Trabajadores sin Trabajo Organizaron Ayer una Manifestación" in *El Día* June 26, 1930, p. 1.

8. This growing repression of the Salvadoran state is often underemphasized in historical accounts of the era. This is likely due to the genocidal repression that took

place in early 1932. The 1932 bloodbath was so massive and overwhelming that the preceding episodes of repression appear miniscule.

9. See *La Prensa* July 7, 1931, p. 1, "Por Medio de Carteles en que Piden se les Permita Efectuar sus Reuniones Subversivas."

10. Anderson (1971) reports a popular disturbance in the city of Santa Ana as late as January 28.

11. Anderson's monograph on the revolt is viewed as both the most objective and exhaustive by Central American historians (see Montes, 1979).

12. This is a quantitative measure for state repression used by Beissinger (2001) in his study of ethnic nationalism in the former Soviet Union.

13. Municipality-level data for coffee production was not generated until 1938 and 1939, when the first national coffee census was administered.

14. Figures for Chalatenango Department's coffee production were estimated from 1930 and 1931 records provided in the same article.

15. The results of this ordered logistic regression analysis of rebellion intensity are available from the author upon request.

16. Though, the odds ratio lessens (from 76 to 18) compared to Table 2 when we control for indigenous population size and amount of coffee cultivation.

17. For processes of community leaders acting as brokers for social movement mobilization see Broadbent (2003). For bloc recruitment dynamics in other kinds of movements see Oberschall (1973) and McAdam (1982).

18. The Pearson correlation between FRT presence and state repression is $r = 0.48$ at the $p < 0.001$ significance level.

19. See *Diario Latino* May 19, 1931, pp. 1 and 4, "Entre los Manifestantes "Rojos" Fue Vista, Dicen, una Persona de Aspecto Distinguido a Caballo."

20. Ching (1997, p. 443) reports only three labor strikes/work stoppages taking place between 1932 and 1939.

21. For example, the radical Islamic guerrilla armies in Algeria's civil war of the 1990s (e.g., the GIA) also emerged from the electoral mobilization of the newly legalized political parties that were banned following their success in municipal and parliamentary elections in the early 1990s.

# ACKNOWLEDGMENTS

The author thanks Dudley Poston and Harland Prechel for extensive comments on the manuscript. In addition, three anonymous reviewers provided many insightful suggestions. This research project also benefited from travel grants awarded by the College of Liberal Arts at Texas A&M University.

# REFERENCES

Almeida, P. D. (2002). Los movimientos populares contra la política de austeridad económica en América Latina entre 1996 y 2001. *Realidad: Revista de Ciencias Sociales y Humanidades, 86*(Marzo-Abril), 177–189.

Almeida, P. D. (2003). Opportunity organizations and threat-induced contention: Protest waves in authoritarian contexts. *American Journal of Sociology*, *109*(2), 345–400.

Almeida, P. D. (2005). Multi-sectoral coalitions and popular movement participation. *Research in Social Movements, Conflicts, and Change*, *26*, 65–99.

Alvarenga, P. (1996). *Cultura y Ética de la Violencia: El Salvador 1880–1932*. San José: EDUCA.

Amenta, E., & Caren, N. (2004). The legislative, organizational, and beneficiary consequences of state-oriented challengers. In: D. Snow, S. Soule & H. Kriesi (Eds), *The Blackwell companion to social movements* (pp. 461–488). Oxford: Blackwell.

Amenta, E., & Young, M. (1999). Democratic states and social movements: Theoretical arguments and hypotheses. *Social Problems*, *46*(2), 153–168.

Anderson, T. (1971). *La Matanza: El Salvador's communist revolt of 1932*. Lincoln: University of Nebraska Press.

Beissinger, M. (2001). *Nationalist mobilization and the collapse of the Soviet State: A tidal approach to the study of nationalism*. Cambridge: Cambridge University Press.

Boswell, T., & Dixon, W. (1990). Dependency and rebellion: A cross-national analysis. *American Sociological Review*, *55*(4), 540–559.

Broadbent, J. (2003). Movement in context: Thick networks and Japanese environmental protest. In: M. Diani & D. McAdam (Eds), *Social movements and networks: Relational approaches to collective action* (pp. 204–229). Oxford: Oxford University Press.

Brockett, C. (1993). A protest-cycle resolution of the repression/popular-protest paradox. *Social Science History*, *17*(3), 457–484.

Bunce, V. (1999). *Subversive institutions: The design and the destruction of socialism and the state*. Cambridge: Cambridge University Press.

Castellanos, J. M. (2001). *El Salvador 1930–1960: Antecedentes históricos de la guerra civil*. San Salvador: CONCULTURA.

Ching, E. (1995). Los Archivos de Moscú: Una nueva apreciación de la insurrección del 32. *Tendencias*, *3*(44), 28–31.

Ching, E. (1997). From clientilism to militarism: The state, politics, and authoritarianism in El Salvador, 1840–1940. Ph.D. Dissertation, University of California, Santa Barbara.

Ching, E. (1998). In search of the party: The communist party, the COMINTERN, and the peasant rebellion of 1932 in El Salvador. *The Americas*, *55*(2), 204–239.

Ching, E. (2004). Patronage and politics under General Maximiliano Martínez, 1931–1939: The local roots of military authoritarianism in El Salvador. In: A. Lauria-Santiago & L. Binford (Eds), *Landscapes of struggle: Politics, society, and community in El Salvador*. Pittsburgh: University of Pittsburgh Press.

Cuenca, A. (Ed.) (1962). *El Salvador: Una Democracia Cafetalera*. Mexico City: ARR Centro Editorial.

Earl, J. (2003). Tanks, tear gas, and taxes: Toward a theory of movement repression. *Sociological Theory*, *21*(1), 44–68.

Edwards, B., & McCarthy, J. D. (2004). Resources and social movement mobilization. In: D. Snow, S. Soule & H. Kriesi (Eds), *The Blackwell companion to social movements* (pp. 116–152). Oxford: Blackwell.

Elam, R. (1968). Appeal to arms: The army and politics in El Salvador, 1931–1964. Ph.D. Dissertation, University of New Mexico.

Fearon, P. (1979). *The origins and nature of the great slump 1929–1932*. Atlantic Highlands, NJ: Humanities Press.

Fish, J. (1995). *Democracy from scratch: Opposition and regime in the New Russian revolution.* Princeton: Princeton University Press.

Francisco, R. A. (1995). The relationship between Coercion and Protest: An empirical evaluation of three coercive states. *Journal of Conflict Resolution, 39*(2), 263–282.

Francisco, R. A. (2005). The dictator's dilemma. In: C. Davenport, H. Johnston & C. Mueller (Eds), *Repression and mobilization* (pp. 58–81). Minneapolis: University of Minnesota Press.

Goldstone, J. A. (1986). Introduction: The comparative and historical study of revolutions. In: J. Goldstone (Ed.), *Revolutions: Theoretical, comparative, and historical studies* (pp. 1–17). San Diego: Harcourt Brace Jovanich.

Goldstone, J. A. (1998). Social movements or revolutions? On the evolution and outcomes of collective action. In: M. Giugni, D. McAdam & C. Tilly (Eds), *From contention to democracy* (pp. 125–145). Lanham, MD: Rowman and Littlefield.

Goldstone, J. A. (2001). Toward a fourth generation of revolutionary theory. *Annual Review of Political Science, 4,* 139–187.

Goldstone, J., & Tilly, C. (2001). Threat (and opportunity): Popular action and state response in the dynamic of contentious action. In: R. Aminzade, J. Goldstone, D. McAdam, E. Perry, W. Sewell, S. Tarrow & C. Tilly (Eds), *Silence and voice in the study of contentious politics* (pp. 179–194). Cambridge: Cambridge University Press.

Goodwin, J. (2001). *No other way out: States and revolutionary movements, 1945–1991.* Cambridge: Cambridge University Press.

Gould, R. V. (1995). *Insurgent identities: Class, community, and protest in Paris from 1848 to the commune.* Chicago: University of Chicago Press.

Gould, J. (2001). Revolutionary nationalism and local memories in El Salvador. In: G. Joseph (Ed.), *Reclaiming the political in Latin American history* (pp. 138–171). Durham: Duke University Press.

Gould, J., & Lauria-Santiago, A. (2004). They call us thieves and steal our wage: Toward a reinterpretation of the Salvadoran rural mobilization, 1929–1931. *Hispanic American Historical Review, 84*(2), 191–237.

Guidos Véjar, R. (1982[1980]). *Acenso del militarismo en El Salvador* (2nd ed.). San José: EDUCA.

Gurr, T. R. (1970). *Why men rebel.* Princeton: Princeton University Press.

Hipsher, P. (1998). Democratic transitions as protest cycles: Social movement dynamics in democratizing Latin America. In: D. Meyer & S. Tarrow (Eds), *The social movement society* (pp. 153–172). Lanham: Rowman & Littlefield Publishers.

Iñigo Carrera, N., & Cotarelo, M. C. (2001). Clase obrera y formas de lucha en la Argentina actual. *Cuadernos del Sur Año, 17*(32), 43–54.

Iraheta Rosales, G., López Alas, V. D., & Escobar Cornejo, M. C. (1971). La Crisis de 1929 y sus Consecuencias en los Años Posteriores. *La Universidad, 96*(6), 22–74.

Javeline, D. (2003). The role of blame in collective action: Evidence from Russia. *American Political Science Review, 97*(1), 107–121.

Jenkins, C. J. C., & Schock, K. (2004). Political process, international dependence, and mass political conflict: A global analysis of protest and rebellion, 1973–1978. *International Journal of Sociology, 33*(4), 41–63.

Jenkins, J. C., & Bond, D. (2001). Conflict-carrying capacity, political crisis, and reconstruction: A framework for the early warning of political system vulnerability. *Journal of Conflict Resolution, 45*(1), 3–31.

Jenkins, J. C., & Form, W. (2005). Social movements and social change. In: T. Janoski, R. R. Alford, A. M. Hicks & M. A. Schwartz (Eds), *The handbook of political sociology: States, civil societies, and globalization* (pp. 331–349). Cambridge: Cambridge University Press.

Johnston, H. (2005). Talking the walk: Speech acts and resistance in authoritarian regimes. In: C. Davenport, H. Johnston & C. Mueller (Eds), *Repression and mobilization* (pp. 108–137). Minneapolis: University of Minnesota Press.

Johnston, H., & Mueller, C. M. (2001). Unobtrusive practices of contention in Leninist regimes. *Sociological Perspectives, 44*(3), 351–375.

Khawaja, M. (1993). Repression and popular collective action: Evidence from the west bank. *Sociological Forum, 8*(1), 47–71.

Kim, H., & Bearman, P. (1997). The structure and dynamics of movement participation. *American Sociological Review, 62,* 70–93.

Kincaid, A. D. (1987). Peasants into rebels: Community and class in rural El Salvador. *Comparative Studies in Society and History, 29*(3), 466–494.

Klandermans, B. (1997). *The social psychology of protest.* Oxford: Blackwell.

Kriesi, H. (1995). The political opportunity structure of new social movements: Its impact on their mobilization. In: J. C. Jenkins & B. Klandermans (Eds), *The politics of social protest: Comparative perspectives on states and social movements* (pp. 167–198). Minneapolis: University of Minnesota Press.

Kriesi, H., Koopmans, R., Duyvendak, J. W., & Giugni, M. G. (1995). *New social movements in Western Europe.* Minneapolis: University of Minnesota Press.

Larín, A. A. (1971). Historia del movimiento sindical de El Salvador. *Universidad, 96*(4), 135–179.

Lauria-Santiago, A. A. (1999). *An Agrarian Republic: Commercial agricultura and the politics of peasant communities in El Salvador, 1823–1914.* Pittsburgh: University of Pittsburgh Press.

Lichbach, M. I. (1987). Deterrence or escalation? The puzzle of aggregate studies of repression and dissent. *Journal of Conflict Resolution, 31*(2), 266–297.

Lindo-Fuentes, H. (1990). *Weak foundations: The economy of El Salvador in the nineteenth century.* Berkeley: University of California Press.

López Vallecillos, I. (Ed.) (1964). *El Periodismo en El Salvador.* San Salvador: Editorial Universitaria.

Lungo, M. (1987). *La lucha de las masas en El Salvador.* San Salvador: UCA.

Markoff, J. (1996). *Waves of democracy: Social movements and political change.* Thousand Oaks, CA: Pine Forge Press.

Marroquín, A. D. (1977). Estudio sobre la crisis de los años treinta en El Salvador. In: P. G. Casanova (Ed.), *América Latina en los años treinta* (pp. 113–190). Mexico City: Instituto de Investigaciones Sociales, UNAM.

Martínez, V. (1987). *Vivir significa luchar.* San Salvador: Ediciones TECOLUT.

McAdam, D. (1996). Conceptual origins, current problems, future directions. In: P. D. McAdam, J. D. McCarthy & M. N. Zald (Eds), *Comparative perspectives on social movements: Political opportunities, mobilizing structures, and cultural framings* (pp. 23–40). Cambridge: Cambridge University Press.

McAdam, D. (1982). *Political process and the development of black insurgency, 1930–1970.* Chicago: University of Chicago Press.

McAdam, D., McCarthy, J., & Zald, M. (Eds). (1996). Preface. In: *Comparative perspectives on social movements: Political opportunities, mobilizing structures, and cultural framings* (pp. xi–xiv). Cambridge: Cambridge University Press.

McAdam, D., Tarrow, S., & Tilly, C. (2001). *The dynamics of contention*. Cambridge: Cambridge University Press.

McClintock, M. (1985). *The American connection: State terror and popular resistance in El Salvador*. London: Zed Books.

Méndez, J. (1932). *Los sucesos comunistas en El Salvador*. San Salvador: Imprenta Funes & Ungo.

Menjívar, R. (Ed.) (1982[1979]). *Formación y lucha del proletariado industrial salvadoreño* (2nd ed.). San Salvador: UCA Editores.

Menjívar, R. (1985). Notas sobre el movimiento obrero Salvadoreño. In: P. G. Casanova (Ed.), *Historia del Movimiento Obrero en América Latina II* (pp. 61–127). Mexico City: Siglo Veintiuno Editores.

Menjívar, R. (1995). *Acumulación originaria y desarrollo del capitalismo en El Salvador* (2nd ed.). San José: EDUCA.

Meyer, D. S. (2002). Opportunities and identities: Bridge-building in the study of social movements. In: D. S. Meyer, N. Whittier & B. Robnett (Eds), *Social movements, identity, culture, and the State* (pp. 3–21). Oxford: Oxford University Press.

Meyer, D. S., & Minkoff, D. C. (2004). Conceptualizing political opportunity. *Social Forces, 82*(4), 1457–1492.

Minkoff, D. C., & McCarthy, J. D. (2005). Reinvigorating the study of organizational processes in social movements. *Mobilization, 10*(2), 289–308.

Monteforte Toledo, M. (1972). *Centro América: Subdesarrollo y dependencia* (Vol. 2). Mexico City: Instituto de Investigaciones Sociales, Universidad Nacional Autónoma de México.

Montes, S. (Ed.) (1979). *El compadrazgo: Una estructura de poder en El Salvador*. San Salvador: UCA Editores.

Montes, S. (Ed.) (1984). *El Salvador: Las fuerzas sociales en la presente coyuntura: Enero 1980 a diciembre 1983*. San Salvador: UCA Editores.

Mueller, C. M. (1999). Claim radicalization? The 1989 protest cycle in the GDR. *Social Problems, 46*(4), 528–547.

Muller, E., & Weede, E. (1994). Theories of rebellion – relative deprivation and power contention. *Rationality and Society, 6*(1), 40–57.

Oberschall, A. (1973). *Social conflict and social movements*. Englewood Cliffs, NJ: Prentice-Hall.

Olivier, J. (1991). State repression and collective action in South Africa, 1970–84. *South African Journal of Sociology, 22*, 109–117.

Opp, K. D. (1994). Repression and revolutionary action: East Germany in 1989. *Rationality and Society, 6*(1), 101–138.

Osa, M. J. (2003). Networks in opposition: Linking organizations through activists in the Polish People's Republic. In: M. Diani & D. McAdam (Eds), *Social movements and networks: Relational approaches to collective action* (pp. 77–104). Oxford: Oxford University Press.

Oviedo, L. (2001). *Una historia del movimiento piquetero: De las primeras coordinadoras a las asambleas nacionales*. Buenos Aires: Ediciones Rumbos.

Paige, J. (1975). *Agrarian revolution: Social movements and export agriculture in the underdeveloped world*. New York: The Free Press.

Paige, J. (1997). *Coffee and power: Revolution and the rise of democracy in central America*. Cambridge: Harvard University Press.

Pérez Brignoli, H. (1995). Indians, communists, and peasants: The 1932 rebellion in El Salvador. In: W. Roseberry, L. Gudmunson & M. Samper Kutschbach (Eds), *Coffee, society, and power in Latin America* (pp. 232–261). Baltimore: The Johns Hopkins University Press.

Polanyi, K. (1944). *The great transformation: The political and economic origins of our time.* Boston: Beacon Press.

Poston, D. L., Jr., & Duan, C. (2000). Nonagricultural unemployment in Beijing: A multilevel analysis. *Research in Community Sociology, 10,* 289–303.

Prechel, H. (2000). *Big business and the state: Historical transitions and corporate transformations, 1880s–1990s.* Albany: State University of New York Press.

Rasler, K. (1996). Concessions, repression, and political protest in the Iranian revolution. *American Sociological Review, 61*(1), 132–153.

Raudenbush, S. W., & Bryk, A. (2002). *Hierarchical linear models: Applications and data analysis methods* (2nd ed.). Thousand Oaks, CA: Sage Publications.

Robinson, W. I. (1996). *Promoting Polyarchy.* Cambridge: Cambridge University Press.

Rule, J. (1988). *Theories of civil violence.* Berkeley: University of California Press.

Schlesinger, J. (Ed.) (1946). *Revolución Comunista: Guatemala en Peligro?* Guatemala City: Editorial Unión Tipográfica.

Schock, K. (2005). *Unarmed insurrections: People power movements in nondemocracies.* Minneapolis: University of Minnesota Press.

Smelser, N. (1962). *Theory of collective behavior.* New York: Free Press.

Snow, D., & Trom, D. (2002). Case study and the study of social movements. In: B. Klandermans & S. Staggenborg (Eds), *Methods of social movement research* (pp. 146–172). Minneapolis: University of Minnesota Press.

Snow, D. A., Soule, S. A., & Cress, D. M. (2005). Homeless protest across 17 U.S. cities, 1980–1991: Assessment of the explanatory utility of strain, resource mobilization, and political opportunity theories. *Social Forces, 83*(3), 1183–1210.

Soule, S. A., McAdam, D., McCarthy, J., & Su, Y. (1999). Protest events: Causes or consequences of state action? The U.S. women's movement and federal congressional activities, 1956–1979. *Mobilization, 4*(2), 239–255.

Tarrow, S. (1998). *Power in movement: Social movements and contentious politics.* Cambridge: Cambridge University Press.

Tilly, C. (1978). *From mobilization to revolution.* Reading, MA: Addison-Wesley.

Tilly, C. (1990). *Coercion, capital, and the European states, AD 990–1990.* Oxford: Blackwell.

Tilly, C. (2003). Inequality, democratization, and de-democratization. *Sociological Theory, 21*(1), 37–43.

Tilly, C. (2004). *Social movements, 1768–2004.* Boulder, CO: Paradigm.

Useem, B. (1985). Disorganization and the New Mexico prison riot of 1980. *American Sociological Review, 50*(5), 677–688.

Van Dyke, N. (2003). Crossing movement boundaries: Factors that facilitate coalition protest by American college students, 1930–1990. *Social Problems, 50*(2), 226–250.

Van Dyke, N., & Soule, S. A. (2002). Structural social change and the mobilizing effect of threat: Explaining levels of patriot and militia organizing in the United States. *Social Problems, 49,* 497–520.

Wickham-Crowley, T. (1989). Winners, losers, and also-rans: Toward a comparative sociology of Latin American guerrilla movements. In: S. Eckstein (Ed.), *Power and popular protest: Latin American social movements* (pp. 132–181). Berkeley: University of California Press.

Wickham-Crowley, T. (1992). *Guerrillas and revolution in Latin America: A comparative study of insurgents and regimes since 1956.* Princeton: University of Princeton Press.

Williams, P. J., & Walter, K. (1997). *Militarization and demilitarization in El Salvador's transition to democracy.* Pittsburgh: University of Pittsburgh.
Williams, R. G. (1994). *States and social evolution: Coffee and the rise of national governments in Central America.* Chapel Hill: University of North Carolina Press.
Wilson, E. A. (1970). The crisis of national integration in El Salvador, 1919–1935. Ph.D. Dissertation, Stanford University.
Wood, E. J. (2003). *Insurgent collective action and civil war in El Salvador.* Cambridge: Cambridge University Press.
Zamosc, L. (1989). Class conflict in an export economy: The social roots of the Salvadoran insurrection of 1932. In: L. J. Flora & E. Torres-Rivas (Eds), *Sociology of developing societies: Central America* (pp. 56–75). New York: Monthly Review.

# APPENDIX

***Table A1.*** Descriptive Statistics: 258 Municipalities of El Salvador in 14 Departments.

| Variables | N | Mean | SD | Minimum | Maximum |
|---|---|---|---|---|---|
| *Level-1 Variables* | | | | | |
| R_1932 | 258 | 0.09 | 0.29 | 0.00 | 1.00 |
| FRTPRES | 258 | 0.07 | 0.26 | 0.00 | 1.00 |
| DUFRTBOR | 258 | 0.26 | 0.44 | 0.00 | 1.00 |
| REPRESS | 258 | 0.05 | 0.22 | 0.00 | 1.00 |
| BOREPRE | 258 | 0.23 | 0.42 | 0.00 | 1.00 |
| LOGPOP | 258 | 8.16 | 0.87 | 6.19 | 11.47 |
| *Level-2 Variables* | | | | | |
| INDIG | 14 | 8.84 | 12.93 | 0.00 | 34.70 |
| PER_CAFE | 14 | 4.28 | 5.39 | 0.08 | 18.80 |

# PART II:
# BUSINESS POLITICS AND GLOBALIZATION

# THE BUSINESS OF ANTI-GLOBALIZATION POLITICS: LESSONS FROM VENEZUELA'S 1998 PRESIDENTIAL ELECTIONS

Leslie C. Gates

## ABSTRACT

*Why might prominent Venezuelan businessmen have supported Hugo Chávez, a presidential candidate widely viewed as a threat to private sector interests, in the 1998 election? A Qualitative Comparative Analysis links the 28 business owners and managers identified by those close to the Chávez campaign as likely contributors to two paths: a structural predisposition to assist the front runner in order to secure access to the state and direct network ties to Chávez which reenforced a structural predisposition to assist a protectionist candidate. These distinct political interests reflect divergent structural incentives for business within an oil-dependent semiperipheral economy.*

On December 6, 1998, Venezuelans overwhelmingly elected Hugo Rafael Chávez Frías, a vocal critic of neoliberal economic reforms and Venezuela's political establishment.[1] His election marked the beginning of a new political landscape in Venezuela; one in which Chávez maintains substantial

Politics and Globalization
Research in Political Sociology, Volume 15, 101–137
Copyright © 2007 by Elsevier Ltd.
All rights of reproduction in any form reserved
ISSN: 0895-9935/doi:10.1016/S0895-9935(06)15004-4

electoral majorities – demonstrated in five votes since 1998 – even as Venezuela becomes increasingly polarized politically – as evidenced by a failed coup attempt in 2002 and over 3 million signatures on a petition which sought to recall Chávez from the presidency. The 1998 election also marked the beginning of a leftward political drift in Latin America. Presidents who distance themselves from the neoliberal reforms favored by the U.S. and which have facilitated the recent mode of world economic integration often called globalization have recently won major elections throughout South America. Understanding how globalization affects politics demands a clearer understanding of the origins of this trend within a region that has historically maintained a deferential relationship with the U.S.. To understand this pivotal election, this study focuses on a factor that has been largely ignored, but which played a key role in electing Chávez: financial assistance from business.[2] This assistance is particularly intriguing given the private sector's prominent role, after the 1998 election, in a debilitating economy-wide strike, mass demonstrations against Chávez and the coup attempt. This study, thus, sheds new light on the rare conditions under which business assists left-leaning politicians as well as the growing political dominance of anti-globalization politics in the region.

Most accounts of Chávez' victory focus on explaining widespread contempt for Venezuela's political establishment (Kelly & Palma, 2004, p. 203): the two multi-class parties (Acción Democrática-AD and Comité de Organización Política Electoral Independiente-COPEI) that had long stabilized Venezuela's democracy (Collier & Collier, 1991) but which rapidly lost popularity as they introduced neoliberal economic reforms.[3] Scholars attribute eroding public confidence in Venezuela's political establishment to several factors: (1) the structural limitations of Venezuela's oil-based rentier economy (Ellner, 2003; McCoy, 1999; McCoy & Smith, 1995) and concomitant social polarization aggravated by neoliberal reforms (Ellner, 2003; Roberts, 2003, p. 2) rigid political institutions which made it difficult to effectively integrate new and critical political actors (Coppedge, 1994; Crisp, 2000; Crisp & Levine, 1998; Crisp, Levine, & Rey, 1995), including the urban poor (Buxton, 2001, p. 222, 2003; Canache, 2004), intellectuals (Hillman, 2004), an emergent civil society (Salamanca, 2004) and junior military officers (Aguero, 1995; Norden, 1996; Tinkunas, 2004); and (3) a series of unfortunate policies, such as social policies in the early 1990s that inadequately addressed the negative effects of neoliberal reforms (McCoy, 2004; McCoy & Smith, 1995; Naím, 1993). This study, however, leaves aside the task of adjudicating the origins of declining confidence in Venezuela's political establishment.

While scholars mention that Chávez received financial assistance from business in passing (Hellinger, 2003, p. 47; Ortiz, 2004, p. 85), there are no scholarly studies of business assistance for Chávez. Yet without business assistance, it may be hard to explain how Chávez, a former military leader who led a failed coup attempt in February 1992, prevailed. Like all of the popular candidates in the 1998 presidential race, Chávez appealed to the electorate's desire, particularly that of the expanding and increasingly politicized urban poor (Canache, 2004; Roberts, 2003), for a political outsider: someone they believed would curb corruption without compromising democracy and improve living standards by rejecting neoliberal reforms and reviving some form of state-led development policy (Gil Yepes, 2004; Kelly & Palma, 2004). Some argue that what distinguished Chávez – and therefore what made him appear most likely to adopt radical political reform (McCoy, 2004, pp. 279, 284; Molina, 2004, p. 170) and to break from neoliberal economic policies (Ellner, 2003) – was that he never accepted endorsement from either of the establishment parties. Nevertheless, business support may have made it feasible for Chávez to eschew establishment party endorsements. Certainly, Venezuela's politicians depended on business support to fund their campaigns throughout the democratic era (Alvarez, 1995); a condition which generally gives business disproportionate political influence (Domhoff, 1967, 1990; Ferguson, 1995; Lewis & Center for Public Integrity, 2004; Mills, 1956). Unlike other candidates, however, Chávez took business support without compromising his reputation as a radical reformer. Indeed, several prominent Venezuelan business leaders appeared to have supported Chávez (Hellinger, 2003, p. 47; Ortiz, 2004, p. 85; Santodomingo, 1999; Zapata, 2000), despite the fact that Chávez denounced "savage capitalism" and was widely viewed as a threat to the private sector.[4]

With a focus on how Chávez financed his campaign, this study responds to the need for more systematic analysis of campaign financing in Latin America (Njaim, 2004; Samuels, 2001a, 2001b) brought on by the greater prevalence of expensive mass-media dominated campaigning in an ever more democratized Latin America (Weyland, 1998). In doing so, it examines a central but less studied mechanism whereby business influences politics not just in Venezuela (Coppedge, 2000; Gómez, 1989; Keller, 1997; Naím, 1984), but in Latin America more generally (Haggard, Maxfield, & Schneider, 1997): informal individual level modes of business representation. Moreover, business assistance for Chávez represents a puzzle. Recent research in Latin America (Samuels, 2001b) confirms conventional wisdom that left-leaning politicians have difficulty obtaining business assistance. Typically we expect business to assist right-leaning politicians that favor fewer regulations on the private sector, more restrictions on unions, lower taxes, constrained wages and reduced government spending on social services. Indeed, business is rarely noted as an important contributor to the recent success of anti-neoliberal presidential candidates throughout Latin America. Rather, this trend is widely interpreted as evidence of the growing influence of social movements representing social sectors disadvantaged by neoliberal reforms.[5]

This study employs journalistic accounts and interviews with those close to the 1998 Chávez campaign to identify and analyze the motivations of 28 business managers and owners likely to have made campaign contributions. It focuses on individual business managers and owners in part because business associations, including Venezuela's umbrella business association the Federation of Chambers and Associations of Commerce and Production (Federación de Cámaras y Asociaciones de Comercio y Producción De Venezuela – FEDECAMARAS), were largely unwilling to publicly support let alone financially assist Chávez. A Qualitative Comparative Analysis (QCA) of the conditions which may have led these 28 business owners and managers to assist Chávez reveals two paths: one in which a structural predisposition to assist any contender with promising chances in order to secure access to the state may have led them to assist Chávez and one in which direct network ties to Chávez reinforced a predisposition to assist a protectionist candidate. These distinct political interests of business reflect the various structural incentives for business within an oil-dependent semi-peripheral economy. As such, they reveal how an economy's insertion into the global economy shapes domestic politics, sometimes in unexpected ways.

## EXPLAINING BUSINESS ASSISTANCE TO AN ANTI-NEOLIBERAL CANDIDATE

An earlier generation of left-leaning Latin American presidents who supported unionization, regulations on business and major social welfare initiatives (Collier & Collier, 1991) received support from business. Research on these populists indicates that some business owners and managers may have *a structural predisposition to favor protectionist policies* – policies that protect domestic producers from global market pressures. Just as certain businesses – oligopolistic firms (Domhoff, 1972; Ferguson & Rogers, 1986; Kolko, 1963; Lindblom, 1977) and/or bankers (Mintz & Schwartz, 1985; Mizruchi, 1982), who tended to be well-connected (Useem, 1984) – appeared to have a structural predisposition to favor the liberal policies of Roosevelt's

New Deal in the U.S., business in certain sectors – weak industrialists who depended on protection from international competitors – appeared to have a structural predisposition to favor the protectionist policies of Latin America's populists. Observers of contemporary Latin American politics confirm this proposition. Many recent studies of successful neoliberal politicians, for example, implicitly acknowledge that some sectors of business have a structural predisposition to oppose neoliberal reforms by emphasizing the importance of forging and sustaining a pro-neoliberal business coalitions (Conaghan & Malloy, 1994; Pastor & Wise, 1994; Schamis, 2002; Silva, 1996; Thacker, 2000). Indeed, Mexican neoliberal reforms had to neutralize anti-neoliberal businesses (Shadlen, 2004) and construct pro-reform business coalitions (Thacker, 2000) in order to carry out one of the region's most aggressive and enduring neoliberal reform agendas.

Building on a long research tradition linking policy preferences to sector interests (Gourevitch, 1986; Rogowski, 1989), Frieden (1991) formalizes concrete predictions about which business sectors we might expect to be predisposed to favor protectionist policies and therefore more likely to assist leftist politicians. He posits that business owners and managers with predominantly fixed assets (those with investments in factories and heavy machinery) have a structural predisposition to favor protectionist trade policies and oppose facile capital flows in and out of the country. They have difficulty in "cashing out" of their investments during crises. In contrast, those with predominantly liquid assets, such as bankers, or those with assets that can be easily converted into cash, like merchants, have a structural predisposition to favor eliminating restrictions on international flows of capital because they have much to gain from a more open market and can more easily protect themselves from the market volatility that accompanies liberalized markets than those with predominantly fixed assets. Silva (1996) further refines Frieden, arguing that fixed asset sectors vary in the degree to which they favor neoliberal reforms depending on their target markets. Those fixed asset sectors that traditionally produce for export (sectors such as mining and oil extraction) or manufacturing sectors with the potential to compete internationally (such as food processing), he argues, do tend to favor reforms. The latter include a select group of manufacturers which have not developed their export potential as a result of trade protections, but which are well situated to do so due to their high level of economic concentration and attractiveness to foreign lenders. This suggests that *being in a fixed-asset non-internationally competitive sector* is a condition that should make businesspeople structurally predisposed to favor protectionist policies and therefore to contribute to the Chávez' campaign.

Evidence that business assistance to Chávez stems from business owners and managers that are structurally predisposed to favor protectionist policies would confirm world systems expectations of private sector political interests in semiperipheral states. Setting aside the rich debate about how best to define semiperipheral states (Arrighi, 1985; Martin, 1990; Nemeth & Smith, 1985; Schwartzman, 1989; Snyder & Kick, 1979; Wallerstein, 1976), I adopt Arrighi and Drangel's (1986) relatively straight forward definition of all states that fall near the middle of the world's distribution of GNP per capita. World systems theory posits that the private sector in semiperipheral or middle-income states not only has competing political interests but also has greater incentives to affect state policy (Wallerstein, 1985, pp. 34–35). It posits that semiperipheral states have a mix of economic activities (Wallerstein, 1974, 1985, p. 34) typical of both core states – those states where "high-profit, high-technology, high-wage diversified production" are concentrated – and peripheral states – those states where "low-profit, low-technology, low-wage, less-diversified production" are concentrated (Wallerstein, 1976, p. 462).[6] This mix of economic activities generates strong competing policy preferences linked to differing modes of insertion into the global economy (Schwartzman, 1989). Furthermore, whereas business in the core may enhance profitability by making changes within the firm, such as restructuring production process, it posits that business in middle-income states is more likely to conclude that changes to state policy are their most expedient means of enhancing profitability. As Wallerstein puts it: semiperipheral domestic property owners "look upon the state as their negotiating instrument with the rest of the capitalist world economy" (Wallerstein, 1976, p. 469).

Yet, studies on campaign financing suggest that some businesses may also be *structurally predisposed to* support left-leaning politicians not because they favor protectionism but because they *prioritize access to the state*. Research on corporate giving through Political Action Committees (PACs) in the U.S., for example, reveals that corporations which depend on government contracts or good working relationships with government regulatory agencies tend to be more likely to support incumbents even if the incumbent favors increased taxes, wages and welfare spending (Gopian, Smith, & Smith, 1984; Grier, Munger, & Roberts, 1994; Handler & Mulkern, 1982). Similarly, Brazilian businesses in sectors that depend on government contracts, namely the construction industry, gave more generously to governors because they awarded the biggest government contracts in Brazil (Samuels, 2001b). This suggests that business managers and owners in sectors that are *dependent on the state*, may be *structurally predisposed to prioritize access to the state* and therefore to support all candidates to some extent, but the candidate most likely to win in particular.

Furthermore, if businessmen in sectors that are dependent on the state are more likely to make contributions to left-leaning politicians because they prioritize state access, then we might also expect business in countries where the private sector as a whole is more dependent on the state to be generally more preoccupied with access to the state and therefore more likely to assist left-leaning politicians. Dependence on oil exports creates peculiarly strong incentives for the private sector to depend on the state (Karl, 1997). Federal governments in oil-exporting economies derive immense resources either by taxing foreign oil companies or by directly controlling the entity producing and exporting oil (i.e. a state-owned oil company). The flood of foreign currency into government coffers allows the government to maintain a favorable exchange rate for domestic consumers. The overvalued domestic currency facilitates imports to satisfy growing consumer appetites and eventually erodes domestic productive capacity in agriculture and industry. The private sector, in this context, struggles to survive in the face of cheap imports. Meanwhile, the cash flush federal government distributes "incentives" to private enterprises in its zealous rush to "sow the oil". In this context, the private sector becomes increasingly dependent on the state to both protect it from exports and to support it through contracts or other forms of direct cash transfers. This phenomenon, first experienced by the Dutch, is often referred to as "Dutch disease".

Thus, states that depend on oil exports (petro-states) may represent a special case of semiperipheral states: a case where inter-sector conflict over various modes of inserting into the global economy may not define the main contours of individual-level political behavior of business. In petro-states, intra-sector competition over access to state resources may overshadow inter-sector conflict over policy agendas and further fragment the political interests of business. Indeed, the high rate of civil war (Collier, 2000; Fearon, 2005; Ross, 2004) and failed democracies (Karl, 1987; Ross, 2001; Smith, 2004) in petro-states appear to stem in part from heightened elite conflict in these countries over access to the state's immense oil-derived resources. In such economies, we might therefore expect business owners and managers to be particularly attuned to both the potential benefits of direct network ties to candidates and the potential risks of candidates who are likely to favor their economic competition in granting contracts and other privileges. Thus, I predict that having *a direct network tie* to Chávez and *distrusting Chávez' political competition* would be a condition that led business owners and managers to assist Chávez.

## DATA AND ANALYTIC STRATEGY

Although laws regulating elections in Venezuela require campaigns to submit records to the National Electoral Commission ((CNE) Comisión Nacional Electoral), they do not require that they report the names of donors (Alvarez, 1995). The records submitted to the CNE from organizations which backed Chávez contain a dated list of amounts deposited in campaign accounts but only one individual name (Sánchez Molina, 2000). Thus, I interviewed those close to the campaign and scoured reports by journalists who have researched the campaign (Santodomingo, 1999; Zapata, 2000) to construct a list of prominent business owners and managers that more than likely assisted Chávez. I will refer to these individuals hereafter as pro-Chávez business owners and managers. Likely assistance included (1) financial contributions, (2) logistical support, such as loaning Chávez a plane, or (3) media support, such as granting Chávez free or heavily discounted access to primetime coverage during the campaign. The study includes those business managers and owners confirmed by at least one of the sources close to the campaign as probable supporters (see Appendix A).[7] Usually my sources were able to confirm a high probability that an individual business manager or owner financially assisted the campaign. Only in a few rare instances, were they actually present when a financial transaction occurred, as this process was shrouded in secrecy. While I may have overlooked some smaller backers, this method yields a list that includes some of Venezuela's wealthiest and arguably most influential business owners and managers in 1998. For example, it includes one of Venezuela's two billionaires, who was rumored to have met with Chávez, arranged for positive media coverage through his market-dominant television network (Santodomingo, 1999, p. 36; Zapata, 2000, p. 69), and donated money to his campaign by mid-1998.[8]

To code each business manager and owner according to their structural predisposition to favor protectionist policies or to prioritize access to the state, I used interviews with sources close to the campaign, secondary accounts of the campaign (Hellinger, 2003, p. 47; Ortiz, 2004, p. 85; Santodomingo, 1999; Zapata, 2000) and an exhaustive search for articles citing each probable supporter in (1) several news files of the LexisNexis News Library (News File, North/South American Sources; Non-English News File, Spanish Sources; and the Business and Finance Sources as well as the Industry News Sources of the Business News File), (2) the Biography File of the Reference Library on LexisNexis, and (3) the only Caracas daily with an electronic database which started as early as 1996 (*El Universal*). The number of articles with information relevant for my coding categories in any of the above electronic sources ranged from 0 for six individuals to 118. I found an average of 11.2 articles with relevant information (although often there were many more without relevant information) for each pro-Chávez business owner and manager.

To assess the conditions associated with pro-Chávez business owners and managers, I used QCA. QCA employs Boolean algebra to establish the various combinations of conditions that lead to a particular event or outcome of interest (Ragin, 1987). It allows researchers to consider how various factors might interact with each other to produce different outcomes, rather than considering each variable's effect independent of others. QCA allows researchers to discern different paths, or configurations of factors, that produce a similar outcome. For example, Cress and Snow (2000) use QCA to identify several combinations of organizational, tactical, framing and political variables that enable organizations mobilizing in the interest of the homeless to attain either organizational resources or benefits for the homeless. I used QCA to derive the combinations of conditions associated with likely contributors to Chávez' 1998 campaign.

## OPERATIONALIZATION

I coded pro-Chávez business owners and managers as structurally predisposed to favor Chávez' protectionist policies (PROTECT = 1), if they were in primarily fixed asset sectors oriented toward domestic markets with little potential to compete internationally. Venezuela's agro-industrialists and most manufacturers fell into this category. Since oil was discovered in 1913, Venezuela's oil exports infused Venezuela's economy with ample foreign currency (Cupolo, 1996; Karl, 1987). Easy access to foreign currency tended to make it cheaper to import both raw materials used in food products as well as already processed food, rather than to produce either domestically (Naím & Francés, 1995). This had made it difficult for producers in agriculture to survive (Karl, 1987; Thorp & Durand, 1997) unless they were protected from cheap grain, cotton and livestock imports. As a result, agriculture declined throughout much of the 20th century (Cupolo, 1996; Jongkind, 1993; Karl, 1987) and suffered even greater losses when the Venezuelan government introduced neoliberal reforms in the 1990s. Thus, agro-industrialists tended to favor protecting their endeavors with high tariffs on imports in conjunction with technical and financial development aid from the state.[9] Indeed, an anonymous source who worked at the association representing agro-industrialists, FEDEAGRO, believes that FEDEAGRO diverted about $2 million of public funds to the Chávez campaign (Sánchez Molina, 2000, p. 105).

Similarly, Venezuela's oil exports dampened demand for domestically produced manufacturing goods (Bitar & Troncoso, 1990; Cupolo, 1996; Jongkind, 1993, p. 66; Naím & Francés, 1995). As a result, the manufacturing sector in general had been anemic until government protected and invested in it historically (Bitar & Troncoso, 1990; Jongkind, 1993; Naím & Francés, 1995; Thorp & Durand, 1997) and it had suffered considerable losses during the 1990s.[10] Indeed, the association representing manufacturers, CONINDUSTRIA, historically opposed trade liberalization.[11]

I coded pro-Chávez business owners and managers as structurally predisposed to favor neoliberalism or *non-protectionist* (PROTECT = 0) if they had predominantly liquid assets or had predominantly fixed assets but were in traditional export sectors or had potential to compete internationally. The latter included a few manufacturing industries which had managed to thrive after neoliberal economic reforms were introduced (Jongkind, 1993, pp. 81–82; Keller, 1997, p. 348). For example, the food processing and paper industries were able to compete domestically with international products (Bitar & Troncoso, 1990) and grew during the 1990s (Jongkind, 1993) after having attracted significant foreign investments (Bitar & Troncoso, 1990). Post-privatization, the cement industry also profited from exports to Florida and other South American countries in the 1990s.[12] The variation in policy preferences across the manufacturing sector may also help explain how Pérez neutralized CONINDUSTRIA's opposition to neoliberal reforms in the early 1990s (Corrales & Cisneros, 1999) and therefore why it did not advocate for or assist Chávez in 1998.[13]

I then coded pro-Chávez business managers and owners according to three possible conditions that might have led them to assist Chávez in order to help ensure that they would have access to the state after the election. First, I coded pro-Chávez business managers and owners as likely to prioritize securing access to the state if they had primary business interests in economic sectors that traditionally relied on large cash transfers to their business from the state and therefore *depended* on the state (DEPEND = 1). Following Samuel's research on Brazil, I coded those in the construction industry or in related industries, such as cement manufacturing, as dependent on the state. However, because Venezuela's oil dependence made a much greater portion of the private sector in Venezuela dependent on the state (Baptista & Mommer, 1989; Briceño-León, 1990, p. 127; Karl, 1997), I also coded bankers and business owners and managers in various telecommunications sector industries as dependent on the state. Venezuelan banks depend on securing contracts as the primary intermediary for government deposits. All of the state's oil revenue is first deposited in Venezuela's central bank after which it is distributed to the different government agencies via private banks, accounting for approximately 60% of bank deposits.[14] Indeed, a banker confessed to a leading expert on elections in 1993 that they needed to know whether a close contender for the presidency that they had not yet financed might have a reasonable chance. If so, they intended to make a contribution in order to help ensure access to the next administration.[15]

Newspaper publishers and radio and TV station owners depended on lucrative advertisement contracts with various government agencies and privileged access to high-level government officials in order to boost circulation.[16] Furthermore, those individuals with significant investments in the telecommunications industry had a keen interest in the outcome of a planned reform of Venezuela's telecommunications law.[17] Industry giants were eager to stream line the process whereby the state regulated the various industries (radio, television, telephone services) within the telecommunications sector in order to better reflect the emerging integration of all forms of media. Those already invested in one part of the sector wanted to have an easier time diversifying into other areas of the sector. A series of reforms to this effect were, indeed, implemented in 2000.[18]

I also considered a second and third condition that might have led any business owner or manager, regardless of their sector interests, to believe that they might have had a good chance of securing access to the state through Chávez. The dependence of much of Venezuela's private sector on the state may have created incentives for all businesses managers and owners to assist those candidates with whom they had network ties or who could defeat those candidates they distrusted. I coded pro-Chávez business managers and owners as having network ties to Chávez (NETWORK = 1) if at least one of my sources close to the 1998 campaign confirmed that the individual had a direct relationship to Chávez. I coded pro-Chávez business managers and owners as having incentives to distrust Chávez' leading contender (DISTRUST = 1) – and therefore as believing that they had a better chance of securing access to the state if Chávez was president – for two different reasons: for being a business competitor or for being closely associated with the prior government's policies that negatively affected them or their close associates.

As of July 1998, Chávez' leading competition was the businessman and former governor of the state of Carabobo, Salas Römer. With 20% of the projected vote, Salas Römer became the candidate in a crowded field of presidential hopefuls with the best chance of defeating Chávez and known as the "darling of the business sector".[19] Yet, the individuals rumored to be associated with a prospective Salas Römer administration were individuals that a number of prominent business owners and managers deeply distrusted due to growing division in the private sector (Santodomingo, 1999; Zapata, 2000, p. 22).[20] Some of those mentioned were individuals who had strong allegiances to particular private enterprises. Ironically, the government had unwittingly unleashed a fierce competition among prominent business owners and managers for market dominance when the state unraveled decades of state mediated market allocation mechanisms with neoliberal economic reforms in the early 1990s (Naím, 1993). The vigorous quest for market dominance among Venezuela's major conglomerates created lasting enmities among the elite, generating strong incentives for some elite to distrust the leading pro-business candidate. Thus, I coded individuals as having incentives to distrust Salas Römer's associates (DISTRUST = 1) for being a *competitor* if that pro-Chávez business owner or manager were one of the main business competitors of a Salas Römer associate or if that pro-Chávez business owner or manager had been involved in a struggle for power over the same company with one of Salas Römer's associates.

Some of those rumored to be close associates of Salas Römer had also been closely associated with the state's selective and retribution oriented handling of Venezuela's devastating bank crisis in 1994.[21] While other countries facing similar bank crises in the 1980s and 1990s adopted a universal strategy such as nationalizing all banks, the Venezuelan government created many enemies. The government selectively distributed emergency aid and rescue packages to some banks while closing and liquidating others.[22] For example, within days of Banco Latino's declaration on January 13, 1994 that it could not pay client checks, the government froze $1.4 billion in Banco Latino savings accounts, affecting 1.3 million depositors throughout Venezuela.[23] The government also sought retribution against Banco Latino, by issuing warrants for 83 Banco Latino executives on February 28, 1994 (see note 23). Meanwhile, the government merely instigated audits of eight other financial institutions to which it distributed emergency aid.[24] The government continued to selectively aid and close banks through January 1995. By mid-June it had become apparent that much of the financial aid was being used to pay off loans held by shareholders or was being "recycled to other weak banks".[25] The government temporarily closed these eight financial institutions on June 14, only to reopen them a few days later to depositors, and liquidate them in August (the second phase of the bank intervention).[26] In August, the government also tried to create incentives for eight more commercial banks to become solvent on their own rather than with the help of government financial assistance.[27] But this strategy also failed. During September and December, the government intervened in yet another round of failing banks, including one of the top three banks in Venezuela (third phase).[28] Finally, the state reluctantly bailed out three of the five banks that faced imminent collapse in January 1995 (fourth phase).[29] All told the state acquired 17 of Venezuela's 50 commercial banks, representing about 70% of the banking sector, and spent an estimated $7 billion, equal to about 75% of government revenue or 11% of Venezuela's 1994 GDP.[30] Thus, those who implemented and who supported this selective and retribution-oriented intervention were suspected of being willing to cut certain business owners and managers off from access to the state.

Close observers of the election argue that some prominent business owners and managers were suspicious of those who had implemented or had publicly supported the government's handling of the bank crisis. They suspected that the government had targeted prominent business owners and managers for "moral cleansing". President Rafael Caldera (1994–1998) had declared that the moral corruption of Venezuela's political system had produced the bank crisis.[31] Some believed that Caldera had sought to capture widespread political discontent with the now disgraced former Venezuelan President, Carlos Andrés Pérez, by selectively seeking retribution against those business owners and managers intimately linked with him. When Salas Römer became associated with those who had implemented the government's bank intervention, such as the former head of the special committee on bank crisis,[32] the former head of the agency administering statized banks[33] and a member of the intervention team of two of the most prominent statized banks,[34] those suspicious of the government's handling of the bank crisis became wary of Salas Römer. Similarly, Salas Römer's rumored association with those who had stoked the flames of public disgust with bankers,[35] and those suspected of spreading rumors of imminent bank collapse (Zapata, 1995, pp. 15, 19–20, 32), also made some businessmen wary of Salas Römer.

In other words, some pro-Chávez business managers and owners may have had good reason to believe their chances of establishing close ties with Chávez were much better than they were with Chávez' leading competition; someone they deeply distrusted because of the individuals with whom he was associated (Santodomingo, 1999; Zapata, 2000, p. 22). Thus, I also coded pro-Chávez business owners and managers as having incentives to distrust Salas Römer's associates (DISTRUST = 1) if that pro-Chávez business owner or manager had a negative association with the bank crisis.

Business owners and managers that had been closely associated with a bank that failed, faced considerable losses, or faced a serious threat of a depositors rush were coded as having a negative association with the bank crisis, as were those that had close network ties to one of the bankers negatively affected by the bank crisis.

## RESULTS OF DATA CODING

Table 1 demonstrates that although *some* pro-Chávez business owners and managers could be considered protectionists (PROTECT = 1), most could not. Only seven of the 28 pro-Chávez business owners and managers had interests in sectors we would expect to favor protectionist policies. Six of them were (or in one case had been) agro-industrialists.[36] The one exception was the owner of an airline (case 2). The airline industry is a fixed asset sector, like agro-industry, that depends in protections from international carriers. But, the majority of pro-Chávez business owners and managers could not be considered protectionist. Notably, 12 (43%) had primary and an additional two (7%) had secondary interests in the financial sector – a liquid asset sector we might expect to support radical neoliberal economic reforms. Even the four pro-Chávez business owners and managers with either primary or secondary manufacturing sector interests were concentrated in the internationally competitive industries which thrived after neoliberal reforms were introduced.[37]

The nine pro-Chávez business owners and managers with interests in the telecommunications and media sector (five with primary interests and four with secondary interests) also did not have a structural predisposition for protectionism. The telecommunications sector is a fixed asset sector that includes a diverse set of industries from the telephone industry, to major radio and television networks, to cable providers. Nevertheless, these enterprises shared an interest in privatizing and deregulating the industry. For example, businesses poised to invest in the telephone service industry advocated privatizing Venezuela's telephone company, CANTV, in the 1990s, in conjunction with foreign multi-nationals. Those in the media, including newspapers, and television networks, oppose tariffs on content and physical materials needed to produce and distribute their product (such as ink and satellite dishes) and supported unregulated access to a strong local currency, the Venezuelan Bolivar (VEB), to help them import these components of their business.[38] Chief among those pro-Chávez owners and managers in the telecommunications sector was the head of one of Latin America's largest

***Table 1.*** Pro-Chávez Business Owners and Managers by their Structural Predispositions.

| Asset Structure | Liquid Asset Sectors | Fixed Asset Sectors | |
|---|---|---|---|
| Market Orientation | Export Oriented | Domestic Oriented | |
| Market Structure | | Potentially Competitive | Non-Competitive |
| *Pro-Chávez business owners and managers by primary interests and structural predisposition* | | | |
| Protectionist | | | Transportation (case 2) Agroindustry (cases 22, 23, 18, 14, 8) |
| Non-protectionist | Banking (cases 1, 4, 5, 7, 11, 12, 13, 16, 17, 19, 24, 28) | Construction (case 9) Cement (case 21) Food processing (case 25) Telecommunications/media (cases 3, 6, 10, 20, 26) Tourism (case 27) | |
| Number of cases | 12 | 9 | 6 |
| As a percent of total[a] | 43 | 32 | 21 |
| *Pro-Chávez business owners and managers by secondary interests and structural predisposition* | | | |
| Protectionist | | | Agroindustry (case 26) |
| Non-protectionist | Banking (cases 6, 15) | Construction (cases 10, 21) Food processing (case 6) Paper (case 28) Telecommunications/media (cases 5, 7, 17, 25) | |
| Number of cases | 2 | 8 | 1 |
| As a percent of total | 7 | 29 | 4 |
| Total number of cases | 14 | 13 | 7 |
| Primary or secondary interests as a percent of total | 50 | 46 | 25 |

[a]Total number of Pro-Chávez business owners and managers = 28. The bottom row does not sum to 100% because one individual only has secondary business interests. This individual (case 15) built a career at a bank but then moved into government in the early 1990s.

media-based conglomerates.[39] His television station gave Chávez positive media coverage and a newspaper in which he had a controlling interest published the first polls indicating Chávez' rise in public opinion (Santodomingo, 1999, p. 34).[40]

Table 2 indicates that there is considerable variation across the cases in the presence or absence of the conditions that might have led them to assist Chávez. Twenty-one of the 28 (75%) pro-Chávez business owners and managers depended on the state for their business profit and were therefore structurally predisposed to prioritize the state. Only eight of the 28 (29%) pro-Chávez business owners and managers had direct network ties to

***Table 2.*** Presence or Absence of Causal Conditions for Business Owners and Managers to Support Chávez.

| Case ID# | PROTECT | DEPEND | NETWORK | DISTRUST |
|---|---|---|---|---|
| 1 | 0 | 1 | 0 | 1[a,b] |
| 2 | 1 | 0 | 0 | 1 |
| 3 | 0 | 1 | 0 | 1[c] |
| 4 | 0 | 1 | 1 | 1[d] |
| 5 | 0 | 1 | 0 | 1[a,b] |
| 6 | 0 | 1 | 0 | 1[b,c] |
| 7 | 0 | 1 | 0 | 1[b] |
| 8 | 1 | 0 | 1 | 0 |
| 9 | 0 | 1 | 0 | 0 |
| 10 | 0 | 1 | 0 | 0 |
| 11 | 0 | 1 | 0 | 0 |
| 12 | 0 | 1 | 0 | 1[d,e] |
| 13 | 0 | 1 | 0 | 1[a,b] |
| 14 | 1 | 0 | 1 | 0 |
| 15 | 0 | 1[f] | 0 | 1[b] |
| 16 | 0 | 1 | 0 | 0 |
| 17 | 0 | 1 | 0 | 1[g] |
| 18 | 1 | 0 | 0 | 0 |
| 19 | 0 | 1 | 0 | 1[d] |
| 20 | 0 | 1 | 0 | 0 |
| 21 | 0 | 1 | 0 | 0 |
| 22 | 1 | 0 | 1 | 0 |
| 23 | 1 | 0 | 1 | 0 |
| 24 | 0 | 1 | 0 | 1[g] |
| 25 | 0 | 1 | 1 | 0 |
| 26 | 0 | 1 | 1 | 0 |
| 27 | 0 | 0 | 1 | 0 |
| 28 | 0 | 1 | 1[h] | 0 |
| Column sum | 6 | 21 | 8 | 13 |
| Column sum as percent of total | 21 | 75 | 29 | 46 |

*Notes:* Column categories: PROTECT = structurally predisposed to favor protectionist policies; DEPEND = structurally predisposed to prioritize access to the state; NETWORK = had network ties to Chávez; DISTRUST = had incentives to distrust Salas Römer associates as those closely associated with the state's bank intervention or as competitors; 1 = presence of condition; and 0 = absence of condition.
[a]Had struggled for power over a business with Salas Römer associate.
[b]Had bank that failed.
[c]Was in direct competition with businesses that Salas Römer associates closely identify with.
[d]Had close network ties to bankers that failed and blamed the spread of rumors on Salas Römer associates.
[e]Had bank that survived, but faced possible rush on deposits when Salas Römer associates allegedly spread rumors that the collapse of their bank was imminent.
[f]Had secondary interest in sector with this structural predisposition.
[g]Had bank that survived with the aid of private sector rescue packages, but only after suffering significant loses.
[h]Had extraordinary success soon after the 1998 election.

Chávez. Meanwhile, 13 (46%) of the 28 pro-Chávez prominent business owners and managers had incentives to distrust Salas Römer either as competitors or for their close association with the government's handling of the bank crisis.

Indeed, six of the 12 pro-Chávez prominent business owners and managers who had primary business interests in the financial sector lost money as a result of the crisis. As indicated on Table 2, four of these six lost their banks (cases 1, 5, 7 and 13) and two suffered significant losses but their banks managed to survive (cases 17 and 24) with the help of private rescue packages.[41] Moreover, the four with primary interests in banking who lost their banks also faced criminal charges for allegedly defrauding depositors. Of the remaining six with primary financial sector interests, one survived an imminent rush on deposits (case 12) and three had close network ties with failed bankers (cases 4, 12 and 19).[42] Both of the prominent business owners and managers with secondary interests in the financial sector were also negatively affected by the bank crisis as a result of their long associations with several banks that failed (cases 6 and 15). In total, all but five of the 17 banks which faced rumors of imminent failure and required special attention from the state had at least one pro-Chávez business owner and manager associated with them.[43]

## RESULTS OF DATA ANALYSIS

In order to assess the combination of factors associated with pro-Chávez business managers and owners, I reduce the multiple configurations present in the data to the simple most common paths. As this study only includes cases of pro-Chávez business owners and managers, I extend a technique recommended by Ragin and Sonnett (2004) for improving parsimony without sacrificing important elements of complexity. They argue that researchers can reduce complexity by including hypothetically possible configurations as "don't care" configurations. QCA will then use these configurations only if they help simplify the paths to a particular outcome (Ragin & Sonnett, 2004, p. 5). But, Ragin and Sonnet urge researchers to use theory in order to determine which hypothetical configurations they should include in the analysis as "don't cares". Researchers may safely assign a "don't care" outcome to configurations that do not exist but would be easy to imagine based on current theory and evidence. Such "easy counterfactuals" are those configurations that posit the presence of a condition that existing theory and evidence suggests is likely to be related to the outcome of interest. However, they argue that configurations which do not exist and which seem hard to imagine should not be coded as "don't care". Such "difficult counterfactuals" are those that posit the lack of a condition may cause a particular of outcome, despite evidence that in the presence of said condition, other cases produced the outcome of interest.

I extend Ragin and Sonnet's logic regarding counterfactual configurations to low-frequency configurations.[44] As Table 3 indicates, there are four configurations represented by more than one case and four configurations represented by only one case. Upper case letters represent the presence of a condition. Lower case letters represent the absence of a condition. I apply Ragin and Sonnet's logic in determining which of the four configurations represented by a single case I might safely recode as having a "don't care" outcome and which ones I should exclude from the analysis. My theory predicts that the presence of any of the conditions are likely to lead business people to assist Chávez, but posits no theoretical reason that the absence of a condition alone or in any combination would be likely to lead businessmen to assist Chávez. Therefore, I recode the two unique configurations that most closely match Ragin and Sonnet's definition of an "easy counterfactual" as "don't cares". However, because these configurations actually exist in my data, I consider these cases "more likely to matter". These are the cases that have at least one of the conditions deemed theoretically likely to lead business people to assist Chávez but which differ from higher frequency configurations in that they have at least one additional condition present. I exclude from the analysis the remaining two cases that have unique configurations because they are more like "difficult counterfactuals". These "less likely to matter" cases are cases in which only one of the conditions deemed theoretically relevant was present.

***Table 3.*** All Configurations Associated with Pro-Chávez Business Owners and Managers.

| Configurations | Number of Cases | Case ID Numbers |
|---|---|---|
| protect · DEPEND · network · DISTRUST | 11 | Cases: 1, 3, 5, 6, 7, 12, 13, 15, 17, 19, 24 |
| protect · DEPEND · network · distrust | 7 | Cases: 9, 10, 11, 16, 20, 21, 25 |
| PROTECT · depend · NETWORK · distrust | 4 | Cases: 8, 14, 22, 23 |
| protect · DEPEND · NETWORK · distrust | 2 | Cases: 26, 28 |
| PROTECT · depend · network · DISTRUST | 1 | Case 2 |
| protect · DEPEND · NETWORK · DISTRUST | 1 | Case 4 |
| PROTECT · depend · network · distrust | 1 | Case 18 |
| protect · depend · NETWORK · distrust | 1 | Case 27 |

The fact that the "more likely to matter" cases were identified by my sources as likely to have been significant contributors to Chávez lends additional credence to including them in QCA's minimization process as don't cares. It further suggests there may be a cumulative effect of combining these conditions. For example, the presence of three of the four hypothesized conditions in case 4 may help explain why he was probably one of Chávez' biggest financial backers who also helped funnel money from other business owners and managers to Chávez (Zapata, 2000, pp. 130, 133).[45] Not only did this individual have direct ties to Chávez forged in his home state of Baranís (Zapata, 2000, p. 98), but as a banker he was also structurally predisposed to prioritize access to the state. Moreover, he had incentives to distrust Salas Römer. The close association of case 4 with two bankers that had strong ties to one of the first banks to collapse probably evoked his empathy for their plight and may even have raised suspicions about his own business practices. The widely known willingness of the owner of an airline (case 2) to lend Chávez a personal jet may have stemmed not just from a structural predisposition to sympathize with Chávez' protectionist convictions but also his incentives to distrust Salas Römer after his airline suffered significant setbacks under Caldera's administration.[46]

The fact that none of the "less likely to matter" cases are likely to have given significant financial assistance further helps to justify excluding them from the analysis. As a minor agro-industrialist, case 18 had a structural predisposition to favor Chávez' protectionism, but could offer little financial assistance.[47] Similarly, a minor hotel operator (case 27) could have given small amounts to the campaign, but his more important contribution to the campaign was undoubtedly his active involvement in the campaign itself.[48]

Table 4 displays the two paths (configurations of conditions) associated with pro-Chávez business owners and managers and the paths employed to produce each path. I used fuzzy set Qualitative Comparative Analysis (fsQCA) to minimize the configurations.[49] The analysis dropped two cases: the two cases in which state dependence (DEPEND) were combined with direct network ties (NETWORK). The fsQCA analysis yields the same results, however, if these two cases are recoded as more likely to matter configurations. This reconfirms their idiosyncratic uniqueness. Both of these individuals reputedly gave generously to the campaign, suggesting that their direct network ties to Chávez reaffirmed their predisposition to assist the front-runner regardless of his policy preferences. As a banker, case 28 would have been eager to secure contracts with government agencies.[50] Indeed, he enjoyed business success in the initial years after the election that appeared to go beyond what the market might otherwise have permitted.[51] By 1998,

**Table 4.**  Paths Taken by Businessmen Identified as Assisting Chávez.

| Paths | Configurations | Code |
|---|---|---|
| 1. protect · DEPEND | protect · DEPEND · network · DISTRUST | 1 |
| | protect · DEPEND · network · distrust | 1 |
| | protect · DEPEND · NETWORK · DISTRUST | – |
| 2. PROTECT · depend · NETWORK · distrust | PROTECT · depend · NETWORK · distrust | 1 |

*Notes:* Upper case letters represent presence of condition. Lower case letters represent absence of condition. Conditions not listed were dropped out of the path because the fsQCA determined they were irrelevant to the outcome. Configurations code refers to how the configuration was coded in fsQCA. Coding Categories: PROTECT = structurally predisposed to favor protectionist policies, DEPEND = structurally predisposed to prioritize access to the state, NETWORK = had direct tie to Chávez, DISTRUST = had incentives to distrust Salas Römer, · = and, + = or, 1 = combination associated with assisting Chávez and − = combination more likely to matter.

case 26 was the president of Venezuela's second largest cable provider and would therefore have had incentives to support the candidate with whom he had direct ties in hopes that he might favorably influence the pending regulatory reforms.

### State Dependence as a Necessary and Sufficient Condition

The dominance of path 1, indicated in Table 4, suggests the potent influence of Venezuela's oil dependence on the political interests of business. Dependence on the state was necessary and sufficient in the absence of protectionist interests for 20 of the 28 pro-Chávez business managers and owners. The analysis determined that both network ties and distrust of Salas Römer were irrelevant to the outcome and were therefore dropped out of path 1. Although 18 of the 20 that took path 1 did not have network ties to Chávez, the case coded as "more likely to matter" which was taken into consideration in determining this path, did have NETWORK ties. Similarly, although 12 businessmen who were structurally predisposed to prioritize access to the state also had incentives to distrust Salas Römer, eight others did not.

Seven businesspeople uniquely matched the configurations of path 1. They included two businesspeople with interests in cement and construction, three newspaper publishers and two bankers. In each of these cases, dependence on the state made them predisposed to assist whichever candidate appeared most likely to win the elections. Indeed, a banker quipped that he assisted Chávez "just in case [he won]" and that he doubted Chávez would end up being that radical or difficult to persuade after being elected.[52] Nevertheless, these cases represented the minority of those who took path 1.

The majority of businessmen that took path 1 (12) were both structurally predisposed to prioritize access to the state and had incentives to distrust Salas Römer's associates. All but one were bankers who also had incentives to distrust Salas Römer for his association with those involved with the bank crisis.[53] The one non-banker was a television network owner (case 3) who had incentives to distrust Salas Römer because of Salas Römer's close personal association with a rival television network owner (Santodomingo, 1999, p. 29). This rival television network owner had historically split the television market with one other network (owned by case 6) until the government approved a third private broadcasting network for case 3 in 1988 (Ortiz, 2004, pp. 80–81). The government made this decision soon after the rival television network had issued harsh accusations of corruption in the current administration. Case 3 and case 6 had reason to believe that the rival television network owner might seek to undermine their current market dominance if he were to gain power via a Salas Römer victory (Ortiz, 2004, p. 86) because cases 3 and 6 had jointly sought to marginalize their rival's market share in the 1990s (Ortiz, 2004, p. 80).

Three bankers (cases 1, 5 and 13) had incentives to distrust Salas Römer's associates as competitors as well as for their involvement with the bank crisis. All three faced massive depositor withdrawals, hostile state interventions and criminal charges. But, they also had incentives to distrust Salas Römer's close economic advisor as a competitor. This economic advisor had taken control of the banks controlled by two of these bankers (cases 1 and 5) in the 1980s.[54] With the help of another banker (case 13), these bankers (cases 1 and 5) won back control over Venezuela's premier bank at the time in 1993 (Zapata, 1995, p. 28).[55] The harsh treatment they received during the bank crisis appeared to both of these bankers to be retribution for having pushed the individual now rumored to be Salas Römer's close economic advisor out.[56] They therefore had reason to believe that they might not prosper during the next presidential administration, if Salas Römer won the election and this advisor gained power.

*Protectionist Interests Necessary in Conjunction with Network Ties*

The second path represented in Table 4 indicates that protectionist economic interests were necessary for some pro-Chávez business owners and managers but only when combined with network ties in the absence of both state dependence and distrust of Salas Römer. A major agro-industrialist (case 8) along with smaller agro-industrialists who grew cotton (case 22) exemplified path 2 taken by four businessmen. Attracted by Chávez' protectionist rhetoric, they promoted a silent pro-Chávez rebellion within the otherwise pro-neoliberal (Giacalone, 1999; Becker, 1990) FEDECAMARAS (Santodomingo, 1999; Zapata, 2000, pp. 31, 96, 97, 132). Policy preferences tied to a protectionist mode of insertion into the global economy were, however, insufficient for these business managers and owners. Path 2 highlights how access to the state can become an over-riding concern in petro-states, even among those who act according to their expected sector-based policy preferences according to world systems theory.

## CONCLUSION

This study contributes to our understanding of private sector political behavior. In particular, it offers new insight into one of the central puzzles regarding campaign financing: why business managers and owners would support a leftist candidate. It does so with a study of the first electoral campaign of one of Latin America's most outspoken critics of globalization: that of President Hugo Chávez in 1998. The analysis of 28 prominent business managers and owners identified by inside sources as likely contributors to Chávez' campaign reveals that for most pro-Chávez business managers and owners it was sufficient to be in a sector which was dependent on the state. The predominance of this path undermines the notion, supported by research on the earlier generation of Latin American leftists and broadly consistent with world systems expectations regarding the political behavior of business in middle-income states, that businesspeople which tend to benefit from protectionist policies would be most likely to assist leftist candidates. Indeed, most of these state-dependent pro-Chávez business managers and owners should have been predisposed to oppose Chávez' anti-neoliberal policy agenda. Instead, these cases confirm recent studies of campaign financing which indicate that business managers and owners in sectors that depend on government contracts are more likely to prioritize access to the state and therefore are more open to supporting leftist political candidates.

Furthermore, although a small number of pro-Chávez business owners and managers were predisposed to share Chávez' enthusiasm for protectionist economic policies, this predisposition was not sufficient. It was associated with pro-Chávez business owners and managers only when combined with the presence of direct network ties. The fact that protectionist predispositions were only associated with pro-Chávez business owners and managers in combination with network ties suggests the need to modify the expectations for political behavior in middle-income states based on world-systems theory and research on prior Latin American populists in certain contexts. It emphasizes how the concern for access to the state may color policy convictions for most business, regardless of sector specific interests, in oil-exporting economies, where the private sector is generally more dependent on the state. As such, these cases support the proposed extension of the reasoning offered by recent campaign finance research for why business-people might assist a leftist candidate beyond sector-based variation to cross-national variation in the private sector's state dependency. The extension posits that incentives to support such a candidate, such as network ties to the candidate, as well as disincentives to support alternative candidates, such as a strong distrust of those closely associated with the candidate, may be more important in determining business' political behavior in economies where business largely depends on the state. Given prior research which indicates that the private sector in oil-exporting states, like Venezuela, may be acutely state dependent, one might expect these incentives and disincentives, independent of sector-specific interests, to play a dominant role in determining the political behavior of business. Indeed, a concern for state access appeared to galvanize those favoring protectionist policies that might otherwise have been apathetic in the 1998 Venezuelan presidential elections, given Chávez lead in the polls. Moreover, most state-dependent pro-Chávez businesspeople also had incentives to distrust Chávez' leading competition. Thus, this general concern for state access also appeared to persuade those who might otherwise have favored the country's further integration into the global economy to assist a radical anti-neoliberal candidate.

This study suggests that future research on the rise to political power of politicians opposed to globalization should consider not just how sector-based interests may shape the political behavior of business managers and owners, but also how the structure of some domestic economies may generate unique opportunities for leftist candidates. If the political behavior of business managers and owners varies according to varying domestic economic structures, we might then expect that the predominant rationale for business to assist anti-neoliberal presidential candidates might vary cross nationally. Clearly oil dependence does not characterize all countries where anti-neoliberal presidents have succeeded. Thus, in countries where the private sector is not as dependent on the state as in petro-states, we would not expect business to prioritize access to the state as they did in Venezuela. We would, instead, expect business assistance for left-leaning candidates in such economies to come from protectionist business owners and managers. Furthermore, given that businesses in protectionist sectors are more likely to be small firms, one might not expect business assistance to figure as prominently in such campaigns. The 2002 election of President Lula de Silva in Brazil, for example, may conform more closely to this scenario.

Alternately, the recent election of South America's newest outspoken critic of neoliberalism, Bolivian President Evo Morales, may confirm the unique opportunities leftist candidates may have in economies with state-dependent private sectors. Like the Venezuelan state, the Bolivian state reaped the majority of its revenue from the extraction and export of natural resources (natural gas, tin and oil among others). Like the Venezuelan private sector, the Bolivian private sector also accounted for a lesser share of the country's investments and much of the private sector depended on the state for subsidies and protections. In such a setting we might expect the private sector to place greater priority on access to the state, making individual businesspeople more susceptible to assisting leftist candidates regardless of their sector-based policy predispositions. If so, then we might expect countries that depend on exporting natural resources to take leadership in defining regional political agendas during periods, such as we face today, when rising anti-American sentiment fosters popular support for left-leaning political leaders.

## NOTES

1. Neoliberal economic reforms typically include: (1) stabilization policies, which constrain wages, lift price constraints and reduce state spending and (2) structural adjustment policies, which liberalize trade along with controls on the flow of capital in and out of a country and privatize state-owned enterprises.

2. A Member of the Finance Committee for Chávez' campaign (interviewed 12/5/2005) described a wide range of fundraising strategies, including various types of fundraising events, that the campaign pursued before soliciting business for campaign contributions. According to several anonymous sources close to the campaign (interviews conducted in late 2005), Chávez also received significant financial assistance from the Cuban government, retired military leaders, MAS governors, old leaders of the communist party, the rector of Venezuela's leading public university and a major narcotics distributor.

3. The Venezuelan president who introduced an aggressive stabilization policy in 1989 by eliminating price controls on gasoline, and restructured the economy to be more oriented toward global markets by privatizing some state enterprises and liberalizing trade, faced widespread riots, a general strike and was impeached in 1993 (Naím, 1993; McCoy & Smith, 1995).

4. Simon Romero, "Coup? Not His Style, But Power? Oh, Yes," *The New York Times*, 4/28/2002, 3, LEXIS, News Library, World News File, North/South America News Sources.

5. For example, Jim Shultz, the executive director of a policy analysis group in Bolivia called Democracy Center, was quoted saying: "There's a common thread that runs through Lula and Kirchner and Chávez and Evo, and the left in Chile to a certain degree, and that thread is a popular challenge to the market fundamentalism of the Washington Consensus." Juan Forero, "Elections Could Tilt Latin America Further to the Left," *New York Times*, 12/10/2005, International, Americas, NYTimes.com

6. Note, however, that "no particular activity (whether defined in terms of its output or of the technique used) is inherently core-like or periphery-like" (Arrighi & Drangel, 1986).

7. My informants, as well as those likely to have made contributions to Chávez, are not identified by name here because of the political sensitivity of the issue. At the time of this publication, Venezuela remains fairly polarized politically and many of those closely associated with the campaign as well as those likely to have assisted Chávez in the past are now firmly opposed to Chávez.

8. "Coup and Counter-coup; Venezuela," *Economist.com*, 4/12//2002, LEXIS, News Library, Business News File, Business and Finance Sources; Simon Romero, "Coup? Not His Style, But Power? Oh, Yes," *The New York Times*, 4/28/2002, 3, LEXIS, News Library, World News File, North/South America News Sources; C. Rodriguez Marturet, "Gustavo Cisneros? Presidente de Venezuela?" in *Soberanía* (2002).

9. "Venezuelan Farmers Go on Strike," *Xinhua News Agency*, 8/19/1997, NEXIS, News Library, World News File, North/South America News Sources.

10. Marita Seara, "A Sector in Crisis: Cinderella: The Textile Industry," *Business Venezuela*, 10/11/1998, LEXIS, News Library, World News File, North/South America News Sources.

11. "Venezuela Trade: Door to Andean Imports Remains Only Half-open," *Latin America Regional Reports: Andean Group*, 9/2/1983, RA-83-07, LEXIS, News Library, World News File, North/South America News Sources; Joseph Mann, "Venezuelans Face Heavy Foreign Exchange Losses," *Financial Times*, 3/7/1989, 1, LEXIS, News Library, World News File, North/South America News Sources.

12. Peter Passell, "Economic Scene; Cement Shoes For Venezuela," *The New York Times*, 9/25/1991, D, LEXIS, News Library, World News File, North/South America News Sources; Raymond Colitt, "Brazil and Venezuela Find Togetherness: Neighbors Overcome Decades of Dissension to Develop Strong Links in Trade and Energy," *The Financial Post*, 7/24/1996, 1, LEXIS, News Library, World News File, North/South America News Sources; Estrella Gutierrez, "Trade-Venezuela: More Liberal Trade with Chile in 1997," *IPS-Inter Press Service*, 12/26/1996, LEXIS, News Library, World News File, North/South America News Sources.

13. Marita Seara, "A Sector in Crisis: Cinderella: The Textile Industry," *Business Venezuela*, 10/11/1998, LEXIS, News Library, World News File, North/South America News Sources.

14. Member of the Finance Committee for Chávez' campaign, interviewed 12/5/2005.

15. Personal email communication with an expert on Venezuelan campaign finance, 11/30/2005.

16. Member of Chávez' public relations team during campaign, interviewed 11/21/2005.

17. Personal email communication with expert on Venezuelan campaign finance, 11/30/2005.

18. Interview with Jesse Chacón, former director of The *National Commission of Telecommunications* (CONATEL) and current Communication and Information Minister published by VenezuelaAnalysis.com 2/13/2004, http://www.venezuelanalysis.com/articles.php?artno=1105.

19. "Venezuela. It's all Chavez," *The Economist*, 7/4/1998, U.S. Edition, World Politics and Current Affairs, The Americas, LEXIS, News Library, World News File, North/South America News Sources; David Paulin, "Chavez Goals Strike Fear in Oil Executives; Venezuela's Poor See Him as Hero," *The Washington Times*, 10/20/1998, LEXIS, News Library, World News File, North/South America News Sources.

20. "Former Bank Chief Convicted," *The Guardian*, 8/4/1998, The Guardian Foreign Page, LEXIS, News Library, General News File, Major Papers Sources.

21. Falling oil prices had compounded a growing sense of insecurity among Venezuela's private sector, following the two 1992 coup attempts and the 1993 impeachment of President Carlos Andrés Pérez. As debtors began to default on their loans, bankers turned to ever more speculative actions, including trading on the Caracas Stock Exchange and buying and selling real estate in order to maintain sufficient liquidity. By early 1994, banks were at their breaking point. See "A Really Big Bank Bust; Venezuela's Crash of the Century is Still Crashing," *The Washington Post*, 3/19/1995, LEXIS, News Library, World News File, North/South America News Sources.

22. Joseph Mann, "Sticks and Carrots for Venezuela's Banks: Selective Assistance and Pressure is on Offer to the Troubled Financial Institutions," *Financial Times*, 8/11/1994a, LEXIS, News Library, Business News File, Business and Finance Sources.

23. "Venezuela: Arrests Begin in the Banco Latino Scandal," *ISP-Inter Press Service*, 3/3/1994, LEXIS, News Library, World News File, North/South America News Sources.

24. Joseph Mann, "Sticks and Carrots for Venezuela's Banks: Selective Assistance and Pressure is on Offer to the Troubled Financial Institutions," *Financial Times*, 8/11/1994a, LEXIS, News Library, Business News File, Business and Finance Sources; "Venezuela: Arrests Begin in the Banco Latino Scandal," *ISP-Inter Press Service*, 3/3/1994, LEXIS, News Library, World News File, North/South America News Sources. These eight financial institutions were Amazonas, Bancor, Barinas, Construcción, La Guaira, Maracaibo and Metropolitano banks and the Sociedad Financiera Fiveca finance company according to "Unexpected Moves in Bank Crisis: Troubled Institutions Closed, Re-opened to Pay Depositors," *Latin America Regional Reports: Andean Group*, 6/30/1994, RA-94-05, LEXIS, News Library, World News File, North/South America News Sources.

25. Joseph Mann, "Sticks and Carrots for Venezuela's Banks: Selective Assistance and Pressure is on Offer to the Troubled Financial Institutions," *Financial Times*, 8/11/1994a, LEXIS, News Library, Business News File, Business and Finance Sources. Some believed this was because Caldera had continued to allow the state-run guarantee fund to allocate emergency aid to the eight banks in trouble without removing the bank boards of directors. See "Venezuelan Banking; Chaos in Caracas," *The Economist*, 6/18/1994, Finance, LEXIS News Library, World News Library, North/South America News Sources.

26. "Venezuelan Government To Liquidate Intervened Banks," *The Associated Press*, 8/11/1994, Business News, LEXIS, News Library, World News File, North/South America News Sources.

27. Joseph Mann, "Sticks and Carrots for Venezuela's Banks: Selective Assistance and Pressure is on Offer to the Troubled Financial Institutions," *Financial Times*, 8/11/1994a, LEXIS, News Library, Business News File, Business and Finance Sources.

28. Joseph Mann, "Sticks and Carrots for Venezuela's Banks: Selective Assistance and Pressure is on Offer to the Troubled Financial Institutions," *Financial Times*, 8/11/1994a, LEXIS, News Library, Business News File, Business and Finance Sources; "Government Takes Over More Banks; Selective Program of Assistance and Pressure," *Latin America Regional Reports: Andean Group*, 9/8/1994, RA-94-07, LEXIS, News Library, World News File, North/South America News Sources.

29. "Venezuela: Review 1996," *Americas Review World of Information*, 11/1995, Comment & Analysis, Country Profile, LEXIS News Library, World News File, North/South America News Sources. According to this article, the government declared it would no longer intervene in troubled banks just hours before three new banks failed and the state intervened on their behalf.

30. Stephen Fidler, "Caracas Takes Over More Banks," *Financial Times*, 12/16/1994, LEXIS, News Library, Business News File, Business and Finance Sources; "Unexpected Moves in Bank Crisis: Troubled Institutions Closed, Re-opened to Pay Depositors," *Latin America Regional Reports: Andean Group*, 6/30/1994, RA-94-05, LEXIS, News Library, World News File, North/South America News Sources.

31. "Venezuela: Arrests Begin in the Banco Latino Scandal," *ISP-Inter Press Service*, 3/3/1994, LEXIS, News Library, World News File, North/South America News Sources.

32. This special Junta de Emergencia Financiera, formed in mid-February 1994, led the campaign to criminally charge bankers. See Zapata (2000, p. 64) and Mann, J. "Venezuela Bank Head Named as Depositors Fume," *Financial Times*, 2/21/1994, p. 6, LEXIS, News Library, Business News File, Business and Finance Sources.

33. See "Cabinet Shuffle Announced." *Union Radio, BBC Summary of Broadcasts*, 5/29/1994, Latin America and the Caribbean; Venezuela, LEXIS News Library, World News File, North/South America News Sources for announcement.

34. A member of both the Banco Latino and Banco de Venezuela intervention teams, this rumored associate took a hard-line approach to bank intervention, as illustrated by his efforts to undermine one of the fallen banks even after it was statized (Zapata, 1997, pp. 42–49).

35. A rival banker who had denounced the extravagance of bankers involved with failed banks (including cases 1, 5, 6 and 7) and an owner of a television network station who publicly blamed the collapse of Banco Latino on two prominent Venezuelan businessmen (cases 6 and 7) were among those rumored to be associated with Salas Romer (Zapata 1995, p. 36). On the former, see Zapata (1995, p. 16) and Kilby, Paul. "Out of the Time Warp," *Latin Finance*, 9/1997, Venezuela Report, p. 41, LEXIS, News Library, World News File, North/South America News Sources. The former publicly denounced case 1 for having "employed 45 personal security guards" and having offices full of artwork that would "put J. P. Morgan to shame". He decried case 5's purchase of a series of huge overpriced ranches and indicated publicly that he thought cases 6 and 7 were to blame for the bank crisis. See "Is Still Crashing," *The Washington Post*, 3/19/1995, p. C03, LEXIS, News Library, World News File, North/South American News Sources.

36. As a former head of Venezuela's agricultural association, FEDEAGRO, this individual (case 26) had historically advocated protectionist policies.

37. For example, case 21 owned a major cement factory (Zapata, 2000, p. 98); case 25 headed a market dominant pasta making enterprise and case 6 was not only Venezuela's CocaCola bottler, but also was the leading bottler in Latin America as well as a competitive beer producer and distributor. See Kenneth Gilpin, "Panamerican Beverages and Venezuelan Bottler to Merge," *The New York Times*, 5/13/1997, D. Lexis, News Library, World News File, North/South America News Sources. In addition, one of the bankers (case 28) profited from manufacturing paper. See "Businessmen Weigh More Than They Own," *Latin America Special Report*, 10/26/1984, Venezuela, LexisNexus News Library, World News Files, North/South America News Sources.

38. Deroy Murdock, "Venezuela's Attack on the Press," *The Washington Times*, 6/15/1995, LEXIS, News Library, World News File, North/South America Sources.

39. Raymond Colitt, "Venezuela's Unfolding Television Drama: CGC Hopes Programming Will Help it Win Latin America's Media War," *Financial Times*, 3/24/1998, Companies and Finance: International, LEXIS, News Library, Business News, Business and Finance Sources. Jo Dallas, "Cisneros' Split Image," *Multinational News International*, 7/1997, LEXIS, News Library, Business News File, Business and Finance Sources.

40. Other television network owners (cases 3 and 17) had provided positive coverage of Chávez' February 4, 1992 coup effort (Zapata, 2000, p. 96) as well as the campaign in 1998 (Zapata, 2000, p. 130).

41. In one of the latter cases, shareholders invested large sums of capital to save the bank. In the other, the bank earned $18 million by selling half of the business to a Colombian bank. See "Venezuela: Review 1996," *Americas Review of Information*, 11/1995, Comment & Analysis, p. 92, LEXIS News Library, News File, North/South America News Sources; "Government Acts on Five Banks," *Facts on File News Digest*, 3/16/1995, F2, Other News, p. 202, LEXIS News Library, News File, North/South America News Sources.

42. Case 4 had close network ties to bankers who had banks which closed (cases 13 and 15). For example, he owed his start in the insurance business to one of these bankers (case 15) (Zapata, 2000, pp. 61–62). The bank with which case 12 was associated had done a significant amount of business with the first bank to fall, Banco Latino (Zapata, 1995, p. 33).

43. The president of another bank that failed, Banco Metropoliana, was not rumored to support Chávez probably because he was president Caldera's son-in-law. See Alison MacGregor, "A Fugitive in Ottawa," *The Ottawa Citizen*, 3/21/1998, LEXIS News Library, World News File, North/South America News Sources. I have been unable to verify whether top ranking officials in four additional banks were pro-Chávez: three of these were banks that were eventually taken over in June 1994 (Amazonas, Construcción and Sociedad Financiera Fiveca) and one was a bank that suffered considerable losses in January 1994 due to rumors of imminent failure (Banco Principal).

44. This method was adopted as per personal correspondence with Charles Ragin, one of the leading scholars on the use of Qualitative Comparative Analysis (12/7, 12/9, 12/14/2005).

45. Member of Chávez' public relations team during campaign, interviewed 11/21/2005.

46. His distress with the previous administration and eagerness to secure a better relationship with the government in hopes that they might help him out of his financial troubles was confirmed by a member of the Finance Committee for Chávez' campaign, interviewed 12/5/2005.

47. Close friend and advisor of Chávez, interviewed 12/2/2005.

48. Member of Chávez' public relations team during campaign, interviewed 11/21/2005 and 12/6/2005.

49. Program accessed at www.fsqca.com, December 2005.

50. Member of Chávez' public relations team during campaign, interviewed 11/21/2005. A close friend and advisor of Chávez, interviewed 12/2/2005, personally took case 28 to meet Chávez and confirmed that he made large donations.

51. John Barham, "Trouble in the Andes," *LatinFinance*, 2000, 9, p. 26, LEXIS News Library, World News File, North/South America News Sources.

52. Personal email communication with an expert on Venezuelan campaign finance, 11/30/2005.

53. "Venezuela: Arrests Begin in the Banco Latino Scandal," *ISP-Inter Press Service*, 3/3/1994, LEXIS, News Library, World News File, North/South America News Sources.

54. Case 1 lost his bank to this individual in 1985. See "Bank post battle," *Latin America Weekly Report*, 12/13/1985, LEXIS, News Library, World News File, North/South America News Sources. Case 5 lost control over his bank to this individual in 1989. See "Venezuela-Finance: Another Large Bank Taken Over by Government," *IPS-Inter Press Service*, 8/8/1994, LEXIS, News Library, World News File, North/South America News Sources.

55. "Buying Positions for the Reform; Hostile Purchase is Crest of Recent Acquisitions Wave," *Latin America Weekly Report*, 11/1/1990, WR-90-42, LEXIS, News Library, World News File, North/South America News Sources.

56. Joseph Mann, "Caldera Critics Face Wave of Security Raids," *Financial Times*, 7/5/1994b, LEXIS, News Library, Business News File, Business and Finance Sources.

# ACKNOWLEDGMENTS

I would like to gratefully acknowledge Liz Borland, Michael Mulcahy, Kati Griffith and the Workshop of the Program on Latin America and the Caribbean at the Maxwell School of Public Affairs, Syracuse University for comments on earlier versions. I would also like to thank the Fulbright Scholar program, the Universidad Central de Venezuela and the Instituto de Estudios Superiores de Administración for making research possible in Venezuela.

# REFERENCES

Aguero, F. (1995). Crisis and decay of democracy in Venezuela: The civil-military dimension. In J. McCoy, A. Serbin, W. Smith & A. Stambouli (Eds), *Venezuelan Democracy Under Stress* (pp. 215–236). Coral Gables FL: North–South Center at the University of Miami.

Alvarez, A. E. (1995). Cuanto Cuesta un Candidato? Estimaciones del Costo de las Campañas Politicas y de las Elecciones en Venezuela. *Politeia 18*, 57–99.

Arrighi, G. (1985). *Semiperipheral Development: The Politics of Southern Europe in the Twentieth Century*. Beverly Hills CA: Sage Publications.

Arrighi, G., & Drangel, J. (1986). The Stratification of the World-economy: An Exploration of the Semiperipheral Zone. *Review 10*, 9–74.

Baptista, A., & Mommer, B. (1989). Renta petrolera y distribución factorial del ingreso. In H.-P. Nissen & B. Mommer (Eds), *Adios a al Bonanza? Crisis de la Distribución del Ingreso en Venezuela* (pp. 15–40). Caracas: ILIS-CENDES, Editorial Nueva Sociedad.

Becker, D. (1990). Business Associations in Latin America: The Venezuelan Case. *Comparative Political Studies 23*(1), 114–138.

Bitar, S., & Troncoso, E. (1990). *Venezuela: The industrial challenge* (M. Shifter, & D. Vera, Trans.). Washington DC: A Publication of the Institute for the Study of Human Issues.

Briceño-León, R. (1990). *Los Efectos Perversos del Petróleo*. Caracas: Fondo Editorial Acta Científica Venezolana; Consorcio de Ediciones Capriles.

Buxton, J. (2001). *The Failure of Political Reform in Venezuela*. Aldershot, England: Ashgate.

Buxton, J. (2003). Economic policy and the rise of Hugo Chávez. In S. Ellner & D. Hellinger (Eds), *Venezuelan Politics in the Chávez Era: Class, Polarization, and Conflict* (pp. 113–130). Boulder CO: Lynne Rienner Publishers.

Canache, D. (2004). Urban poor and political order. In J. McCoy & D. Myers (Eds), *The Unraveling of Representative Democracy in Venezuela*. Baltimore MD: Johns Hopkins University Press.

Collier, P. (2000). *Economic Causes of Civil Conflict and their Implications for Policy*. Washington DC: World Bank.

Collier, R. B., & Collier, D. (1991). *Shaping the Political Arena: Critical Junctures, the Labor Movement, and Regime Dynamics in Latin America*. Princeton NJ: Princeton University Press.

Conaghan, C., & Malloy, J. (1994). *Unsettling Statecraft: Democracy and Neoliberalism in the Central Andes*. Pittsburgh PA: University of Pittsburgh Press.

Coppedge, M. (1994). Prospects for Democratic Governability in Venezuela. *Journal of Interamerican Studies and World Affairs 36*(2), 39–64.

Coppedge, M. (2000). Venezuelan parties and the representation of elite interests. In K. Middlebrook (Ed.), *Conservative Parties, the Right, and Democracy in Latin America* (pp. 110–136). Baltimore MD: The Johns Hopkins University Press.

Corrales, J., & Cisneros, I. (1999). Corporatism, Trade Liberalization and Sectoral Responses: The Case of Venezuela, 1989–1999. *World Development 27*(12), 2099–2123.

Cress, D., & Snow, D. (2000). The Outcomes of Homeless Mobilization: The Influence of Organization, Distruption, Political Mediation, and Framing. *The American Journal of Sociology 105*(4), 1063–1104.

Crisp, B. (2000). *Democratic Institutional Design*. Stanford CA: Stanford University Press.

Crisp, B., & Levine, D. (1998). Democratizing the Democracy? Crisis and Reform in Venezuela. *Journal of Interamerican Studies and World Affairs 40*(2), 27–61.

Crisp, B., Levine, D., & Rey, J. C. (1995). The legitimacy problem. In J. McCoy, A. Servin, W. C. Smith & A. Stambouli (Eds), *Venezuela Democracy Under Stress*. New Brunswick NJ: Transaction Books.

Cupolo, M. (1996). *Petróleo y Política en México y Venezuela*. Caracas: Equinoccio; Ediciones de la Universidad Simon Bolivar.

Domhoff, G. W. (1967). *Who Rules America?* Englewood Cliffs NJ: Prentice-Hall.

Domhoff, G. W. (1972). *Fat Cats and Democrats: The Role of the Big Rich in the Party of the Common Man.* Englewood Cliffs NJ: Prentice-Hall.

Domhoff, G. W. (1990). *The Power Elite and the State: How Policy is Made in America.* New York: A. de Gruyter.

Ellner, S. (2003). Introduction: The search for explanations. In S. Ellner & D. Hellinger (Eds), *Venezuelan Politics in the Chávez Era* (pp. 7–26). Boulder CO: Lynne Rienner Publishers.

Fearon, J. (2005). Primary Commodity Exports and Civil War. *Journal of Conflict Resolution* 49(4), 483–507.

Ferguson, T. (1995). *Golden Rule: The Investment Theory of Party Competition and the Logic of Money-driven Political Systems.* Chicago IL: University of Chicago Press.

Ferguson, T., & Rogers, J. (1986). *Right Turn: The Decline of the Democrats and the Future of American Politics* (1st ed.). New York: Hill and Wang.

Frieden, J. (1991). *Debt, Development and Democracy: Modern Political Economy and Latin America, 1965–1985.* Princeton NJ: Princeton University Press.

Giacalone, R. (1999). *Los Empresarios Frente al Grupo de los Tres: Integración, Intereses e Ideas.* Caracas: Nueva Sociedad.

Gil Yepes, J. A. (2004). Public opinion, political socialization, and regime stablization. In J. McCoy & D. Myers (Eds), *The Unraveling of Representative Democracy in Venezuela.* Baltimore MD: Johns Hopkins University Press.

Gómez, E. (1989). *El Empresariado Venezolano: A Mitad de Camino entre Keynes y Hayek.* Caracas: Alltolitho.

Gopian, D. J., Smith, H., & Smith, W. (1984). What Makes PACs Tick? *American Journal of Political Science* 28(2), 259–281.

Gourevitch, P. (1986). *Politics in Hard Times: Comparative Responses to International Economic Crisis.* Ithaca NY: Cornell University Press.

Grier, K., Munger, M., & Roberts, B. (1994). The Determinants of Industry Political Activity, 1978–1986. *American Journal of Political Science* 88(4), 911–926.

Haggard, S., Maxfield, S., & Schneider, B. R. (1997). Theories of business and business-state relations. In S. Maxfield & B. R. Schneider (Eds), *Business and the State in Developing Countries* (pp. 36–60). Ithaca NY: Cornell University Press.

Handler, E., & Mulkern, J. R. (1982). *Business in Politics: Campaign Strategies of Corporate Political Action Committees.* Lexington MA: Lexington Books.

Hellinger, D. (2003). Political overview: The breakdown of *Puntofijismo.* In S. Ellner & D. Hellinger (Eds), *Venezuelan Politics in the Chávez Era: Class, Polarization, and Conflict* (pp. 27–54). Boulder CO: Lynne Rienner Publishers.

Hillman, R. (2004). Intellectuals: An elite divided. In J. McCoy & D. Myers (Eds), *The Unraveling of Representative Democracy in Venezuela* (pp. 115–129). Baltimore MD: Johns Hopkins University Press.

Jongkind, F. (1993). Venezuelan Industry Under the New Conditions of the 1989 Economic Policy. *European Review of Latin American and Caribbean Studies* 54, 65–93.

Karl, T. L. (1987). Petroleum and Political Pacts: The Transition to Democracy in Venezuela. *Latin American Research Review* 22(1), 63–94.

Karl, T. L. (1997). *The Paradox of Plenty: Oil Booms and Petro-states.* Berkeley CA: University of California Press.

Keller, A. (1997). Las fortalezas aparentes: El caso de los actores politicos Venezolanos frente a los procesos de democratización y de reformas económicas. In M. M. Araujo (Ed.), *Los Actores Sociales y Políticos en los Procesos de Transformación en América Latina*. Buenos Aires: CIEDLA.

Kelly, J., & Palma, P. A. (2004). The syndrome of economic decline and the quest for change. In J. McCoy & D. Myers (Eds), *The Unraveling of Representative Democracy in Venezuela* (pp. 202–230). Baltimore MD: Johns Hopkins University Press.

Kolko, G. (1963). *The Triumph of Conservatism: A Re-interpretation of American History, 1900–1916*. New York: Free Press of Glencoe.

Lewis, C., & Center for Public Integrity. (2004). *The Buying of the President, 2004: Who's Really Bankrolling Bush and his Democratic Challengers – and What They Expect in Return* (1st ed.). New York: Perennial.

Lindblom, C. E. (1977). *Politics and Markets: The World's Political Economic Systems*. New York: Basic Books.

Martin, W. G. (1990). Introduction: The challenge of the semiperiphery. In W. G. Martin (Ed.), *Semiperipheral States in the World-economy*. New York: Greenwood Press.

McCoy, J. (1999). Chavez and the End of 'Partyarchy' in Venezuela. *Journal of Democracy* *10*(3), 64–77.

McCoy, J. (2004). From representative to participatory democracy? Regime transformation in Venezuela. In J. McCoy & D. Myers (Eds), *The unraveling of representative democracy in Venezuela* (pp. 263–296). Baltimore MD: Johns Hopkins University Press.

McCoy, J., & Smith, W. C. (1995). Democratic Disequilibrium in Venezuela. *Journal of Interameircan Studies and World Affairs 37*(2), 113–179.

Mills, C. W. (1956). *The Power Elite*. New York: Oxford University Press.

Mintz, B., & Schwartz, M. (1985). *The Power Structure of American Business*. Chicago IL: University of Chicago Press.

Mizruchi, M. S. (1982). *The American Corporate Network, 1904–1974*. Beverly Hills CA: Sage.

Molina, J. (2004). The unraveling of Venezuela's party system: From party rule to personalistic politics and deinstitutionalization. In J. McCoy & D. Myers (Eds), *The Unraveling of Representative Democracy in Venezuela* (pp. 152–180). Baltimore MD: Johns Hopkins University Press.

Naím, M. (1984). La empresa privada en Venezuela: Que pasa cuando se crece en medio de la riqueza y la confusión? In M. Naím & R. Piñango (Eds), *El Caso Venezuela: Una Ilusión de Armonía* (pp. 152–183). Caracas: Ediciones IESA.

Naím, M. (1993). *Paper Tigers and Minotaurs*. Washington DC: Carnegie Endowment for International Peace.

Naím, M., Francés, A. (1995). The Venezuelan private sector: From courting the state to courting the market. In L. W. Goodman, J. M. Forman, M. Naím, J. S. Tulchin & G. Bland (Eds), *Lessons of the Venezuelan Experience* (pp. 165–192). Washington DC: The Woodrow Wilson Center Press.

Nemeth, R. J., & Smith, D. A. (1985). International Trade and World-system Structure: A Multiple Network Analysis. *Review 8*, 517–560.

Njaim, H. (2004). Financiamiento político en los países Andinos: Bolivia, Colombia, Ecuador, Perú y Venezuela. In S. Griner & D. Zovatto (Eds), *De las Normas a las Buenas Prácticas*. San José: Organización de los Estados Americanos/IDEA.

Norden, D. (1996). The Rise of the Leuitenant Colonels: Rebellion in Argentina and Venezuela. *Latin American Perspectives 23*(30), 74–86.

Ortiz, N. (2004). Entrepreneurs: Profits without power? In J. McCoy & D. Myers (Eds), *The unraveling of representative democracy in Venezuela* (pp. 71–92). Baltimore MD: Johns Hopkins University Press.

Pastor, M., & Wise, C. (1994). The Origins and Sustainability of Mexico's Free Trade Policy. *International Organization 48*(3), 459–489.

Ragin, C. C. (1987). *The Comparative Method: Moving Beyond Qualitative and Quantitative Strategies.* Berkeley CA: University of California Press.

Ragin, C. C., & Sonnett, J. (2004). Between complexity and parsimony: Limited diversity, counterfactual cases, and comparative analysis. In S. Kropp & M. Minkenbert (Eds), *Vergleichen in der Politickwissenschaft.* Wiesbaden: VS Verlag fur Sozialwissenschaften.

Roberts, K. (2003). Social polarization and the populist resurgence in Venezuela. In S. Ellner & D. Hellinger (Eds), *Venezuelan Politics in the Chávez era: Class, Polarization, and Conflict* (pp. 55–72). Boulder CO: Lynne Rienner Publishers.

Rogowski, R. (1989). *Commerce and Coalitions: How Trade Affects Domestic Political Alignments.* Princeton NJ: Princeton University Press.

Ross, M. L. (2001). Does oil hinder democracy? *World Politics 53*(3), 325.

Ross, M. L. (2004). How Do Natural Resources Influence Civil War? Evidence from Thirteen Cases. *International Organization 58*(1), 35–70.

Salamanca, L. (2004). Civil society: Late bloomers. In J. McCoy & D. Myers (Eds), *The Unraveling of Representative Democracy in Venezuela* (pp. 93–114). Baltimore MD: Johns Hopkins University Press.

Samuels, D. (2001a). Does Money Matter? Credible Commitments and Campaign Finance in New Democracies: Theory and Evidence from Brazil. *Comparative Politics 34*(1), 23.

Samuels, D. (2001b). Money, Elections, and Democracy in Brazil. *Latin American Politics and Society 43*(2), 27–48.

Sánchez Molina, Y. (2000). *Quienes fueron los financistas del candidato Hugo Chávez Frias? El origin de los fondos financieros de la campaña presidencial del abandera del MVR.* Unpublished undergraduate thesis, Caracas: UCAB.

Santodomingo, R. (1999). *La Conspiración 98: Un Pacto Secreto para Llevar a Hugo Chávez al Poder.* Caracas: ALFA Grupo Editorial.

Schamis, H. (2002). *Re-forming the state: The Politics of Privatization in Latin America and Europe.* Ann Arbor MI: University of Michigan Press.

Schwartzman, K. (1989). *The Social Origins of Democratic Collapse: The First Portuguese Republic in the Global Economy.* Lawrence KS: University Press of Kansas.

Shadlen, K. (2004). *Democratization without Representation: The Politics of Small Industry in Mexico.* University Park PA: The Pennsylvania State University Press.

Silva, E. (1996). *The State and Capital in Chile: Business Elites, Technocrats, and Market Economics.* Boulder CO: Westview Press.

Smith, B. (2004). Oil Wealth and Regime Survival in the Developing World, 1960–1999. *American Journal of Political Science 48*, 232–246.

Snyder, D., & Kick, E. (1979). Structural Position in the World-system and Economic Growth, 1955–1970: A Multiple Network Analysis of Transnational Interactions. *American Journal of Sociology 84*, 1096–1126.

Thacker, S. (2000). *Big Business, the State, and Free Trade: Constructing Coalitions in Mexico.* Cambridge MA: Cambridge University Press.

Thorp, R., & Durand, F. (1997). A historical view of business-state relations: Colombia, Peru and Venezuela compared. In S. Maxfield & B. R. Schneider (Eds), *Business and the State in Developing Countries.* Princeton NJ: Princeton University Press.

Tinkunas, H. (2004). The military: From marginalization to center stage. In J. McCoy & D. Myers (Eds), *The Unraveling of Representative Democracy in Venezuela* (pp. 50–70). Baltimore MD: Johns Hopkins University Press.

Useem, M. (1984). *The Inner Circle: Large Corporations and the Rise of Business Political Activity in the U.S. and U.K.* New York: Oxford University Press.

Wallerstein, I. (1974). *The Modern World-system: Capitalist Agriculture and the Origins of the European World-economy in the Sixteenth Century.* New York: Academic Press.

Wallerstein, I. (1976). Semi-peripheral countries and the contemporary world crisis. *Theory and Society, 3*(4), 461–483.

Wallerstein, I. (1985). The relevance of the concept of semiperiphery to Southern Europe. In G. Arrighi (Ed.), *Semiperipheral Development. The Politics of Southern Europe in the Twentieth Century* (pp. 31–39). Beverly Hills CA: Sage Publications.

Weyland, K. (1998). The Politics of Corruption in Latin America. *Journal of Democracy 9*(2), 108–121.

Zapata, J. C. (1995). *Los Ricos Bobos.* Caracas: Alfadil Ediciones.

Zapata, J. C. (1997). *Las Intrigas del poder: Quien Manda en Venezuela.* Caracas: Alfadil Ediciones.

Zapata, J. C. (2000). *Plomo más Plomo es Guerra: Processo a Chávez.* Caracas: Alfadil Ediciones.

# APPENDIX A. PROBABLE DONORS BY CONFIRMATION SOURCE

| Case ID# | Campaign Sources | | | Journalists | | Expert | Other Sources |
|---|---|---|---|---|---|---|---|
| | A | B | C | D | E | F | |
| 1 | Yes | No | ? | p. 127 | | Yes | |
| 2 | Yes | Yes | Yes | p. 132 | | Yes | |
| 3 | Yes | Yes | Yes | p.127, 130 | | Yes | |
| 4 | Yes | Yes | Yes | p. 96 | | Yes | • Lopez Ulacio (Sánchez Molina, 2000, p. 101) • Anonymous FEDEAGRO source (Sánchez Molina, 2000, p. 97) • Multinacional Seguro receipt to pay consultores 21 (Sánchez Molina, 2000) |
| 5 | Yes | No | No | p. 98 | p. 30 | Yes | Sánchez Molina (2000, p. 114) |
| 6 | Yes | Yes | Yes | pp. 69, 127, | pp. 34–36, 45, 132 | Yes | Economist.com 4/12/02 "Coup and Counter-coup" Römero, S. "Coup? Not his style ..." 4/28/02, NYT |
| 7 | Yes | Possible | Yes | pp. 65–70 | p. 29 | Yes | |
| 8 | Yes | Yes | Yes | pp. 70, 97, 133 | | Yes | |
| 9 | ? | ? | Yes | pp. 96, 127 | | Yes | |
| 10 | Yes | N/A | Yes | p. 98 | | N/A | |
| 11 | Yes | N/A | Yes | pp. 97, 132 | | | |
| 12 | Yes | Possible | Yes | pp. 96, 98, 133 | | Yes | |
| 13 | Yes | No | ? | p. 127 | | Yes | |
| 14 | Yes | No | Yes | p. 127 | | Yes | |
| 15 | Yes | Possible | Yes | pp. 98, 133 | | Yes | |

## APPENDIX A. (Continued)

| Case ID# | Campaign Sources | | | Journalists | | Expert | Other Sources |
|---|---|---|---|---|---|---|---|
| | A | B | C | D | E | F | |
| 16 | Yes | Doubtful | Yes | p. 96 | | Yes | |
| 17 | Possible | Yes | Yes | p. 98 | | Yes | |
| 18 | Yes | Yes | Yes | pp. 96, 133 | | Yes | |
| 19 | Yes | Yes | Yes | pp. 37–38, 70 | | Yes | |
| 20 | Yes | Yes | Yes | pp. 96, 132 | | Yes | |
| 21 | Yes | Yes | Yes | pp. 132, 45, 96 | | Yes | |
| 22 | Yes | Yes | Yes | p. 132 | | Yes | Anonymous FEDEAGRO source (Sánchez Molina, 2000) |
| 23 | Yes | Yes | Yes | p. 132 | | Yes | |
| 24 | ? | Yes | Yes | p. 127 | | Yes | Bank with which this individual was associated was listed as donor in records of Chávez' party submitted to the National Elections Commission (Sánchez Molina, 2000) |
| 25 | Yes | Yes | Yes | p. 132 | | Yes | |
| 26 | Yes | Yes | ? | p. 96 | | Yes | |
| 27 | Yes | N/A | Yes | p. 98 | | N/A | |
| 28 | Yes | Yes | Yes | | p. 89 | Yes | Barreto, a journalist who remains loyal to government doubts it (Sánchez Molina, 2000, p. 104) |

*Sources*: A, member of Chávez' public relations team during campaign; B, close friend and advisor of Chávez; C, member of the Finance Committee for Chávez' campaign; D, Juan Carlos Zapata – journalist; E, Roger Santadomingo – journalist; F, political scientist, expert on Venezuelan campaign finance.

# APPENDIX B. ACRONYMS

| | |
|---|---|
| AD | – Democratic Action (Acción Democrática) |
| COPEI | – Committee for Independent Electoral Politics (Comité de Organización Política Electoral Independiente) |
| FEDECAMARAS | – Federation of Chambers and Associations of Commerce and Production (Federación de Cámaras y Asociaciones de Comercio y Producción De Venezuela) |
| QCA | – Qualitative Comparative Analysis |
| FEDEAGRO | – National Confederation of Agricultural Producers (Confederación Nacional de Asociaciones de Productores Agropecuarios) |
| CONINDUSTRIA | – Confederation of Venezuelan Industrialists (Confederacion Venezonala de Industriales) |
| RCTV | – Radio Caracas TV |

# CONFLICT, COOPERATION, CONVERGENCE: GLOBALIZATION AND THE POLITICS OF DOWNTOWN DEVELOPMENT IN MEXICO CITY ☆

Diane E. Davis

## ABSTRACT

*This paper uses a case study of the political struggles over an urban mega project for downtown Mexico City to examine questions about the impact of urban politics on globalization as well as the role ascribed to conflict versus cooperation in determining built environmental outcomes in global cities. It addresses the question of which urban political structures make it possible for urban residents, socially or economically marginal and otherwise, to struggle for or against changes in the city wrought by global forces and conditions. It further asks if political alliance-building and conflict among those both advantaged and disadvantaged by globalization*

☆ An earlier version of this paper was presented at a May 2005 workshop on Globalization and Urban Space in the Sociology Department of the University of Chicago. It is a revised version of a talk initially prepared for a lecture series titled *Globalization and the Refiguring of Urban Space*, organized by Ravi Arvind Palat and held at Binghamton University in May 2003.

Politics and Globalization
Research in Political Sociology, Volume 15, 139–174
ISSN: 0895-9935/doi:10.1016/S0895-9935(06)15005-6

*is part of the process of struggle, then around which political issues and which local political institutions will such alliances or conflicts emerge. The paper concludes by arguing that struggle over the globalization of Mexico City involved both cooperation and conflict within and between advantaged and disadvantaged urban constituencies. It also suggests that the virulence of conflict over the redevelopment of downtown, despite the successful implementation of the urban megaproject, laid a foundation for violence and sustained urban conflict that hold the potential to thwart the upscale redevelopment of the area, thereby calling into question the convergence thesis in the global cities literature.*

## CITIES, GLOBALIZATION, AND CONFLICT

As processes of globalization[1] accelerate and deepen, scholars are moving beyond the initial preoccupation with larger patterns of national and international economic restructuring to explore globalization's social, political, and spatial impacts. The city has been a good place for such studies because command and control functions fueling global circuits of capital have made many urban locales central to economic globalization processes (Sassen, 2001, 1996). In David Harvey's (1982) words, a concrete "spatio-temporal fix" enables disembedded capital to flow more easily; and a grid of world cities helps fuel this process as various locales compete to "absorb global capital [and] undertake major infrastructure and urban development projects to improve their global image and become a node in this network" (Pizarro, Wei, & Banerjee, 2003, p. 14).

In recent years, scholars have spawned a variety of new concepts to express the dynamic inter-relationship between cities and globalization, ranging from "world cities" and "global cities" to "global city regions" (Friedmann, 1986; Knox & Taylor, 1995; Clark, 2003; Scott, 2002; Sassen, 2000, 2001, 2002c; Simmonds & Hack, 2001; Andersson & Andersson, 2000). Although there is some disagreement on the definitional clarity of these concepts, and whether quantitative versus qualitative indicators of global "citiness" are better able to capture what some insist is a process rather than a state of being, one thing is clear: fundamental transformations in the social composition and built environment of major cities around the world are seen as reflecting the changing global economic dynamics of the past two decades (Sassen 2003, pp. 4–5; Pizarro et al., 2003; Short & Kim, 1999). As a result, almost every large city or major metropolitan agglomeration and its fragments is now being conceptualized as "global" in some way or another (Crane & Daniere, 1996; Keil, 1996; Al-Sayyad, 2000; Taylor & Walker, 2001; Scott, 2002), while the most conventional topics long studied by urbanists, ranging from the development of suburbs (Muller, 1997) and "midtowns" (Ford, 1998) to real estate (Haila, 1999, 2000), and urban governance (Brenner, 1999; Yusuf & Wu, 2000) are now routinely examined in global context.

Implicit in most of this research is the assumption that globalization, as a single and increasingly hegemonic process, is drawing ever more major cities into its orbit, and that little can be done to stop the process. Many also have claimed that these global dynamics are leading to ever more convergence in urban land use and employment patterns within cities around the world (Savitch & Kantor, 2002, pp. 267–271). A second prevailing assumption, perhaps related to the first, is that globalization is creating a relatively efficient socio-spatial pecking order of inter- and intra-urban functions as well as shared cultural values that help legitimize these urban land use and employment transformations. As Ananya Roy (2004, p. 73) puts it, the notion of globalization "conjures up images of socio-spatial homogeneity, even equilibrium" as cities increasingly become "hitched to the global scale" and start sharing common features within and among themselves. Notions like "articulation" and "hybridization" or even "integration" are becoming more popular in the global city literature, and with it the sense that seemingly antagonistic global and local dynamics are mixing in form if not function to create entirely new and visually legible patterns of urbanism and cosmopolitanism. Jordi Borja and Castells (1997, pp. 16, 37) have even claimed that the new "articulation of the global and the local" frequently presents itself as a "mixture of historical time periods and a superimposition of functions and cultures in a single space."

The question, however, is whether the transformative processes that have been identified as producing new social and spatial patterns in global cities, understood broadly as locales increasingly integrated into global circuits of capital and investment by virtue of their open economies, free markets, and regional command and control functions, can really be understood through the theoretical lenses of harmony, integration, or functional economic logic that now dominate much of the literature. Or, is *conflict* a better characterization of the process; and if so, what type of conflict, over what, and with whose involvement? After all, most of the cities now identified as enveloped in a global orbit are characterized by their remarkable expansion in space, coupled with a growth of highly developed, high-rent financial center and service economy, known to displace poor residents and/or exacerbate social, spatial, and economic polarization (Smith, 2001; Marcuse & Van Kempen,

2000). These are precisely the social and spatial dynamics that created urban conflicts in past epochs (Fainstein, 1997; Massey, 1997; Smith, 1997; Kowarick, 1994). If such spatial outcomes were hotly contested in urban struggles of prior periods, why would we use a different conceptual lens – that of globalization – to understand them now; and what difference might that make to our understanding of these conflicts and contemporary urban outcomes?

Such questions are not merely empirical; they also entail a more careful consideration of the theory and epistemology of the global cities literature. They force consideration of whether the urban land use transformations now evident in so many large cities around the world owe to novel actions or pressures imposed by new global forces and conditions, as opposed to old-style, garden variety local political dynamics (see Beauregard & Haila, 2000), and whether it is conflict and struggle as opposed to cooperation and consensus that characterize the relationship between these differentially scaled forces and conditions.

Granted, to imply that functionalism or harmony have fully eclipsed conflict in today's global cities, or to suggest that contemporary globalization scholars are more likely to epistemologically embrace a version of Durkheim or Parsons than Marx or Weber, may seem a caricature of the cities and globalization literature. As research on cities and globalization becomes more sophisticated in framing and theoretical reach, we do see more and more writing about globalization's "discontents" and the growing problems of social and spatial inequality in global cities (Sassen, 1998). World Bank pronouncements aside, many scholars and multilateral agencies now openly recognize globalization to be a "contradictory process ... characterized by contestation, internal differentiation, and continuous border crossings" (Habitat, 2001, p. 75). Clearly, the specter of conflict is not completely absent from the global city literature. This is not only evident from the work of scholars like John Walton (1994), Andre Drainville (2004), and Andre Sorenson (2003), who have posed important questions about social struggles in cities as a result of globalization. It also is a key assertion of one of the field's leading globalization scholars, Saskia Sassen (2002a, p. 19), who argues that in the era of globalization large cities "are far more concrete places for social struggles than the national political system."

Even so, with the exception of Sorenson's (2003) recent work, most of the contemporary literature on global cities says very little about the specific character of the conflict that emerges in global cities as social and spatial conditions change, let alone who is most likely to be involved in such battles and with what impact.[2] Nor is much said about whether conflicts in contemporary global cities are better understood through the lens of new concepts, actors, or processes associated with globalization than with long-standing theoretical and methodological frameworks of the past that called attention to urban political conditions and the class and social power (im)balances in cities (Fainstein, 2001; Merrifield & Swyngedouw, 1997; Castells, 1978, 1983). The unspoken assumption in much of today's literature is that once cities become "global," urban political dynamics will necessarily be different. Even in the handful of studies where globalization is actually identified as mattering in urban conflict, the preoccupation with globalization is more likely to be seen as a discursive tool – not a tangible process – used to rhetorically privilege the same old forces that have always been involved in land use struggles: big property developers against local residents (Sorenson, 2003).[3] Owing to this, very few studies have demonstrated whether and how urban conflict, when it occurs in a so-called global city or invokes globalization as an enabling political discourse, has made the built environment of cities *different* than in prior periods when cities were less integrated into global circuits of capital.

## FROM CONFLICT TO URBAN POLITICS: WHITHER THE SILENCES?

The fact that we know little about the answers to these questions may owe to the fact that local politics has been a neglected subject of study in the literature on cities and globalization (Davis, 2005, p. 102). This state of affairs has led scholars like Alan Mabin to herald the call for "much more exploration of specifically urban politics – the kind of politics which David Harvey locates in tensions within particular spaces and in which those who are dependent on particular geographies of production and circulation co-alesce or come into conflict around projects to promote or defend their positions or aspirations" (Mabin, 2005, p. 126). Yet despite this admonition, the failure to seriously examine urban politics persists even among the leaders in the field who have already started to explore the potential for conflict in global cities, perhaps because rather than examining formal political institutions and practices, economic conflict continues to be their main point of departure. Saskia Sassen's work is illustrative of both the possibilities and limits of this approach.

Sassen (2003, p. 16) claims that globalization produces new social and economic actors who converge in the "new frontier zones emerge(nt) in the global city" and thus hold the potential to greatly impact the city's future through their actions. This holds especially true, she further suggests, for the so-called disadvantaged actors whose very segregation and exclusion from the upper-level circuits of finance capital, and the downtown areas of global cities where these economic activities locate, comes as a result of globalization. For Sassen, in fact, it is precisely the newly cast social marginality or economic *exclusion* from global circuits and spaces that gives poor and disenfranchised urban populations a unique presence in the course of waging their struggles (Sassen, 2003, p. 16). These forces may be powerless in formal political terms, she further notes, but their economic and social "presence" allows them to "escape the boundaries of the formal polity" even as it "signals the possibility of a politics" (Sassen, 2002b, p. 23). In its most powerful form, moreover, this newfound "presence" will sustain new forms of citizenship that can further empower the urban disenfranchised in land use struggles in ways that eluded them in earlier epochs (Sassen, 2002b, p. 23; see also Holston, 1999).[4]

Such a proposition about the "possibility of a politics" is intriguing, to be sure, even if it is presented more as utopian promise than anything else. But as a scholarly claim it begs the empirical question of what local conditions make such opposition politics possible, let alone likely or effective. How could the so-called subaltern struggles determine outcomes in an environment where other more affluent local actors, not to mention their national or international allies who are visibly active supporters of globalization, are both "present" and politically powerful in local politics or governance institutions. It is one thing to note that globalization is contradictory, and brings clear winners and losers who should be in conflict over the future of the city. It is quite another to suggest that those urban residents *most* economically disenfranchised or socially excluded from globalization processes will, because of that exclusion, serve as key protagonists in determining the future of either the city or globalization. Would this always be the case? And would not a city's history and the character of its urban political institutions have something to do with how open it was to the claims of these forces?

To be sure, Sassen is trying to make a claim about the *informal* political power of folks on the street. She and others are right that low-income, economically marginal residents are frequently ignored by analysts whose preoccupation with formal politics makes them focus on national political systems of party politics and electoral representation, in which the most excluded and marginal citizens generally have little say. The fact that national-level institutions are losing power as global actors bypass the nation-state also factors into the sense that formal politics is not as significant as it used to be. But to assume that formal politics only happens nationally and that urban political institutions and practices will not matter in struggles over globalization – whether waged by global investors or poor citizens or both – is a debatable proposition. Local political conditions in cities, formal and otherwise, are part of everyday urban life. They can set limits on the willingness and capacity of citizens to mobilize behind urban demands, and they can make socially or economically "weak" forces political powerful if the historical or institutional conditions are right. Thus, they cannot be ignored if we want to understand conflict, cooperation, and the dynamics of change in so-called global cities.

The question is *which* urban political structures or processes make it possible for urban residents, marginal and otherwise, to struggle for or against changes in the city wrought by global forces and conditions? If political alliance building or conflict among those both advantaged and disadvantaged by globalization is part of this process, then around which political issues and through which local political institutions and practices will such alliances or conflicts emerge? And can these urban political dynamics bring urban outcomes unanticipated by the globalization literature; or will they merely serve as the mechanism through which expected changes do materialize?

## STRUGGLES OVER DOWNTOWN DEVELOPMENT IN MEXICO CITY: A CASE STUDY

In seeking answers to these questions about urban politics, the socially and economically disadvantaged, and globalization as well as the larger theoretical concerns about the role ascribed to conflict versus cooperation in determining urban outcomes in global cities, we turn to Mexico City, a burgeoning metropolis of more than 9 million.[5] The Mexico City metropolitan area, which holds a population of close to 20 million, is one of Latin America's largest and most rapidly growing megalopolises. It is also the nation's capital and home to the largest concentration of the nation's economic investments and financial institutions. Mexico City has been identified by several leading scholars as a global city by virtue of the important role it plays in mediating foreign capital and investment flows within Mexico, throughout the Americas, and across the globe (Sassen, 2003 p. 18; Parnreiter, 2002).

The origins of these capital flows and investment connections trace to the colonial and mercantile development of the urban economy, and were strengthened throughout the 20th century via direct foreign investment by US firms and through strong trading (of people and goods) relations between Mexico and its northern neighbor. The country's recent embrace of economic liberalization in the 1980s, its adoption of the North American Free Trade Agreement (NAFTA) in the 1990s, and the 2000 election of a fiscally conservative pro-liberalization president, who served as the vice-president of Coca Cola's Latin American markets division before assuming national office, have further catapulted Mexico City into the global limelight. At present, many in the capital see it as poised on a trajectory of entering the ranks of the world's even more affluent global cities, if it is successful in becoming a Mecca for new and ever more expanded flows of global investors, firms, and tourists. Toward these ends, over the past several years private and public sector forces have thrown their support behind several high profile infrastructure projects, including support for a new international airport located, designed to contribute to Mexico City's global "citiness" by increasing the ease of international connections and investment flows so as to enhance the city's role and visibility in the global economy (Davis & Rosan, 2004).[6]

One of the most controversial of these infrastructural projects has been the Alameda project, a high profile urban mega project initially proposed in 1989, and then again in 1991, 1994, and 2001. Designed to sit on a key boulevard facing an attractive green space (*Parque Alameda*) in the city's historic center, developers hoped this hotel and upscale commercial and residential complex would attract new international flows of visitors, global corporate headquarters, and foreign investors. From the very beginning, support for this project was premised on the expectation that a healthy dose of "urban renewal" would materialize in areas immediately surrounding the Alameda Park, bringing the displacement of low- and moderate-income residents, the demise of small-scale commercial businesses, and the rise of high-end residential complexes and entertainment venues to this key part of the historic center. The project's promoters envisioned it as changing Mexico City land use and urban servicing patterns not just by drawing new international firms and global corporate headquarters to downtown areas, but also by facilitating the residential return of middle and upper-income populations to the city center. Both goals were enshrined in the project's promotional materials, and later reiterated as the centerpiece of an August 2001 plan intended to "rescue" Mexico's historic center, which in 1987 was declared as world historical national patrimony by UNESCO.

Although the specter of citizen opposition from those slated for displacement loomed large from the very beginning, local officials originally supported the plan. Mexico City's increasingly precarious budgetary situation – also a product of liberalization and globalization to a great extent – made this high profile urban mega project especially appealing. Ever since the Federal Government enacted fiscal decentralization policies in the early 1980s, Mexico City authorities faced difficulties covering the city's large operating expenses with local revenues. With the more open borders produced by NAFTA, many of the manufacturing firms that used to locate in the capital city began moving to northern regions near cheaper sources of labor and foreign partners guaranteed by nation's *maquiladora* programs, further limiting local tax revenues. To the extent that the Alameda project held the potential to counterbalance these losses by helping generate new tax revenues, key local officials – including the mayor – signed onto the plan. With public sector go-ahead in place as early as 1989, investors made considerable financial commitments, and a contract was signed.

However, political conflict emerged almost immediately, stalling the Alameda project for almost a decade despite the support from both public and private sectors, globally linked and otherwise. In the upcoming pages, we focus on the political struggles over this project. We examine the role played by local residents slated for displacement by the massive upscale development. We also explore the impact of formal politics, which changed dramatically in this same period. Between 1991 and 2001, as globalization and liberalization of the economy intensified, Mexico pursued a path of democratization, which changed the political landscape and the principal cast of characters involved in the conflict. In 1991, Mexico City's mayor was hand-appointed by the President, who stood at the pinnacle of a regime dominated by one-party rule for close to 80 years. By 2001, when the project finally took hold, Mexico City citizens held democratic rights and privileges that guaranteed their capacities to directly elect a Mayor and city council members. Accordingly, this case study not only offers an opportunity to determine what type of conflict emerged over the project and who exactly was involved. It also allows us to ask whether fundamental changes in urban political structures and conditions were as important as the social struggles fueled by economic globalization in determining the origins and outcome of conflict over the project.

This project also offers a unique opportunity to analyze the political role played by socially and economically disadvantaged sectors, primarily because of the project's spatial location. Although this particular redevelopment project perched squarely in the middle of an appealing historic area destined for "rescue" because of its monumental colonial palaces, churches, governmental buildings, and lovely green spaces, it also sat a stone's throw away from a rundown, low-income neighborhood called Tepito, home to many of the city's informal sector workers and site for most of the metropolitan area's wholesale and retail commercial transactions. Because this overly crowded and physically dilapidated area also hosted wholesale and retail distributors of goods as diverse as shoes, clothes, electronics, plastic consumer goods, and furniture, it held the low-income, socially marginal, and disenfranchised forces and informal sector actors that Sassen and others identify as being socially excluded or spatially displaced by employment, investment, and urban land use changes accompanying globalization.[7] Its unique history[8] gave Tepito and its residents a formidable "presence" that was easily marshaled in support or opposition to the Alameda project.

## POLITICS AND DOWNTOWN DEVELOPMENT *BEFORE* GLOBALIZATION: WERE THE ACTORS DIFFERENT?

The desire to renovate downtown Mexico City by constructing high-rise commercial or residential buildings to displace dilapidated low-density buildings devoted to retail use, or by using these projects to spark a thriving downtown property market, was by no means a new aim. For decades, public officials and private investors toyed with the idea of destroying the deteriorating colonial-era buildings in downtown areas and constructing a modernist façade for Mexico's capital, as occurred in so many other major cities of Latin America. In order to understand the novelty of the Alameda project, and to ascertain whether *new* forces or conditions associated with globalization help explain the timing and implementation of the project, we should attempt to understand what happened with these very similar projects in "pre-globalization" periods.[9] Were the same actors involved, and what facilitated or impeded their success?

As early as 1930, the city's leading architect-planner, Mario Pani, sought to redesign downtown areas around the French modernist Le Corbusier's vision, going so far as to secure private investment and preliminary government approval for the project before having it abruptly tabled by local officials. This and other large-scale downtown development projects of the 1930s failed because Pani and other property developers faced daunting opposition from a broad class-grouping of local residents, who ranged from individual property owners who relished their access to the city's main retail markets, cultural sites, government offices to the resident urban poor who worked in retail and commercial activities that dotted downtown streets.

During the 1940s, middle-class residents of downtown areas began departing for suburban areas, leaving a much less influential class of lower–middle and lower classes in properties near the center of the city. With the social composition of downtown changing dramatically between 1940 and 1960, architects, urbanists, private investors, and city planners yet again sought to introduce urban development projects that would transform these key downtown areas through greater densification of land use, rationalization of transport (including street widening), and the forced removal of ambulant vendors who hawked their wares on downtown sidewalks.[10] Yet, by and large, city planners again failed in their efforts to redevelop, renovate, or remove the activities and buildings that give downtown its special cultural and economic profile as home to petty commodity production and trading. Few of these urban redevelopment plans came to fruition because local residents in downtown areas, especially Tepito, actively fought government intervention in neighborhood affairs – at all levels, but particularly at the scale of the built environment. An almost unparalleled social solidarity and resilience in the face of official planning efforts helped earn Tepito its nickname as the "barrio bravo." Their well-organized and vocal opposition to urban redevelopment insured that downtown areas maintained a mixed industrial, service, and residential land use dominated by small-scale firms and individual vendors.

Nonetheless, struggles waged by local vendors and *comerciantes* against developers or city officials who promoted urban renovation cannot fully account for the failures to transform downtown Mexico City in pre-globalization periods. Public sector actors with considerable formal political clout also joined the struggle to preserve Mexico City's traditional character. Mexico City Mayor Ernesto Uruchurtu was particularly influential in these regards. A presidentially appointed mayor who governed the city from 1952 to 1966, Ernesto Uruchurtu catered to the desires of the city's middle classes, turning much of his attention to the development and maintenance of parks, gardens, and all variety of public spaces available for strolling and consuming the city's history and culture. Mayor Uruchurtu was particularly protective of downtown areas, where many middle classes still lived and worked during the 1960s and 1970s. He worked hard to economically sustain the medium- and large-scale commercial and retail activities on the western and southern perimeter of the Zocalo, many of which were suffering from competition from small scale retailers and street vendors in contiguous lower income areas like Tepito (which sat on the eastern and northern perimeter of the Zocalo). Of all Mexico City's mayors, Uruchurtu was perhaps the strongest opponent to urban redevelopment plans, and the most vocal supporter of the importance of maintaining the traditional middle class character of downtown. Although Uruchurtu was forced to resign in large part because of this stance, his political leadership at a critical juncture in the city's urban growth and development (1952–1965) effectively forestalled any massive urban renovation projects, with the exception of the subway, on which construction began the month after he was forced from office.

To summarize, in early struggles over downtown development projects, the oppositional role of the socially disenfranchised combined with the actions of formal political institutions and actors to keep property speculators and big investment capital out of downtown Mexico City.[11] The results were three-fold: (1) a legacy of mixed land use downtown, evident in both social class and building composition; (2) a built environment peppered with historic Colonial and Independence structures dating to centuries earlier as well as a significant splattering of monumental buildings from the pre- and immediate post-revolutionary period inspired by the Beaux Artes and Art Deco schools; and (3) a deteriorating physical environment, itself a product of the failure to implement upscale urban redevelopment plans combined with a depression in the urban property market (brought both by the failure to invest and the existence of rent control). These three conditions set the stage for particularly divisive conflicts over the city's urban transformation in later periods, and ultimately, for the success of the downtown redevelopment forces in 2001.

## THE 1985 EARTHQUAKE AND NEW OPPORTUNITIES FOR DOWNTOWN DEVELOPMENT

The first serious cracks in the unity of the citizen-local state alliance against downtown redevelopment came in October 1985, when Mexico City suffered a massive earthquake reaching over 7 on the Richter scale. The 1985 earthquake served as a watershed moment in the transition to a more liberalized urban property market and a more globally linked urban economy in Mexico City, producing both short- and long-term effects on the city's property market and in its governance (Davis, 2004). In the short term, the earthquake destroyed hundreds of the city's precarious buildings, killing hundreds and displacing hundreds of thousands. Many of these buildings were in Tepito or in downtown areas surrounding Tepito. More often than not, residents of these central areas refused to leave downtown, which served as the source of their social life and economic livelihood. Many citizens also mobilized in social movements, demanding the government respond to their claims for housing, and for tenancy. The changed political atmosphere posed new pressure on the local government to democratize and be more responsive to citizen's urban policy demands.

Complicating matters, the earthquake also brought a new group of protagonists onto the scene: absentee landowners who had collected rents for years without upgrading their buildings, and who now saw the opportunity to wrest control of potentially valuable properties (especially if the buildings were destroyed or slated for removal). The ensuing struggles over tenancy pitted owners against occupiers, also placing local and national government authorities in a very difficult position. That owners now openly identified themselves, after being absent from the scene for years, meant the possibility of future public revenues from taxation. Yet citizens in these downtown areas were an important political constituency for the local *Partido Revolucionario Instituciona* (PRI), and their dissatisfaction with initial earthquake recovery efforts made them highly critical of the government. Governing officials thus found themselves caught between those investors wanted to take advantage of the new window of opportunity for downtown land speculation and property development, and those local residents who only wanted their homes rebuilt and original lifestyles returned to them.

Public authorities responded by creating a new housing program (*Renovación Habitacional Popular*) that was also intended to transfer property rights to many longstanding downtown residents, who were subsequently given title to their homes. The short-term consequences of this program were reduced public protests against authorities and a slow but steady reconstruction of low- and middle-income housing in downtown areas. The medium-term consequence was a re-strengthening of local community organizations and citizen networks, as this type of community-level social solidarity became a pre-requisite for demand-making about tenancy and for the distribution of property titles in destroyed neighborhoods. The long-term consequence of this program was to breathe new life into the urban property market, which in turn helped fuel the slow-burning fires of urban real estate speculation, thus opening the door for more global capital.

The effects of these changes in downtown real estate speculation were not obvious immediately; but within a few years after the initiation of this new housing program, private investors began pressuring local government officials to introduce new urban policies that would jump-start a renovation of downtown, either directly through new developments or indirectly by moving low-income folks out of traditional neighborhoods. This is best evidenced by a slate of new efforts to push downtown development projects starting within a year or two after the transfer of property titles began. As early as 1989, Mexico City's presidentially appointed mayor, Manuel Camacho (1988–1994), took steps to begin the urban redevelopment process by inviting several Mexican architectural firms to propose new plans for the

Alameda area. Soon thereafter, Mayor Camacho created a *fideicomiso* (public–private trust) to aid in the development of new projects targeted toward key sections of downtown, mainly in western ends where private capital saw a potentially lucrative real estate market. However, such urban redevelopment projects had difficulties flourishing without additional foreign capital, given the limited internal resources for such speculation.

In an attempt to widen their financial bases of support and tap into global economic resources, in 1991 pro-urban development forces from Mexico City organized under the auspices of Grupo Danho (a private urban real estate development firm) joined with an American firm from Dallas to develop a new plan for downtown. They jointly participated in the creation of Fidalameda Trust, a fiduciary organization named as such because it targeted areas around the Alameda. Their proposal to local authorities received tacit approval. Yet word about the project leaked before construction started, and organized political opposition from neighborhood groups and local community organizations who decried the project stalled its completion. Among residents' concerns were the fact that the proposal did not contain sufficient housing for current residents and that it was too oriented toward luring upscale residents and foreign visitors.[12] With strong citizen opposition, Fidalameda (which became absorbed by yet another public–private trust called *Servicios Metropolitanos*, or SERVIMET) dropped the Alameda plan and turned its attention to property development in other parts of the city, distant from the socially well-organized and relatively activist downtown areas. In this instance, again, citizen stalled the Alameda project's success, despite the strong alliance between local and global capital behind its implementation.

But supporters of urban redevelopment in city government did not give up so easily, and the idea of redeveloping the Alameda stayed on the agenda. Mexico City's Mayor Camacho had early in his term identified property development as a potential goldmine of revenues for the city, which after several years of fiscal decentralization was under increasing pressure to finance its own development. He also expected such activities to be beneficial for the nation, which was suffering from the exhaustion of import-substitution industrialization and eager for continued foreign investments and export earnings. As a key spokesman for the country's ruling party (*Partido Revolucionario Institucional*, or PRI), and a public official who owed his appointment to the President, Camacho sought a project that would fulfill both urban and national aims. Toward these ends, Camacho spent much of his time in office trying to establish a political foothold among neighborhood-level political leaders in central Mexico City who long had been opposed to changes in downtown land use. Camacho was well known for creating new working relationships with downtown-based street vendor organizations of the city, by negotiating new market spaces for their relocation with the aim of freeing up downtown streets in areas like Tepito. His administration, moreover, was so committed to a change in this particular neighborhood that on occasion it restored to the use of violent force, taking many by surprise because previous mayors usually tread quite gently in this key neighborhood. Camacho's 1990 "Tepitazo," in which militarized police forces were sent into Tepito to dislodge sellers of illegal goods (*fayuca*) who were charged with fiscal evasion and trafficking in contraband, was one of the most high profile indicators of his new resolve.

With Camacho supportive of efforts to transform downtown areas, it did not take long for a new round of foreign investors to try again. In 1991, an internationally influential private property developer, Reichmann Brothers, known for its global investment firm specializing in recuperation of dilapidated properties in anticipation of their redevelopment or renovation potential,[13] proposed a construction project for several blocks surrounding the Alameda. Keenly aware of the potential revenues to the increasingly cash-strapped city, Mayor Camacho worked diligently to set the stage for the project's success. With new promises of foreign capital and firms eager to invest in downtown projects, and with Mayor Camacho appearing to hold sufficient domestic political sway – both formal and informal – to negotiate with many longstanding downtown residents, local authorities advanced several new plans for a tourist and convention complex for downtown. One of the most important of which was designed by the world-famous Mexican architect Ricardo Legoretta. Sights were set high for making Mexico City a more global city, replete with transformations in the built environment to seduce global investors and global headquarters.

However, even with concerted effort on the part of global investors, local elites, and Mexico City's mayor, new political events and conditions stalled the planned redevelopment. For one thing, the early 1990s was a period marked by growing urban social movements in support of democratizing the city, whose governance by a presidentially appointed mayor generated considerable public outcry as a violation of basic democratic principles. Part of Camacho's responsiveness to citizens' demands owed to the fact that the absence of formal democracy in the city (in the name of a single party that had governed Mexico since 1929) made him even more vulnerable to charges of ruling elite bias, an image he sought to counter. Moreover, many urban residents were still fuming over what was seen as government failure in the wake of the 1985 earthquake. While the housing tenancy program had made some headway, there were still thousands of residents who remained home-less, with a large number living in damaged buildings that remained in pre-carious condition. The Contributing to his accommodating response to Mexico City citizens was the fact that Mayor Camacho was considered a strong party loyalist and an up and coming political leader with presidential as-pirations. He would need all the citizen support he could get if he were to win the 1994 presidential elections, and with Mexico City the largest and most important city in the nation, he could ill afford to alienate its residents. In this charged political environment, Mayor Camacho held back on many of the major redevelopment projects for the city, waiting until the political situation stabilized and a new round of foreign funding made such projects more economically viable.

## ECONOMIC LIBERALIZATION, DEMOCRATIZATION, AND DOWNTOWN DEVELOPMENT: NEW POSSIBILITIES MEET OLD LIMITS

The year 1994 brought dramatic changes in the political and economic sit-uation of both the city and the nation, raising anew the possibility that pro-Alameda forces might finally be successful. A key element of this changed landscape was the NAFTA, approved by Mexico (plus the US and Canada) in 1994. To the extent that liberalization is frequently conceived as the "handmaiden of globalization" (Roy, 2004, p. 74), many in and outside Mexico expressed the hope that economic liberalization processes set in motion by the NAFTA might finally open the city and country to foreign capital and investors sufficiently to break the stalemate over downtown. But the actual effects of the NAFTA on the viability of the Alameda project were quite the opposite.

For one thing, protests in the city and countryside against the free trade agreement scared foreign investors and thus put on hold many investment projects relying on foreign capital, with urban redevelopment plans for downtown Mexico City no exception. For another, in response to the high levels of violence in Chiapas by antiglobalization Zapatista rebels, federal officials asked Mayor Camacho to serve as the chief negotiator with the rebels. That Camacho was a highly popular politician with national visi-bility who had already his demonstrated responsiveness to citizen mobili-zation in the capital city made him a perfect candidate for the job. But with

Camacho absent from the city, many of the urban renovation plans he had advocated were put on the back burner, including the Alameda project.

The tabling of the Alameda project also owed to unstable social and political conditions in the capital city itself, where a groundswell of support for the Zapatista rebels materialized. To the extent that many Mexico City citizens sympathized with the Zapatista cause of countering the glaring social inequities in the Mexican polity and economy, the political viability of pushing forward an upscale redevelopment project in one of the poorer sections of the city fell in further jeopardy. Moreover, once the Zapatistas tied their antiglobalization rhetoric to a critique of the Mexican political system, social movement organizations in the capital city also began to link questions of economic globalization to the failures of political democratization for the city's poorest and most disenfranchised.

But the NAFTA-generated protests of 1994 did more than reduce the enthusiasm of foreign investors and empower antiglobalization opponents to the Alameda project. It also contributed to the declining legitimacy of the local and national political system. Indeed, the protests generated by the NAFTA, themselves coming on top of post-earthquake movements pressing for a democratic opening, helped alter the political climate in the city. Governing officials soon succumbed to citizen demands for substantial democratic changes in formal political institutions and processes, leading to congressional approval of a democratic reform for Mexico City in 1995. This reform legislatively empowered local residents in the city council (which previously had been primarily consultative), even as it called for the eventual election of Mexico City's mayor.[14] These two factors held the potential to create problems down the road for any large-scale urban development projects agreed upon before the upcoming elections.

Specifically, with democratic structures and practices in place in Mexico City, developers showed reluctance to push for projects for which they could not count on local officials to support their efforts, or in which they did not even know who these officials would be. The financial crisis that accompanied the post-NAFTA mobilization fallout further heightened developers' concerns about local political and economic stability. All this meant that although political and economic liberalization may have increased the private sector's desire to invest in projects like the Alameda redevelopment plan in the abstract, in the concrete these changes also made the political situation much more precarious, as it was unclear what position residents would take on downtown development plans and whether they would use this issue at the ballot box when electing a mayor for the first time. Both sets of factors increased the local government's political reluctance to push the project.

Equally important, conditions on the ground for the city's poorest citizens were worsening. The steady liberalization of the Mexican economy throughout the 1990s changed the employment possibilities and political orientations of those citizens who had the most to lose from the increased globalization of Mexico City. This was particularly the case for those whose employment prospects and lifestyles would be altered by the potential transformation of the city's downtown areas into a location more oriented toward upscale financial services and corporate headquarters. Many of the small- and medium-sized industrial firms in Mexico City that had flourished under decades of protectionism went bankrupt with the post-1994 removal of tariff and trade barriers. Their closing pushed ever larger numbers of the city's labor force into the informal sector. Also, the character and nature of the city's informal sector itself began to undergo a major transformation. Without heavy tariffs and other protectionist barriers, many of the goods sold on downtown streets by informal sector vendors declined dramatically in cost – in part because they could be purchased almost anywhere now, including in big commercial chains like Walmart or its Mexican equivalents. The reduced demand for informally sold goods occurred even as the aggregate number of sellers pushed into this precarious form of employment increased, thereby reducing the per capita income of informal sector workers as a whole. In Sassen's terms, with globalization of the economy, many low-income workers had become even more disenfranchised and excluded.

But rather than becoming invisible, they became even more visible, as they spilled out of neighborhoods like Tepito and packed into crowded corners of busy thoroughfares, desperate to find new locations for hawking their goods. Moreover, the closing of small manufacturing firms, under the pressure to survive in a more competitive liberalizing economy, pushed some low income factory workers into informal jobs, thereby increasing the competition within and among the existent ranks of informal sector workers. Nowhere was the burgeoning of the informal sectors seen more dramatically than in the downtown barrio of Tepito. This was not just because Tepito had long been considered to be home to most of the city's vibrant informal sector. It also owed to the fact that many of the goods sold in Tepito were known to be illegal, and street vendors in Tepito had long developed networks of production and consumption that revolved around the informal and illegal trade of goods.

While for many decades what comprised "illegal goods" was nothing more harmful than contraband electronics or illegally produced brand name items, with the lifting of trade and tariff barriers and other liberalization measures, many goods that used to be illegal were now completely legal – because they were sold everywhere and available on open markets. One consequence of this transformation was that after 1994 trading and retail networks in Tepito began to shift toward the importation and sales of new types of informal and illegal commodities, which increasingly meant pirated CDs and DVDs as well as guns and drugs. Sales of these goods not only linked certain Tepito merchants to different commodity chains in the global economy, as with was the case with the CDs and DVDs, and other contraband petty retail goods produced in East Asia (Hello Kitty purses, Gucci watches, etc.). These transformations within the informal sector also brought some local residents into ever more dangerous and violent international networks in which drugs and guns were the preferred means of exchange and/or coercion.

Both sets of networks began to change this critical downtown locale, but from within, even as they transformed community leaders' powers vis-a-vis local political institutions and actors, including the newly elected representative assembly and the Mayor's office. This is made clear by the example of immigrant South Koreans who, after 1994, moved into the neighborhood for the first time and created their own competing social organizations, a state of affairs which called into question the informal, top–down political authority of the community's existent leadership structure. The presence of South Koreans, and the overall transformation of the informal sector to host within its ranks a small but powerful cadre of highly dangerous gun and drug traders, created new sources of community disunity and conflict that threatened to destroy the unity of the neighborhood from within. As longstanding local leaders lost their authority, owing to the splits in the community, and as some prior political leaders became ever more involved in violent and dangerous trade, the neighborhood itself became a place of growing public insecurity. When the streets of Tepito became ever more insecure, residents whose livelihood was not tied to these dangerous activities also began to resent the economic and physical transformation of their . neighborhood into a violence-wracked hotbed of illegal activities. They not only felt insecure in their daily lives but also the new conditions of violence and insecurity scared off potential customers for their less dangerous small scale informal, retail, and commercial activities.

By 1997, just as Mexico City was prepared to vote in its first democratically elected Mayor in almost 70 years, the security situation reached a new low. Crime rates had been skyrocketing since 1994 (Davis & Alvarado, 1999), and violence was now seen a part of everyday urban life – especially on downtown streets in and around Tepito. On one occasion, federal judicial police sent into the neighborhood to arrest those involved in illegal activities were met by armed gunfire from local merchants, leading to an escalation of social and political conflicts between the most dangerous Tepito-based trade organizations and government authorities. These same battles exploded into violence on several other occasions, leading one newspaper to label Tepito as a "no man's land."

It is worth noting that some of the initial conflict between Tepito residents and government officials revolved around new plans to revitalize this part of downtown with renovated housing, extensive street widening (as ever more ambulant vending made access by vehicles and even pedestrians virtually impossible), and the construction of several "modern" markets/mini malls for the sale of small-scale commercial goods so as to restore some order to the neighborhood streets. Mexico City's new democratically elected mayor, Cuauhtémoc Cárdenas, of the left-leaning *Partido de la Revolución Democrática* (PRD), promoted these urban reforms because he saw his mandate as that of addressing the concerns of the city's most impoverished residents. He also took a principled position against upper-end downtown real estate development in Tepito or other parts of downtown, and he openly shunned the high-rise financial, commercial, and convention center complex for the Alameda promoted by Camacho just a few years earlier. Instead, he sought to preserve Tepito's character as a vibrant urban neighborhood with mixed residential and commercial land use, and he did so by supporting the types of small-scale economic activities and usable public spaces that were missing from the Alameda project.

Still, even with Mayor Cárdenas' desire to protect this low-income community from the onslaught of upscale property development, and an active commitment to supporting Tepito's own infrastructure needs as an alternative, he made little headway. The basic problem was that it was difficult to de-link the built environment of this poor, low-income neighborhood from its economic character, and especially from the growing predominance of globally linked illegal trading networks. While many residents did relish the promise of new housing and the plans to reestablish some sort of physical and social order in the street vending neighborhood, those residents who had the economic and coercive power to reject these plans were those involved in ever more illicit illegal activities, like drugs and guns, who were benefiting from Tepito's status as a dangerous and inaccessible location where even local police feared to enter. As such, even the most equitable and carefully designed urban infrastructure plans remained stalled, experiencing from the opposite end of the socio-economic spectrum the same fate as those promoting more luxurious upscale development for the Alameda.

With violence on the rise in Tepito and continuing pressure from global investors to redevelop the Alameda project, the years from 1998 to early 2001 represented a stalemate between these two competing urban visions for downtown Mexico City. This was so despite the fact that city planners of the administration in power (Cárdenas, 1997–2000) favored redeveloping Tepito over the upscale property development of the Alameda area. Although there was strong pressure from globally linked international property developers to push forward the Alameda plans, the project's promoters were unsuccessful because Cárdenas' loyalties lay more with the poor and disenfranchised than wealthy developers, either local or foreign, and the new democratic process allowed their voices to be heard. With the PRD also winning a majority of seats in the newly democratized local representative assembly, the Mayor and his allies counted on citizens to legislatively sustain his opposition to these plans. This new political balance of power within the formal political institutions of governance prevented the Alameda project supporters from prevailing, as had been the case during the Camacho administration when the absence of democracy allowed the mayor to strike deals with the private sector.

However, the local government's responsiveness to the poor and disenfranchised did not mean that Cárdenas was politically strong enough to insure the successful implementation of his infrastructure plans for Tepito. Even if Cárdenas was successful in opposing the Alameda project, he was unsuccessful in redeveloping Tepito along the lines desired by much of his constituency. This owed to the fact that the community itself was divided between illegal mafia-run informal activities and the more traditional street sellers. The ranks of the latter expanded because of shifts in the formal economy owing to liberalization, but their political power paled in comparison to the former, precisely because alternative networks of (illegal) globalization economically strengthened them. These networks of global networks of economic and coercive power (i.e. monopoly over guns and violence), made it almost impossible for the Mayor to politically outmaneuver mafia smuggling rings, who continued to call the political shots in Tepito. Stated differently, although global networks of capital sustained the Alameda project proponents, and were responsible in part for the project's initial wide-ranging support from public and private sector actors, after 1994 new global networks of (illegal) capital sustained the activities and political power of opponents to land use changes in Tepito, as well. Thus, when Mayor Cárdenas left office in late 2000 very little had changed with respect to the built environment in downtown Mexico City, either in Tepito or the Alameda. If anything the entire downtown area was becoming more dilapidated and insecure, owing to the failure of both projects.

## URBAN DEVELOPMENT, SECURITY, AND COOPERATION ON DOWNTOWN DEVELOPMENT

Scarcely a year later, however, in 1991, the Alameda project was approved for construction, and done so by a newly elected mayor from the same political party as Cárdenas. What explains this reversal of fortune for the project? What happened to the opposition from citizens in the areas surrounding the Alameda Project, or to the objections from the Tepito-based "competing globalizers" – those economically and politically powerful mafia forces, themselves linked to global trading networks, who had opposed prior efforts at downtown development?

Part of the answer lies in the deteriorating security environment in the capital – itself a result of decades of inaction on the urban redevelopment front. As downtown buildings and streets deteriorated, citizens ventured less frequently to these areas for shopping and strolling, reducing the income accruing to local residents and limiting their visibility and salience in the community. This occurred as mafia forces increased their economic and political salience, through drug, gun, and contraband activities that expanded through global supply networks. With these mafia forces ever more likely to use violent means to protect their clandestine activities and market shares, security conditions worsened. The situation devolved into low-grade warfare among mafias and gangs who moved around Tepito and ever larger contiguous downtown areas with near impunity. By the time Andres Manuel López Obrador assumed the mayorship in late 2000, citizens identified the city at a crisis point. The new mayor soon faced growing citizen mobilization and opposition party demands to end the problems of urban violence, much of which emanated from mafia activities in downtown areas. In response, López Obrador turned to the Alameda project as a way of rescuing his party's precarious political legitimacy in the face of the deteriorating urban and security conditions, many of them driven by economic and social changes associated with liberalization and globalization.

But if political legitimacy concerns of the PRD were so critical to this outcome, why did López Obrador pursue different urban polices than Cárdenas, who came from the same party, and who also governed a city increasingly wracked by violence? This is where both formal political conditions and informal political alliances enter the analysis. Cárdenas was the first opposition mayor to be elected in Mexico City, and he came to office in 1997 with considerable citizen support and goodwill. He also tried to deal with the security problem by attempting to clean up the police department. After three years in office, he failed with the latter goal, and citizens were also more demanding of the PRD because progress on citizen participation was less advanced that many had hoped (Davis & Alvarado, 2004). Indeed, in the 2000 elections the PRD won, but with a much reduced electoral mandate than in 1997. When López Obrador came to office in 2000, he needed to compensate for these failures. Equally critical, however, was the fact that López Obrador counted on slightly different electoral bases and several different political allies and alliances than did Cárdenas.

One of the López Obrador's key political bases of support was a leading urban social movement organization, called the *Asamblea de Barrios*, that had emerged during the earthquake and counted strongly on residents from Tepito and historic downtown areas as their rank-and-file (Massolo, 1986). One of the major gains accruing to citizens involved with the *Asamblea de Barrios* was the transfer of property owning titles (from absentee landlords to them) in the aftermath of the earthquake (Gamboa de Buen & Revah Locoutery, 1990). Thus, these groups were stakeholders not only in the López Obrador government, but also in the downtown urban property market.

Still, rather than using this community-based political alliance to advocate for the urban redevelopment of Tepito and other low-income areas of the city, as did Cárdenas and as might be expected in urban patronage politics, López Obrador took a counter-intuitive step and turned his attention to the "rescue" of the more upscale downtown areas surrounding the Alameda project. This again, is where liberalization and globalization also made a difference. Indeed, with Mexico City democratized and the social movements protesting NAFTA absent from the political scene, global investors remained eager to pour funds into Mexico City. As a leftist mayor in competition with a President from a different party (PAN), the city budget had long been a point of political contention for López Obrador. He was eager to find tax revenues to govern the city, and a downtown development project that appealed to global investors offered such a possibility. This was the same fiscal logic that guided Camacho in the early 1990s in the wake of fiscal decentralization.

But even more important, unlike Camacho, López Obrador was able to successfully follow through on these aims because he counted on sufficient political connections in Tepito to battle project opponents through political favors and negotiation, rather than by displacing them through the urban redevelopment of Tepito. In addition, unlike either Camacho or Cárdenas, López Obrador argued that the Alameda project would actually be good for

Tepito, because by raising land prices generally the benefits would accrue to Tepito property owners, even as the upscaling of downtown areas might reverse the fears of violence and bring new customers to downtown streets. In short, Mayor López Obrador forged new formal and informal political alliances within and between marginalized low-income groups in Tepito *and* upscale investors (including both foreign and domestic capitalists interested in the globalization of the urban economy and the redevelopment of a downtown property market), and convinced both that they could gain from the upscale development of the Alameda.[15]

The argument was that the planned rescue and renewal of the Alameda area would not only benefit large-scale property developers who were investing in downtown service activities and upscale commercial and residential buildings, it also would give the small number of Tepito residents who owned property a way to valorize their own investments, because of the neighborhood's spatial contiguity with the targeted redevelopment area. This possibility was especially appealing to those whose livelihood had been hurt by the growing violence of the area, and who had been politically unable to thwart the informal political power wielded by other Tepito residents involved in illegal commercial activities. Remember, the latter set of forces wanted to keep Tepito an under-developed "no man's land" where police, developers, and government officials would not dare to tread. In contrast, the development of the Alameda would slowly and stealthily invigorate the downtown property market in ways that could advantage Tepito property owners in the long run, without starting an all-out battle with illegal mafias over displacement and a more direct transformation of the neighborhood. This strategy worked, moreover, because even those poor and economically disenfranchised Tepito residents who were not property owners saw some potential gain. This was so because the Alameda-based downtown development project also held potential to provide a newly renovated and safer area for street vending, where consumer goods could be sold to tourists and other resident pedestrians that feared to enter Tepito because of the crime and violence.

In sum, the planned redevelopment of the Alameda held potential benefits for a considerable number of low-income, socially and economically marginal residents from Tepito and nearby downtown areas, both street vendors and a small number of property owners. Building on this idea, and on concern over deteriorating security conditions, López Obrador creates a broad-based political coalition of united forces who in past periods were divided over the Alameda project but who now were united. And by linking the interests of low-income, socially disenfranchised sectors with those of global property developers, this mayor was the first one capable of implementing this long-contested downtown development project. His success, then, owed not so much to globalization as to politically astute alliance building advanced within the right combination of social, economic, electoral, and security conditions.

His actions with the Alameda project were only the beginning of the story. By jump-starting the Alameda project and redeveloping downtown areas through concentrated investments in infrastructure, parks redevelopment, policing, and other urban policies intended to make central city streets safer, López Obrador gave a signal to global investors that redeveloped properties would be both secure and financially viable. His actions started a process that held the potential to transform the entire downtown property market. It also meant that headway could be made in displacing the globally linked smuggling mafias that had long prevented him and prior governing officials from upgrading Tepito. This was so not only because the successful transformation of the Alameda and its surrounds entailed "gating" and security measures – via new police services and the installation of surveillance cameras on downtown streets – that spatially marginalized those involved in illegal commerce of Tepito, potentially isolating them enough to control their activities.[16] It also owed to the fact that the more successful the Alameda project in real estate terms, the greater the investment potential of the downtown urban property market, a dynamic that itself would lead to a more fundamental transformation of downtown land uses in and around the Alameda.

In spatial terms, this cycle would not only drive more property investment in ever larger concentric circles around the Alameda project and a renovated downtown core, thereby bringing the more extensive urban land use transformations normally associated with global "citiness." These same changes were seen as eventually displacing or expelling low-income informal sector workers who now lived in Tepito and whose political support for López Obrador helped him implement the globalization project in the first place.

## GLOBALIZATION AND DOWNTOWN DEVELOPMENT IN THEORY AND PRACTICE: A SUMMARY OF FINDINGS

To a great extent, these conclusions about land use changes wrought by the Alameda project are consistent with the contemporary urban globalization literature, which identifies social polarization and fragmentation as part of the modern global city. But what is most important about this case are its findings with respect to the *processes* through which these urban transformations were eventually set in motion. The key actors and conditions – and more specifically, the struggles they waged and the alliances they forged – were constantly in flux, with downtown development the subject of ongoing struggle for an extended period of time. Indeed, rather than coming as a automatic market response to the ways that globalization brought new capital resources, new investment potential in downtown property markets, and new economically powerful protagonists (both domestic and foreign) willing to promote or support projects to change downtown land use, the Alameda project's success resulted from concerted political actions guided by a skilled political entrepreneur, Mayor López Obrador, who built a cross-class urban political coalition of forces both advantaged (upscale property developers) *and* disadvantaged (i.e. those pushed into informal sector work by the loss of competitive manufacturing jobs) by economic globalization.

Formal changes in political institutions and structures, wrought by the newfound democratization of Mexico City governance in the mid-1990s, explain part of his success. But so too did the more informal political relations and alliances crafted by López Obrador. His strong connections to key sectors of socially and economically disenfranchised residents of Tepito explain why he was took a different stance than his democratically elected predecessor Cárdenas, and why he was successful in marshaling their support for the Alameda project. After all, the project's successful outcome owed primarily to *cooperation* between key sectors of the disenfranchised in Tepito and more upscale developers, and only López Obrador was able to forge this consensus. Such alliances between those advantaged and disadvantaged by globalization are rarely identified in the globalization literature, in large part because socially and economically people disenfranchised negatively affected by globalization (and its employment and built environmental effects) are assumed to be natural opponents to projects that benefit pro-globalizing forces, like the Alameda project promoters. In Mexico, this clearly was not the case.

Another key difference, at least with respect to what the globalization literature suggests, was the fact that this unusual political coalition crafted by López Obrador as well as his willingness to promote downtown redevelopment also emerged in response to growing *conflict* among different factions of the urban disenfranchised, whose employment and lifestyles had been transformed by globalization, but in different ways. These splits owed to economic to tensions between illegal mafia forces who peddled globally imported drugs, guns, and other illicit contraband and the community's more traditional low-income residents whose street selling activities were harmed by the liberalization of the economy. Overall, then, this case study not only shows that patterns of conflict *and* cooperation were simultaneously at play in the drama over the Alameda project and its eventual approval, it also suggests that both conflict and cooperation were produced in the orbits of globalization *and* politics.

Mayor López Obrador made the most of the unique conditions at his disposal. He developed strong formal and informal political connections within and between speculating and low income forces advantaged and disadvantaged by globalization, and he used these alliances to create political room to maneuver vis-à-vis the globally linked smugglers who had long shunned the real estate transformation of downtown areas and who preferred to remain outside formal party politics. Through these actions, he set Mexico City on a path toward becoming a financial, real estate, and service center firmly ensconced in a global network of investment flows and multinational services.

But what does all this say about the built environmental impact of the project on the city itself, and whether urban outcomes were different given the unique domestic and global political alliances and conditions that eventually brought approval in 2001. Were changes in the city produced by this upscale development project different than they would have been in pre-globalization eras – as for example in 1989 when Camacho tried unsuccessfully to implement these transformations without the aid of global capital? The answer is both yes and no. No matter its origins or timing, the building of the Alameda project would have revalorized the downtown Mexico City property market and made more likely the displacement of low-income folks from central city locations to the further outreaches of the urban periphery. However paradoxical this may seem under the watch of a leftist mayor, a similar outcome most probably would have occurred had the project been introduced in 1989 or any time thereafter, and no matter which party was in power. The high probability of social and spatial polarization in fact, is precisely why Cárdenas rejected the plan in 1997.

Still, had the Alameda project been implemented in 1989, 1991, or 1994 as desired by Camacho, one might have seen much less active isolation or "gating" of the Alameda area, and less evidence of the extreme social and economic polarization between this area and the poorer surrounding areas of Tepito than is evident now in 2006. This owes not just to the fact that the liberalization and globalization have increased income inequality in the city and the nation to a much greater degree now than a decade ago (with these income patterns reflected in real estate markets and citizen buying power). It also owes to the fact that globalization's impact on the informal sector economy over the last decade has resulted in more illicit activities and huge flows of illegal money pouring into downtown. Because this occurred as other informal sector workers in the same neighborhood spiral down into poverty (though more intra-sector competition and the numeric expansion of the informal sector), we see more internal income differentiation even within "poor" areas like Tepito in 2001 than in 1989.

Stated differently, in 1989 and even in 1991 and pre-NAFTA 1994, when most low-income folks downtown were linked to the same production and consumption supply chains (many of them domestic and not globally situated), income differences within the community were not as great as they were after 2001, when the Alameda project was finally approved and the country had experienced more than a decade of economic liberalization and the first stages of a global economic restructuring. Also, because in this earlier period the global drug and trade was not so well established, those living in these low-income areas would not have been seen as quite so dangerous. Thus the need for gating or security isolation would have been less, and we might have seen less overall fragmentation and spatial polarization of the historic center than is apparent now with this project in place.

## FROM COOPERATION AND COMPETITION TO CONVERGENCE? SOME CONCLUDING REMARKS

With Mexico City's urban economy and downtown land uses transforming along the lines predicted in the literature on globalizing cities, even if through a different process than anticipated, the final question is whether this study gives evidence to support the convergence thesis that is gaining popularity among many global city theorists. At first glance, recent progress on the "rescue" of downtown Mexico City seems to imply that this may be the case. Night life and youth activities are on the upswing in ways unthinkable a mere five years ago, and ever more modern building projects dotting the skyline in ways that could make this city a cosmopolitan rival to other more affluent, globally connected cities around the world. Still, the fate of downtown remains uncertain.

For one thing, the massive property development projects started in 2001 and 2002 have stalled considerably because the security situation has not improved enough for middle- and upper-income residents to move large in numbers to the redeveloped parts of the city, and because many low-income residents insist on remaining downtown. With many low-income residents and small commercial firms unwilling to deport from these strategic central locations, which continue to serve them well in an expanding metropolis of 20 million, many developers have hit a glass ceiling in terms of the revenues to be generated through investment in an upscale downtown property market. For another, a steady inflow of street vendors and other underemployed service workers into the new areas has filled downtown streets beyond capacity, reproducing the old-style informality and a mix of rich and poor more associated with past epochs and "traditional" third world cities than a modern, globalizing metropolis. These physical conditions also put a damper on upscale investment and redevelopment, as they limit the potential market appeal of new downtown properties.

The basic source of these problems is the persistence of illegal and informal activities in Tepito, and the continued violence and public insecurity associated with the forms of employment and service activities in this area of the city. Although considerable progress has been made on the upscale development part of the picture in targeted areas surrounding the Alameda project, Tepito remains dangerous and volatile, with murders and assassinations relatively unchecked, and with Mexico City police remaining fearful at times of entering the neighborhood. It is somewhat paradoxical that it was precisely this violence and public anxiety about illegal activities in Tepito that helped create political space for Mayor López Obrador to craft a political coalition of informal sector residents and property developers in support of downtown development in the first place. But even with the project approved and downtown land use and property transformation under way, the violence and anxiety that emanate from Tepito are not gone. If anything, the successes of the Alameda project may be driving illegal forces in Tepito to further entrench their activities and reassert their control over downtown neighborhoods and streets, in order to maintain the spatial conditions of social marginality that over the years have allowed their illegal and economically "marginal" activities to flourish.

What makes this state of affairs particularly intriguing, if not paradoxical, is the fact that many illegal mafia forces have themselves been empowered through globalization, albeit through a very different network of global flows and activities than those responsible for bringing the pro-Alameda property development forces into the picture. One could even say that continued conflict over Mexico City's downtown development, even in the face of the Alameda project's recent approval, owes to "competing globalizations" – defined as the struggle between two "economies," or divergent networks of economic forces who draw their economic strength from entirely

different complexes of global actors and investors, yet whose uneasy co-
existence in a delimited physical space turns them into ruthless competitors
to control land use and the character of downtown. We could identify these
two distinct global networks as "liberal" and "illiberal" rather than merely
legal and illegal, because the former are defined as a "legitimate" in the eyes
of economic liberalization proponents, primarily because they are constituted by a relatively accountable network of investors who operate in a
world of regulations, property rights, and formal contract law. This label
would encompass investors in the Alameda project, other upscale properties
for tourists, residential housing, corporate headquarters, and most global
firms and investors. The latter are defined as illiberal because they are considered socially "illegitimate" partakers of the global economy, given that
they are constituted by networks of investors whose global supply chain
revolves around illicit, black market, and violence-prone activities where the
rule of law remains elusive (i.e. global investors in the marketing and distribution of drugs, guns, and other forms of contraband).

These "competing globalizers" have divergent spatial aims and downtown
development visions. The former desire an upscale renovation of downtown
with open spaces and pristine architectural environments. The latter prefer
the dilapidated, informal, and inaccessible back alleys and streets where
their clandestine activities can remain hidden from view. And with these
liberal and illiberal global forces in struggle over the character and built
environment of downtown, the violence and conflict that now destabilize
Mexico City are as much about control over space as about the direction, or
globalization, of the economy. It is not just a question of whose global
network is going to prevail in what physical space. Precisely because this is a
conflict about economic livelihood as well, and it involves "illiberal" forces,
it is a particularly virulent conflict and not easily remedied by urban politics,
primarily because the source of profitability for both groups is at stake. For
these reasons, we see continued conflict between these "competing" globalizers playing itself out in the streets of the city and on the terrain of security
practices as much as formal political deliberation and dialogue.

If these divergent visions for downtown continue to collide without resolution, the stakes will accelerate, leading to new forms of violence and
anxious public and private efforts to control it. The Alameda area is already
protected by a special police force even as it remains surrounded by dilapidated areas hosting informal sector activities, and high tech surveillance
cameras and private security guards that characterize the new upscale residential buildings of the areas. More such efforts are likely to be used to
create mobility barriers between the upscale redeveloped parts of the

Alameda and Tepito. The result would be that Mexico City could face even greater socio-economic and spatial polarization (both within Tepito and between it and other key downtown locations). Such spatial outcomes may sustain the theoretical propositions advanced in the urban globalization literature (Moulart, Salen, & Werquine, 2001), and suggest a certain convergence in land use patterns across global cities. But they also suggests an extreme form of social and spatial polarization, mediated by violence, that we would not expect to see in other global cities like London, Tokyo, and Singapore. Complicating matters, the short-term implications of this pattern may in fact undermine the long-term path toward convergence. Extreme polarization and violence will set clear limits on further upscale property development and circumvent any movement toward global "convergence" in urban land uses across the Mexico City metropolitan area, as well as when compared to other global cities.

Right now Mexico City stands at the crossroads, in the process of being transformed by globalization and poised on the precipice of major changes that could change the built environment of downtown in ways that have eluded the city for most of the century. But where it will be a few years from now is still unclear. Whether its built environment, land use, and employment patterns will converge with other global cities depends entirely on the status of the conflict between Mexico City's competing globalizers, and who wins out in the battle over downtown space. Mexico City may have its own political, spatial, and historical peculiarities, which have made its globalization and these urban processes particularly contested, complex, and violent. But it may be that other cities of the global south also share some of these historical legacies (Beavon, 1998). The persistence and growth of an informal sector throughout periods of industrialization, the spatial contiguity of various social classes, the vibrancy of commercial and downtown life, the politics of urban clientelism, and the expanding networks of illegal activities that hovered in the background of this story are also characteristic of other developing country cities seeking to integrate into a global orbit: Johannesburg, Buenos Aires, Rio de Janeiro, Manilla (see Gugler, 2004; Lo & Yeung, 1998). So in addition to recognizing the importance of urban politics to the fate of these "wanna be" global cities in the developing world, we might do well to begin looking for common patterns of conflict and cooperation, as well as violence, that will facilitate or impede the globalization of cities in the global south and elsewhere. The end result could be a more theoretically rich and empirically nuanced understanding of how global cities emerge, whether different patterns and processes govern cities of the global north and south, and how stable their status as such will be.

# NOTES

1. There is much debate over how to define globalization, whether it is a new or old phenomenon, and how to distinguish international from global dynamics. One broad definition of globalization is "the stretching of similar economic, cultural, and political activities across the globe" (Short & Kim, 1999, p. 3), although within this mélange of activities, and in this paper's study of land use transformation, I treat economic activities (via the formation of global production, global markets, and global finance) as the central driving force for change. It has long been my contention that global dynamics have been relevant for cities in the developing world, like Mexico City, for decades if not centuries (Davis, 2005). However, I also concur with the prevailing sentiment in the literature that we have entered a new stage of globalization, ushered during the 1980s by the time–space compression produced though telecommunications and information technologies. This paper focuses precisely on that period when Mexico City was faced with a new and altogether different opportunity to integrate into alternative global networks of capital and investment.

2. In fact, in much of the literature where cities are identified as a central location for the emergence of struggles over globalization, as with Walton's (1994) research on urban food riots spurred by IMF-imposed stabilization measures, conflicts are more likely to be theorized as anti-liberalization or anti-globalization movements than as conflicts in and about the city.

3. For example, in Andre Sorenson's (2003) study of conflict over downtown development in Tokyo, globalization is relevant mainly to the extent that property developers used the discourse of global competitiveness and global citiness to triumph in their struggle against local resident vis-a-vis imposed building volumes and heights in special regeneration areas of the city.

4. In making this argument, Sassen compares the invisibility of low-income populations in periods of urban renewal with a much increased "presence" or visibility in the social and economic spaces of global cities.

5. When I use the nomenclature Mexico City I am referring to the Distrito Federal, or Federal District, which holds approximately 9 million residents and is administered by an elected mayor (technically, the *Gobernador del Distrito Federal*) with a planning staff. In theory, the Federal District Governor also works in collaboration with an elected city council (*Asamblea Legislativa del Distrito Federal*).

6. Conflict over the airport project was so great that eventually it was cancelled. For more on the ways that the airport's opponents and proponents both sought to use globalization rhetoric and a global network of supporters to advance their position, see Davis and Rosan (2004).

7. Although Tepito forms part of the 9.7 square kilometers of downtown area declared as historic national patrimony by UNESCO in 1980, authorities did not include it in the downtown "rescue" project. This is so despite the fact that it is only a few blocks from the area targeted for renovation.

8. The neighborhood of Tepito is the location made famous by Oscar Lewis in his classical study of the culture of poverty, *The Children of Sanchez*.

9. When I use the term "pre-globalization" in this text I mean in the periods from 1930 to 1980, before the recent increase in speed and density of globalization as a worldwide phenomenon. Obviously, in a developing country like Mexico global

networks were relevant even in these periods; but that is not to say that the country engaged liberalization and globalization in the ways it did wholeheartedly starting in the late 1980s and 1990s.

10. During the late 1950s and 1960, the city built several Corbusier-inspired high-density housing projects in downtown areas, the most famous of which was the Tlatelolco Housing Estate, built by Pani. This housing complex provided government-subsidized housing for middle-class government employees and others eligible for housing assistance. But because it was a government-financed project whose residents were more modest income folk whose tenure was linked to their employment, this project did very little to change downtown land use dynamics, especially in the commercial and retail sectors. If anything, the existence of government funded high-rise housing projects merely enforced the demand for the lower-end retail sector activities that persisted in much of the downtown areas, especially those concentrated in Tepito.

11. The only massive urban infrastructure project that was successfully implemented was the construction of a subway in 1966, with central stations downtown and lines extending south and westward. Yet even this project did not valorize a downtown property market or change downtown land use in the ways its promoters hoped, give the existent political power of local residents and others who opposed the physical transformation of the city. For more on why downtown Mexico City retained its traditional social and spatial character, see my *Urban Leviathan: Mexico City in the Twentieth Century* (Temple University Press, 1994).

12. For more on the Alameda development project, and the ways that community organization stalled large developer plans, see Martínez Leal de De la Macorra (1998).

13. Reichmann Brothers is perhaps best known for their development of Canary Wharf in London. For more on the evolution of the firm's global strategy, and its investments in Mexico, see "A Developer Back from the Brink," *New York Times* (2003), Business Section (p. 2), February 21.

14. For more on the ways that social conflict and protests in the post-1985 period led to the partial and then full democratization of Mexico City, see Davis (1994, 2002).

15. One of the López Obrador's key allies in his downtown redevelopment plans was Carlos Slim, Mexico's richest man and globally known billionaire owner of Telmex, the country's telephone company, and other major commercial firms. Slim's conglomerate, which in recent years expanded to found its own property development division, has given considerable resources to the government for urban infrastructure renovation and helped foot the bill for Rudolph Giuliani's visit to the city to develop a public security plan for downtown.

16. A key component of the redevelopment project initiated by López Obrador, with financial support from Carlos Slim, was the implementation of Rudolph Giuliani's zero tolerance policing recommendations. For more the relationship between policing proposals and the urban redevelopment of downtown areas, see Davis (2006).

# ACKNOWLEDGMENT

The author would like to thank the anonymous reviewers of *Research in Political Sociology* for their valuable comments and suggestions.

# REFERENCES

Al-Sayyad, N. (2000). *Global norms and urban forms: Identity, hybridity, and tradition in the contemporary built environment.* London: E & FN Spon.

Andersson, A., & Andersson, D. (Eds) (2000). *Gateways to the global economy.* MA, USA: Elgar Publishing Limited.

Beauregard, B., & Haila, A. (2000). The unavoidable continuities of the city. In: P. Marcuse & R. van Kempen (Eds), *Globalizing cities: A new spatial order* (pp. 22–36). New York: Blackwell Publishers.

Beavon, K. (1998). Johannesbur: Coming to grips with globalization from an abnormal base. In: F. Lo & Y. Yeung (Eds), *Globalization and the world of large cities* (pp. 352–385). Tokyo: United Nations University Press.

Borja, J., & Castells, M. (1997). *Local and global: Management of cities in the information age.* London: Earthscan Publications.

Brenner, N. (1999). Globalisation as reterritorialisation: The re-scaling of urban governance in the European Union. *Urban Studies, 36*(3), 431–451.

Castells, M. (1978). *City, class, and power.* New York: St. Martin's Press.

Castells, M. (1983). *The city and the grassroots: A cross cultural theory of social movements.* Berkeley: University of California Press.

Clark, D. (2003). *Urban world/global city* (2nd ed.). New York: Routledge.

Crane, R., & Daniere, A. (1996). Measuring access to basic services in global cities: Descriptive and behavioral approaches. *Journal of the American Planning Association, 62,* 203–221.

Davis, D. (1994). *Urban leviathan: Mexico City in the twentieth century.* Philadelphia: Temple University Press.

Davis, D. (2002). Capital city politics in Mexico: The local–national dynamics of democratization. In: H. A. Dietz & D. J. Myers (Eds), *Capital city politics in Latin America: Democratization and change.* Boulder, CO: Lynne Rienner.

Davis, D. (2004). Reverberations: Mexico City's 1985 earthquake and the transformation of the capital. In: L. Vale & T. Campanella (Eds), *The resilient city.* Oxford: Oxford University Press.

Davis, D. (2005). Cities in global context: A brief intellectual history. *International Journal of Urban and Regional Research, 29*(1), 92–109.

Davis, D. (2006). The Giuliani factor: Crime, zero tolerance policing, and the transformation of the public sphere. In: G. A. Jones (Ed.), *Public space and public sphere in Mexico.* (forthcoming).

Davis, D., & Alvarado, A. (1999). *Descent into chaos: Liberalization, public insecurity, and deteriorating rule of law in Mexico City.* Working Papers in Local Governance and Democracy 99/1, pp. 95–107.

Davis, D., & Alvarado, A. (2004). Citizen participation, democratic governance, and the PRD in Mexico city: The challenge of political transition. In: B. Goldfrank & D. Chavez (Eds), *Left in the city: Progressive and participatory local governance in Latin America.* London: Latin America Bureau.

Davis, D., & Rosan, C. (2004). The 'Power of distance' and social movements in a globalizing Latin America: Lessons from the Mexico City airport controversy. *Mobilization, 9*(3), 279–294.

Drainville, A. (2004). *Contesting globalization: Space and place in the world economy.* London, NY: Routledge.

Fainstein, S. (1997). Justice, politics, and the creation of urban space. In: A. Merrifield & E. Swyngedouw (Eds), *The urbanization of injustice* (pp. 18–44). New York: New York University Press.

Fainstein, S. (2001). *The city builders: Property development in New York and London, 1980–2000*. Oxford: University of Kansas Press.

Ford, L. R. (1998). Midtowns, megastructures, and world cities. *The Geographical Review*, *88*(4), 528–547.

Friedmann, J. (1986). The world city hypothesis. *Development and Change*, *17*, 69–83.

Gamboa de Buen, J., & Revah Locoutery, J. A. (1990). Reconstrucción y politica urbana en la Ciudad de Mexico. *Foro Internacional*, *30*(5), 677–694.

Gugler, J. (2004). *World cities beyond the West: Globalization, development, and inequality*. Cambridge: Cambridge University Press.

Habitat. (2001). *Cities in a globalizing world*. Sterling, VA: Stylus Publishing.

Haila, A. (1999). City building in the East and West: United States, Europe, Hong Kong and Singapore compared. *Cities*, *14*(4), 259–267.

Haila, A. (2000). Real estate in global cities: Singapore and Hong Kong as property states. *Urban Studies*, *37*(2), 2241–2256.

Harvey, D. (1982). *The limits to capital*. Chicago: University of Chicago Press.

Holston, J. (1999). Spaces of insurgent citizenship. In: J. Holston (Ed.), *Cities and citizenship* (pp. 155–173). Durham, NC: Duke University Press.

Keil, R. (Ed.) (1996). *Local places in the age of the global city*. London: Black Rose Books Ltd.

Knox, P., & Taylor, P. (1995). *World cities in a world system*. Cambrdige: Cambridge University Press.

Kowarick, L. (1994). *Social struggles and the city*. New York: Monthly Review Press.

Lo, F., & Yeung, Y. (1998). *Globalization and the world of large cities*. Tokyo: United Nations University Press.

Mabin, A. (2005). Review of Josef Gugler (Ed.), "World cities beyond the west: Globalization, development, and inequality." *Society in Transition*, *36*(1), 123–126.

Marcuse, P., & Von Kempen, R. (Eds) (2000). *Globalizing cities: A new spatial order?* Massachusetts: Blackwell Publishers.

Martínez Leal de De la Macorra, C. (1998). *Innovative community projects and their role in the urban development of Mexico City*. Doctoral thesis, Oxford Brookes University (London), December 1998.

Massey, D. (1997). Space/power, identity/difference: Tensions in the city. In: A. Merrifield & E. Swyngedouw (Eds), *The urbanization of injustice* (pp. 100–116). New York: New York University Press.

Massolo, A. (1986). Que el Gobierno Entienda, la primera es la vivienda. *Revista Mexicana de Sociología*, *48*(April–June), 195–239.

Merrifield, A., & Swyngedouw, E. (Eds) (1997). *The urbanization of injustice*. New York: New York University Press.

Moulart, F., Salen, E., & Werquine, T. (2001). Euralille: Large scale urban development and social polarization. *European Union Urban and Regional Studies*, *8*(2), 145–160.

Muller, P. O. (1997). The suburban transformation of the globalizing American city. *The Annals of the American Academy of Political and Social Science*, *551*(May), 44–58.

New York Times. (2003). A developer back from the brink, *New York Times*, Business Section, February 21, p. 2.

Parnreiter, C. (2002). Mexico City: The making of a global city. In: S. Sassen (Ed.), *Global networks, linked cities* (pp. 145–182). New York: Routledge.

Pizarro, R., Wei, L., & Banerjee, T. (2003). Agencies of globalization and third world urban form: A review. *Journal of Planning Literature, 18*(2), 111–130.

Roy, A. (2004). Global histories: A new repertoire of cities. In: E. Morss (Ed.), *New global history and the city*. Newton Center, MA: New Global History Press.

Sassen, S. (1996). Cities and communities in the global economy. *American Behavioral Scientist, 39*(5), 629–639.

Sassen, S. (1998). *Globalization and its discontents: Essays on the new mobility of people and money*. New York: The New Press.

Sassen, S. (2000). *Cities in a world economy*. Thousand Oaks: Pine Forge Press.

Sassen, S. (2001). *The global city: New York, London, Tokyo* (2nd ed.). Princeton: Princeton University Press.

Sassen, S. (2002a). Globalization or denationalization? *Items and Issues, 4*(1), 15–20.

Sassen, S. (2002b). The repositioning of citizenship: Emergent subjects and spaces for politics. *Berkeley Journal of Sociology, 46*, 4–25.

Sassen, S. (2002c). *Global networks, linked cities*. New York: Routledge.

Sassen, S. (2003). Reading the city in a global digital age: Between topographic representation and spatialized power projects. *Revista: The Harvard Review of Latin America, II*(2), 12–16.

Savitch, H. V., & Kantor, P. (2002). *Cities in the international marketplace: The political economy of urban development in Western Europe and the United States*. Princeton: Princeton University Press.

Scott, A. (2002). *Global city-regions: Trends, theory, policy*. Oxford: Oxford University Press.

Short, J., & Kim, Y. (1999). *Globalization and the city*. London: Longman, Ltd.

Simmonds, R., & Hack, G. (2001). *Global city regions: Their emerging forms*. London, NY: Spon.

Smith, M. P. (2001). *Transnational urbanism: Locating globalization*. Oxford: Blackwell.

Smith, N. (1997). Social justice and the New American urbanism: The Revanchist City. In: A. Merrifield & E. Swyngedouw (Eds), *The urbanization of injustice* (pp. 117–136). New York: New York University Press.

Sorenson, A. (2003). Building world city Tokyo: Globalization and conflict over urban space. *The Annals of Regional Science, 37*(3), 519–531.

Taylor, P., & Walker, D. R. J. (2001). World cities: A first multivariate analysis of their service complexes. *Urban Studies, 38*(1), 23–47.

Walton, J. (1994). *Free markets and food riots: The politics of global adjustment*. Cambridge, MA: Blackwell.

Yusuf, S., & Wu, W. (2000). *Local dynamics in an era of globalization: 21st century catalysts for development*. New York: Oxford University Press.

# PART III:
# THE POLITICS OF TRADE POLICY AND GLOBALIZATION

# FAST TRACKING TRADE POLICY: STATE STRUCTURES AND NGO INFLUENCE DURING THE NAFTA NEGOTIATIONS

Tim Woods and Theresa Morris

## ABSTRACT

*In this paper, we assess the relative influence of business, labor, and environmental organizations on the development of the North American Free Trade Agreement (NAFTA). Incorporating an historical contingency theory of the state, we argue that an understanding of the fast track and the resulting relationship between Congress and the Executive Branch that it established is instrumental in understanding the differential influence of nongovernmental organizations on the trade-policy process. Further, a detailed case study of the NAFTA policy-formation process highlights the importance of state structures not only as mechanisms that serve to unify business influence, but also as mechanisms used to exclude opposition groups.*

## INTRODUCTION

The development of the North American Free Trade Agreement (NAFTA) provides an illustration of significant changes to the organizational structures

Politics and Globalization
Research in Political Sociology, Volume 15, 177–204
Copyright © 2007 by Elsevier Ltd.
All rights of reproduction in any form reserved
ISSN: 0895-9935/doi:10.1016/S0895-9935(06)15006-8

defining global trade. The NAFTA was historically unique in two ways. First, in the post-WWII era, the U.S. trade policy agenda was focused on the development and expansion of multilateral trade talks on a global scale (i.e., the General Agreement on Tariffs and Trade (GATT)). The NAFTA contradicted this trend by establishing a regional trade alliance among the U.S., Canada, and Mexico. Second, the NAFTA represents an important shift in class alliances surrounding trade policy. Within specific industries, capital and labor had previously agreed on trade-policy issues. However, by the 1980s, this coalition had fallen apart, resulting in class-wide conflict over trade policies such as the NAFTA. Further complicating the class alliances surrounding NAFTA was the appearance of a myriad of environmental groups attempting to influence the trade policy process. In order to understand the developing effects of global trade on labor, the environment, and business, it is important for sociologists to first develop explanations of the political processes that resulted in the NAFTA.[1]

Most previous research on the NAFTA policy process relies on two theoretical perspectives. From one perspective, a relatively autonomous Executive Branch brokers trade policy in the "nation's interest" (Cameron & Tomlin, 2000; Maxfield & Shapiro, 1998). In this state-centered model, the formal rules governing trade policy and/or the international environment in which it takes place, affords the Executive Branch with the autonomy and, therefore, power to devise trade policy, insulated from the influence of business and other groups external to the state. The second perspective, the power structure model, suggests that powerful corporate actors influence or control trade policy through an elite network of corporate and state ties (Dreiling, 2000, 2001; MacArthur, 2000). While both conceptions highlight important aspects of the trade policy process, they are built largely upon conventional models of the state–society relationship and thus reflect the weaknesses of these models. The state-autonomy explanation is unable to account for the significant influence of the largest American corporations on the NAFTA negotiations. The power structure model accounts for the influence of corporations over labor and environmental groups, but pays relatively little attention to whether the state's organizational context facilitates business control over trade policy. What is missing from both theories is a conceptualization of the extent to which historical contingencies and state structures affect the capacity of state managers and classes and groups outside the state to exercise power.

We argue that sociologists' understanding of the political processes surrounding NAFTA is advanced by the incorporation of recent developments in state theory (Prechel, 1990; Hicks & Misra, 1993; Amenta & Poulsen,

1996; Skidmore & Glasberg, 1996; Amenta & Halfmann, 2000). The central emphasis shared by these researchers is the importance of understanding state policy as the result of the intersections of state institutions and corporate actors within specific historical contexts. By incorporating theoretical conceptions from this research into the empirical study of trade policy, we develop a more thorough understanding of the NAFTA than has been presented in previous trade-policy research. Thus this case study serves two goals. First, it directs sociologists' attention toward the relatively neglected but increasingly important research area of foreign trade policy. Second, it makes the important theoretical point that state policy should include analyses of class relations and the organizational relationships between state structures through which corporate influence occurs.

## PREVIOUS EXPLANATIONS OF NAFTA POLITICS

### *State-Centered Model*

Established as an effort to "bring the state back in" through the study of the effects of internal state structures on policy formation (Evans, Rueschemeyer, & Skocpol, 1985), state-centered theories conceptualize foreign policy as developed independent from the influence of groups external to the state (Krasner, 1978; Ikenberry, Lake, & Mastanduno, 1988). State-centered analyses of U.S. trade policy during the late 19th and early 20th centuries conclude that the state is an independent actor in developing and maintaining trade policy and that the state formulates foreign trade policy "despite resistance from society" (Lake, 1988, p. 57). Responding to international sources of trade constraints, state managers formulate trade policy in "the national interest" (Goldstein, 1993). The fact that the formulation of trade policy takes place almost exclusively within the Executive Branch is of key importance to state-centered researchers. They argue that it is the autonomous nature of the Executive Branch that allows trade policy to be formulated in the broad national interests instead of the interests of specific domestic groups that too easily pressure Congress for protection (Haggard, 1988; Goldstein, 1993, p. 1153).

Researchers using a state-centered model have asserted that the NAFTA is best understood as a product of the Bush and Clinton administration's foreign policy agendas and/or the competing international interests of the U.S., Canada, and Mexico. Along this line, Cameron and Tomlin (2000) focus on the international dimensions of the NAFTA negotiations.

According to their research, state managers within the U.S. trade bureaucracy as well as top-level cabinet members from both the Bush and Clinton administrations bargained with respective members of Canadian and Mexican governments in an effort to maximize collective American interests. As a result, the NAFTA was "critically shaped by three factors: (1) asymmetries of power between the three states; (2) sharply contrasting domestic political institutions; and (3) differences in the ... heads of government and their chief negotiators"(Cameron & Tomlin, 2000, p. 15).

Maxfield and Shapiro (1998) present a more nuanced state-centered perspective in their explanation of the NAFTA. While they do not ignore the role of corporate influence, they nonetheless conceptualize U.S. negotiators as autonomous agents led by institutional principles or ideas surrounding appropriate trade-policy strategies. Thus they conclude that the NAFTA policy process falls "in line with patterns of post-WWII American–foreign policy for U.S. Trade negotiators to be more intransigent about international trade principles than about defending particular economic sectors" (Maxfield & Shapiro, 1998, p. 117). In summary, in the state-centered research, powerful societal groups, while potentially present in the background, are overshadowed by the agendas and ideologies of specific state managers and the institutions within which the policy process takes place.

*Power Structure Model*

The power structure model (Domhoff, 1970, 1990) overcomes the weakness of state-centered theory by conceptualizing state policy as a process wherein powerful societal groups influence foreign trade policy. Domhoff's (1970, 1990) work recognizes that during the 1960s capitalists were divided between an internationalist segment seeking free-trade and a nationalist segment seeking trade protection. The unification of the internationalist and nationalist segments around a single trade policy is tied to networks of individuals and organizations (especially the Committee for Economic Development) operating both external to and within the state. Domhoff (1990, pp. 217–224) explains that the resulting 1962 Trade Act reflected an agreement by both segments that the act include measures to expand free-trade arrangements for the internationalist sector and provide sector-specific protectionist measures for the nationalist textile and chemical manufacturers.

Several researchers have adopted a power-structure perspective to explain the politics of the NAFTA (e.g., Korten, 1995; Dreiling, 2000, 2001;

MacArthur, 2000). The significance of this research is its ability to show the effects of collective corporate action on the NAFTA policy process. Thus, Korten (1995, pp. 141–148) explains that the NAFTA was a result of influence placed on the state by American business. The Business Roundtable organized corporate pressure in support of the NAFTA by founding USA*NAFTA. Composed of the nation's largest business interests, USA*NAFTA then served as an organization to mobilize a unified corporate political response in support of the NAFTA (Korten, 1995, p. 145).

Dreiling (2000, 2001) provides the most extensive sociological account of the NAFTA policy process from a power-structure perspective. Focusing on inter-corporate unity in defense of the NAFTA, he finds that the presence of an extensive network among the nation's largest corporations, business organizations (e.g., Business Roundtable, USA*NAFTA), and trade-advisory committees within the Executive Branch. Dreiling's (2000, 2001) research points to the magnitude of unified corporate influence in the later stages of the NAFTA, but is limited to that stage of the policy-formation process following NAFTA's formal negotiation. While this explanation of the negotiated NAFTA agreement is important, focusing on this stage of the policy-formation process leaves unexamined the political process that set the stage for the NAFTA negotiations.

Further, while state structures are sometimes discussed within power-structure analysis of trade policy, this research tends to underconceptualize the influence of state structures on the policy process. For example, Dreiling (2000, 2001) operationalizes the effects of state structures as the presence of pro-NAFTA capitalists on trade-advisory committees within the state. However, he spends little time discussing why business influence operated through Executive Branch trade-advisory committees and not some other state structure (e.g., Congress). This leaves unanswered the question of why some state structures are more important in the trade policy process than others and why capitalists have greater influence over some state structures than they have over others. We argue that in order to answer these questions, one must take seriously the historically contingent nature of the role of organizational relations between state structures and between state structures and interest groups. Thus, we analyze the fast track as a set of organizational rules and regulations that structures the trade–policy relationship between Congress, the Executive Branch, and capitalists and other interests groups in society. Our main point is that the fast-track organizational structure is instrumental in understanding the relationship between state and society during the developments of the NAFTA.

## Historical Contingency Approach

Following years of debate and little resolution as to the nature of state–
society interaction, theorists such as Prechel (1990, 2000) and Akard (1992)
introduced a historical contingency argument into state theory. State
autonomy and class unity are best seen as ideal types that rarely exist at the
empirical level, but whose empirical forms are contingent upon the historical
conditions within which a state policy is developed (Prechel, 1990). Thus,
the degree to which the state is more or less autonomous, as well as the
degree of class unity, shifts depending upon the specific historical conditions
characterizing a given time period. For Prechel, the dominant historical
contingency determining the relative degree of state autonomy and class
unity is capital accumulation. In contrast to state-centered models that
attempt to separate these organizational structures from their societal
contexts,[2] Prechel (1990, 2000) shows that, in addition to varying with
class unity, state autonomy varies in relationship to the expansion of state
structures governing the policy-formation process (see also Guthrie &
McQuarrie, 2005). During specific historical periods, state organizational
structures become the basis for a "more prominent, less autonomous" state
(Prechel, 1991). Thus, as Prechel (1990) concludes:

> [A]s the states authority is expanded over more areas of economic activity and more
> complex enforcement structures are established (e.g., laws, rules, procedures), state au-
> tonomy may decline because these new structures provide class segments with legitimate
> mechanisms within which to exercise their political power (p. 651).

Concentrating on the analysis of state structures and their effects on corporate
influence, this research uses the historical contingency model to explain the
political process of the NAFTA. We contend that the organizational structure
commonly called "fast track" was a key factor in linking state and society
during the NAFTA trade policy process. The origins of the fast track are in
the Reciprocal Trade Act of 1934, which has been shown to be a product of
the influence of internationalist corporate influence in New Deal trade policy
(Woods, 2003). The fast track is especially relevant to the historical contingency framework because of the fact that the fast track has always been a
temporary structure. As Woods (2003) shows, the only way that the internationalist segment and the Executive Branch obtained the fast-track authority in its original form was to agree that this authority be temporary.

   This dimension of the organizational structure of the state is important theoretically and empirically because it redefined the relationships between branches of government (i.e., Congress and the Executive Branch) and

between the state and societal groups. Once Congress establishes fast track for a given trade policy, the rules and procedures set forth by this organizational structure greatly influence the trade-policy process. Once a political structure is enacted, it becomes the potential base of class power, depending on the contingencies of class unity and capital accumulation agendas (Prechel, 1990, 2000).

We find that the fast track was a significant factor in mediating both business unity and class conflict over trade policy. Because business unity developed in part around the fast-track issue and, once passed, the fast track provided the organizational rules and procedures governing trade policy, this organizational structure played an instrumental role in the development of the NAFTA. However, the fast-track structure did not insulate state managers from the demands of societal groups as the state-centered perspective would predict. Alternatively, once invoked as the structure in which trade policy takes place within the state, the fast track allowed for the dominance of corporate influence and the exclusion of other societal groups. The fast-track rules specified that the NAFTA negotiations take place almost exclusively within the Executive Branch trade bureaucracy. As a result, business organizations with access to the bureaucracy's advisory committee structure were able to dominate the policy process to the exclusion of labor and environmental groups.

In this research, we present a case study of the NAFTA political process. Focusing on the influence of business, labor, and environmental groups, and state agendas within the context of the fast-track organizational structure, we analyze three distinct periods in the development of the NAFTA. First, we present a historical overview of the U.S. economy in the 1970s and 1980s to situation the discussion of trade policy formation within the economic context. Second, we discuss the presence of class conflict and business divisions preceding the origination of the NAFTA and explain how the fast-track structure played an important role in the unification of business segments on trade policy. Third, we move to the negotiations of the NAFTA in an effort to show how the rules and procedures of the fast track provided business groups with access to the Executive Branch advisory committees whereby they influenced the NAFTA negotiations relatively insulated from the demands of labor, environmental groups, and Congress. Fourth, we move to the Congressional debates over the approval of the Executive Branch negotiations and the ways in which the fast-track structured Congressional influence during this final stage. Finally, we examine the outcomes of the NAFTA policy on labor and environmental groups, the excluded groups in the NAFTA policy-formation process.

# NAFTA CASE STUDY

*Historical Background: 1980s Trade Policy and Business Divisions*

At center stage in the demise of the post-WWII political economy was heightened international competition. During the 1970s and 1980s, U.S. business faced strong competition from abroad. The value of U.S. manufactured imports relative to domestic production increased from less that 14 percent in 1969 to 38 percent in 1979 (Harrison & Bluestone, 1988, p. 8). Domestic manufacturers found themselves competing not only against the European and Japanese producers, but also an emerging group of newly industrializing countries (NICs) (Reich, 1991; Hartland-Thunberg, 1985, p. 17). The increased competition from abroad and the general failure of global institutions ensuring U.S. dominance (such as the Bretton Woods monetary system) sent the U.S. economy into a tailspin. Initially, the economic slowdown took the form of overproduction as domestic markets became flooded with multiple alternative goods from abroad. Charles Sabel explains that the "fundamental cause of the slowdown of the 1970s was the saturation of domestic markets for consumer durables and hence [the] exhaustion of new investment opportunities in the business lines that had been the mainstay of the post-war expansion" (in Harrison & Bluestone, 1988, p. 10).

The economic decline documented above was responsible for a widening gap in the divisions between business segments. During the 1970s and 1980s the nationalist segment (e.g., steel, textiles) multiplied its political pressure on the state to pass protectionist trade policy. Most importantly, the nationalist segment directly opposed the internationalist agenda of trade expansion. Escalating international competition from Japanese and European imports in the 1970s and 1980s combined with declines in capital accumulation to place this segment at increasing odds with the internationalist segment's agenda to expand foreign trade. When the Executive Branch failed to respond to the nationalist segment's demands for policies of trade protection, corporations and industry groups (e.g., steel) filed anti-dumping and countervailing duty complaints in an attempt to force the state to protect their interests (Prechel, 1990, pp. 658–659). When they were unsuccessful in influencing the Executive Branch, they turned to Congress (U.S. Congress, Senate, 1987). Suffering from "unfair" competition by Japanese and European producers, this segment emphasized to Congress the need for immediate protectionist policies in the 1980s. For example, Ford Motor Company recommended to Congress the establishment of state policy that would force reductions in the number of foreign autos that Japanese and European producers imported to America (U.S. Congress, Senate, 1987, p. 195).

In opposition to the nationalist segment, the internationalist business segment, led by multinational financial and banking capital, desired free trade and investment policy on a global scale through the extension of GATT at the Uruguay Round.[3] The internationalist segment's strategy during the late 1980s was reflected in the policy objectives of the Institute for International Economics and other corporate policy planning organizations. In 1989, the Institute called for the extension of GATT and concluded that the "U.S. pursuit of the bilateral or regional option would be counterproductive ... and would *undermine* the major U.S. interest in rapid further liberalization of world markets" (U.S. Congress, Senate, 1989, p. 65, emphasis in original). In May 1990, corporations within the internationalist segment organized the Multilateral Trade Negotiations (MTN) Coalition in an effort to consolidate their influence over trade policy (Farnsworth, 1990). Comprised largely of American corporations with extensive international operations (e.g., IBM, Honeywell, 3M, and American Express), MTN Coalition members set as their single goal the mobilization of political support for GATT trade expansion.

In summary, as economic competition increased in the 1970s and 1980s foreign trade emerged as a central issue in business-state relations and the desire of both business and the state to promote capital accumulation. While disagreeing on trade policy, both business segments pressured the state to develop trade-policy remedies. Just as the conflict between the two business segments came to head over the ongoing Uruguay Round of the GATT, Mexican President Carlos Salinas approached the Bush administration with the possibility of developing a NAFTA regional alliance.

### The Fast-Track Debates

Trade officials within the Bush administration initially reacted with the perception that the proposed NAFTA would be a diversion to the GATT talks. The administration and the United States Trade Representative (USTR) had spent too many resources on the emerging Uruguay Round to suddenly shift gears toward a regional alliance. However, the administration quickly realized the potential that the NAFTA created for forging business unity on foreign trade policy. President Bush, along with Secretary of State James Baker and Secretary of Commerce Robert Mosbacher, all Texans with strong ties to Mexico, included the creation of the NAFTA along side the GATT as the administration's official trade agenda for the 1990s.

Business, too, was becoming increasingly unified in support of the NAFTA. Many corporations within the nationalist segment, particularly automobile producers, overwhelmingly approved of the NAFTA. To these corporations, the NAFTA provided the optimal trade-policy choice. A regional alliance with Mexico would allow these corporations to expand their consumer and labor market to Mexico, while simultaneously providing them with regional protection from Asian and European producers. Further, with the GATT talks seemingly stalled over agriculture subsidies and related issues, the internationalist segment began to endorse the NAFTA. In statements before Congress, the Business Roundtable argued that the NAFTA would not only give the U.S. leverage vis-à-vis other regional trade blocs, it could also be designed as one step toward global trade if the GATT failed (U.S. Congress, House, 1991a, pp. 125–131).

On March 1, 1991, the administration cemented business unity for the NAFTA by requesting fast-track authority from Congress for both the GATT and the NAFTA under a single request. Fast-track authority refers to a procedure that transfers from Congress to the Executive Branch authority to negotiate trade agreements. Once negotiated by the President, the agreement is submitted to Congress for an up or down vote, with no amendments permitted. If passed as a single request in Congress, fast-track authority would allow the administration to negotiate both the NAFTA and the Uruguay Round of the GATT. Once the success of both NAFTA and GATT were dependent upon a single fast-track vote, the administration and business felt assured of fast-track's extension in Congress.[4] One of many organizations participating in big business' push for fast track was the U.S. Council of the Mexico–U.S. Business Committee (U.S. Congress, House, 1991b). Created by 59 of the largest U.S. financial and manufacturing businesses in the U.S., this organization was sponsored by the Council of the Americas as well as the U.S. Chamber of Commerce. The 1990 membership roster included American Express, Bank of America, Chase Manhattan Bank, Solomon Brothers, Shearson Lehman Hutton, Ford, General Motors, Chrysler, Exxon, General Electric, Du Pont, Coca-Cola, and AT&T, among others (U.S. Congress, House, 1991b, p. 645). Other business organizations supporting the fast track included the Business Roundtable, National Foreign Trade Council, and the National Association of Manufacturers, among others. Testifying before the House Ways and Means Committee, Thomas Enders, Chair of the Committee and zan Investment Banker at Salomon Brothers, Inc., asserted unified business support for the fast-track procedure (U.S. Congress, House, 1991b, pp. 637–639).

However, despite the unification of business support around a single fast-track vote and Executive Branch support for the NAFTA, Congressional opposition would place the fast track in jeopardy. Aware of the fast track's potential to exclude them from negotiations, labor and environmental groups quickly mobilized pressure on Democratic Congressional representatives to vote against fast-track extension.

## Labor Opposition
The American Federation of Labor-Congress of Industrial Organization (AFL-CIO) vowed to make the defeat of fast track its number one political priority for 1991 (Congressional Quarterly, Inc., 1991a). Labor's argument was that a U.S.–Mexico free-trade agreement would increase the movement of jobs to low-wage Mexico, resulting in a loss of jobs for U.S. workers. As Thomas Donahue, Secretary-Treasurer of the AFL-CIO, testified before Congress, "The [NAFTA] agreement would pave the way for the loss of hundreds of thousands of jobs that will be exported to Mexico, and the debasing of American wages" (U.S. Congress, House, 1991a, p. 97). Labor's opposition to the NAFTA reflected a major shift in class conflict surrounding U.S. trade policy. In fact, the NAFTA represents the first major trade-policy debate in which labor organized as a class against capitalists (McKeown, 1999). Three main factors were responsible for this shift. First, in the 1980s, the Reagan administration significantly cut funding for trade-displaced workers through the Trade Adjustment Assistance (TAA) program. Second, many U.S. corporations began downsizing their American workforce and accelerating the movement of factories overseas in response to increasing foreign competition and a declining domestic economy (Harrison & Bluestone, 1988; Reich, 1991; Harrison, 1994; Barnet & Cavanagh, 1994). And third, trade policy increasingly was being expanded to encompass foreign-investment policy. Perceiving that the inclusion of foreign-investment provisions within trade agreements were being used by U.S. corporations as devices for the acceleration of moving jobs overseas, labor organizations strongly opposed all trade agreements, especially those aimed at liberalizing trade with less-developed nations such as Mexico.

## Environmental Opposition
The NAFTA was also significant because it represents one of the first national debates on the effect of trade expansion on the environment. The majority of environmental organizations mounted a campaign in Congress against the 1991 approval of the fast-track procedure. While opposition to the NAFTA varied across environmental organizations, the most commonly

voiced position differed from that of organized labor in its "wait-and-see" attitude. Representatives of the environmental organizations Friends of the Earth and The National Wildlife Federation testified in the fast-track hearings that due to the possibility that expanded trade with Mexico could result in increased pollution, they could not support the fast track or the NAFTA "at this time" (U.S. Congress, House, 1991b, p. 214). However, they were willing to support a trade agreement with Mexico if it included provisions reflecting the groups' environmental concerns.

*Business Opposition*
Opposition to fast track was also found among some business sectors. For example, fruit, vegetable, and textile producers wanted to eliminate the GATT. The central focus of the Uruguay Round of the GATT centered on the elimination of agricultural and textile subsidies. One of the Bush administration's central goals of the GATT negotiations was to decrease agricultural subsidies, especially in the European Community (Congressional Quarterly, Inc., 1993, p. 166). The administration saw multilateral agreements that reduced or eliminated subsidies as the only way to decrease the federal payments of price and income support payments to U.S. farmers (Congressional Quarterly, Inc., 1993, p. 166). Such agreements would also reduce subsidies paid to nations purchasing agriculture exports.

For the textile industry the extension of the fast track was a highly debated policy. The Multi-Fiber Arrangement (MFA), the existing multilateral regime providing some protection for the U.S. textile industry, was to expire in 1991. One of the aims of future GATT rounds was to incorporate provisions regulating textiles and clothing within the GATT structure, allowing the phasing-out provisions for the MFA. Textile producers viewed the MFA as less than optimal because its complex structure of quotas was often difficult to enforce. However, as a representative of the American Textile Manufacturers Institute explained, U.S. producers saw the Uruguay Round textile provisions as threatening "the very existence of the U.S. textile and clothing industry" (U.S. Congress, House, 1991a, p. 183). From the industry's perspective, the proposed phase-out of the MFA and its incorporation into the GATT would likely result in open competition between textile producers in the U.S. and developing countries. Therefore, textile producers lobbied in opposition to the fast-track extension (U.S. Congress, House, 1991c, pp. 148–150).

In sum, following the President's request for fast track, labor, environmental, and a few business groups mobilized pressure on Congress against Executive Branch trade authority. House majority leader, Richard Gephart, along with Ways and Means Chair, Dan Rostenkowski, and Senate Finance Chair, Lloyd Bentsen, came under intense pressure from labor and environmental groups to lead the charge against fast track (Congressional Quarterly, Inc., 1993, p. 189). All three leaders voiced cautious support for the extension, but demanded that labor and environmental issues be at the forefront of any policy. While the relationship between labor and environmental groups was relatively new, their mobilization in Congress was successful. Not having predicted the strength of the opposition, both the administration and business groups were slow to react to the situation.

By the beginning of 1991, the administration was suddenly faced with a Congress prepared to turn down its fast-track requests and thus derail the administration's entire trade agenda. There was even some talk within the House of Representatives of a possible separate vote on the two trade agreements, leaving the future of the NAFTA on shaky ground (Congressional Quarterly, Inc., 1991b, p. 661). In response to the dire situation, Carla Hills, USTR, stated, "I think we are going to have a very tough fight to retain fast track" (Auerbach, 1991).

*The Administration's Response*
In response to Congressional opposition over labor and environmental concerns, the Executive Branch officials met to develop a plan to revive the fast track. While it was clear that labor's opposition could not be changed, a few environmental groups had spoken of the possibility of working with the administration on the NAFTA if environmental issues were included in the negotiations. As a result, Carla Hills, USTR, testified before Congress that the administration was now willing to discuss social issues, including workers rights and the environment, in return for fast-track authority (U.S. Congress, House, 1991b).

In late February and early March 1991, Administrative officials from the USTR office and the Environmental Protection Agency (EPA) began meeting with environmental groups. The head of the EPA, Bill Reilly, was the former President of the World Wildlife Fund and, thus, was included in an effort to persuade more conservative environmental groups to support the fast-track extension (Mayer, 1998, p. 80). In return for the administration's inclusion of representatives from the environmental groups on the USTRs trade-advisory committees, some moderate environmental groups (e.g., National Wildlife Fund, Natural Resources Defense Council) changed their position to support the fast track.

On a more general level, following its meetings with environmental groups and discussions with Democratic Congressional leaders, the administration issued an "action plan" to assure Congress and the American people that Executive Branch negotiations would be sensitive to labor and environmental interests. In the action plan "the administration avoided making ironclad pledges and reiterated its contentions that the agreement would not threaten jobs and would help the environment. But, at virtually every step, it also conceded that the doomsayers had legitimate concerns" and that these groups' interests would be represented in the NAFTA negotiation process (Congressional Quarterly, Inc., 1993, p. 189).

After the development of the administration's action plan and the development of support by some environmental groups, many formerly undecided Congressional members switched their position to cautious support of fast track. At the same time, business increased its pressure on Congress by creating a new National Foreign Trade Council to coordinate efforts between the nationalist segment and the MTN Coalition (Mayer, 1998, p. 87). Further, some Congressional members maintained that Congressional support for fast-track authority did not entail an approval of the NAFTA and that if the final agreement did not protect labor and the environment, it could be voted down in its final form. Therefore, the House Ways and Means Committee drafted and the full House approved a resolution emphasizing that Congress could reject the final policy if the administration did not keep its promise to workers and the environment (Congressional Quarterly, Inc., 1991a). On May 23 the House and on May 24 the Senate approved the extension of Executive Branch fast-track authority.

In summary, the initial stages of NAFTA must be understood as a combination of business pressure, state agendas, and political structures (i.e., fast track). Because the NAFTA posed a potential solution to business disagreement over foreign trade policy and a Congressional extension of fast track would apply to both the GATT and the NAFTA, business unified in support of fast-track extension. While nationalist and internationalist business segments proposed different trade policies during the late 1980s, by March 1991 both business segments unified their support for the Congressional approval of Executive Branch trade authority. Further, the Executive Branch was instrumental in its ability to gain Congressional support for the fast track by splitting the environmental community. Without the administration's action plan, Congress was unwilling to provide fast-track authority to the Executive Branch.

The Bush administration and business were ultimately successful in advancing the NAFTA during this initial stage of the policy process. In order to get fast-track authority, though, they were forced by Congressional politics to include an action plan to respond to the demands of labor and environmental groups. However, once put in motion, the organizational rules and procedures set forth by the fast track greatly restricted the actual influence of Congressional representatives, labor, and environmental groups on the NAFTA negotiation stage. In this manner, the fast-track organizational structure continued to frame the influence of societal groups on the formal negotiation of the NAFTA.

## Formal NAFTA Negotiations

The fast-track procedure granted the Executive Branch the authority to negotiate foreign trade policy, relatively independent from Congressional control. Carla Hills, USTR, handled the formal negotiation of the NAFTA and, while Congress continued to hold hearings on the NAFTA, Congressional members were not directly involved in the negotiations. However, it would be a mistake to assume that because the fast track ensured that Executive Branch officials could negotiate the NAFTA independent from Congressional control that the same relationship occurred between the Executive Branch and societal groups. In fact, one of the most important aspects of the fast-track organizational structure is the influence it allows to large businesses groups. Business segments used Executive Branch trade-advisory committees in order to develop a unified NAFTA policy to benefit both segments and exclude the interests of labor and environmental groups.

### Advisory Committees and Business Influence

Research on advisory committees has one fundamental conclusion: "federal advisory committees facilitate the permanent institutionalization of linkages between [private] interests and the national Executive" (Petracca, 1994, p. 211). Numerous researchers have documented advisory committees as organizational mechanisms through which private interests (usually large corporations) affect specific state policies or policy agendas (Wolanin, 1975; Domhoff, 1978, 1990; Useem, 1984, pp. 76–80; Petracca, 1994; Moore, Sobieraj, Whitt, Mayorova, & Beaulieu, 2002). State managers also acknowledge the significant role that advisory committees play as structures of business influence over foreign-trade policy. For example, Stephen Strauss (1982), Acting Deputy Assistant Secretary of Commerce, explains that business representatives "contributed substantially to the final wording" of the GATT code on international subsidy practices (p. 1). Further, J. Michael Farren (1991), U.S. Secretary for International Trade, states that private sector advisors are "truly full partners in the U.S. negotiating team" (p. 24).

The Executive Branch office of the USTR and its advisory committees provided business organizations a direct and powerful channel through which to influence the trade-policy process. In the case of the NAFTA, there were two highly influential Executive Branch advisory committees: the Advisory Committee for Trade Policy and Negotiations (ACTPN) and the Industry Policy Advisory Committee (IPAC). Of the total 80 members on these two advisory committees, 71 were representatives (usually CEOs) of large corporations, 3 were representatives of business organizations (e.g., National Cattlemen's Association), 2 were labor representatives, 2 were environmental representatives; and 2 were representatives of other organizations (e.g., consumer organizations) (U.S. President, 1992a, 1992b).

It was through the Executive Branch advisory committees that very specific business demands, such as the regionalist business segment's demands for protection, were incorporated into the NAFTA trade policy. The September 1992 IPAC report provides general approval of the NAFTA process, but also contains numerous policy objectives that are industry, firm, or even product specific (U.S. President, 1992b). The policy-formation process leading to the NAFTA rules of origin provides a significant example of how business organizations used their position on advisory committees to influence the negotiated provisions of the trade policy. Rules of origin are those laws that mandate the proportion of North American-produced content that a particular good must have in order to qualify for NAFTA tariff schedules. The general objective of the rules of origin from business' standpoint was to "prevent Mexico and Canada from becoming platforms for penetration of the U.S. market by third country producers" (U.S. President, 1992b, p. 4). However, domestic industries that had incurred damaging foreign competition (e.g., automobile producers) sought particularly heightened rules of origin in order to protect themselves from Japanese and European producers.

Business organizations made known their specific demands regarding the NAFTA rules of origin through their participation in the IPAC and its related sub-committees. The IPAC was divided into smaller sub-committees, each representing a specific industrial sector. One sub-committee was the Industry Sector Advisory Committee for Trade in Transportation, Construction, and Agriculture Equipment (ISAC-16). ISAC-16 consisted of 18 members, all of which were representatives of large businesses (e.g., Ford Motor Company, General Motors) or large business associations (e.g., Motor Vehicle Manufacturers Association) (U.S. President, 1992c, pp. 516–517). Early in the negotiation process, members of the ISAC-16 advocated to the USTR that a 65 percent minimum level of regional content for automotive production be incorporated into the NAFTA (U.S. President, 1992c). The regional content provisions would protect auto producers already in Mexico (e.g., Chrysler, Ford, General Motors) from foreign competitors who did not already have plants in Mexico (e.g., Honda, Toyota). As Eden and Molot (1996, p. 529) conclude, "the Big Three were influential in shaping the auto provisions of the NAFTA in ways advantageous to themselves."

Members of the IPAC further supported the demands of this subcommittee by encouraging the USTR to incorporate sector-specific rules of origin and investment liberalization into the NAFTA (U.S. President, 1992b). As a result of business' influence over the USTR advisory process, the committees' requests were incorporated into the NAFTA provisions. The final NAFTA policy stipulated a 62.5 percent regional content provision for automotive goods and established a two-tier system providing a more rapid decrease in tariffs for those producers already manufacturing in Mexico, providing significant levels of sector-specific trade protection for U.S. automotive producers (Eden & Molot, 1996, p. 529; U.S. President, 1992c).

Further, statements given to Congress by James D. Robinson III, Chair of Advisory ACTPN, Chair of the Business Roundtable, and CEO of American Express, support the contention that business organizations with assess to Executive Branch advisory committees were able to influence the NAFTA negotiation process at every turn. He reported to Congress that at the beginning of the negotiations the ACTPN and the Business Roundtable issued their objectives for the NAFTA to the USTR (U.S. Congress, Senate, 1992, p. 102). With this communication, the groups "made it clear that we expected the administration to consult with us on an ongoing basis so that we would be part of the process" (U.S. Congress, Senate, 1992, p. 102). He goes on to say that the administration fulfilled this expectation:

> The U.S. Trade Representative, her staff, and others in the administration met with the private sector representatives – both official advisors, as well as trade associations – nearly 1,000 times over the course of the negotiations. We had regular, detailed, substantive input into the process (U.S. Congress, Senate, 1992, p. 102).

In summary, the fast track provided the Executive Branch with authority over the trade negotiation process. At the same time, the organizational structure of fast track provided business organizations with important channels through which to dominate the trade policy negotiation process. The NAFTA negotiation process confirms much of the literature on advisory committees. Business organizations used the advisory committees to ensure that their interests were reflected in the trade policy. However, this channel of influence was selective in that only business groups were able to use the advisory committees to influence the policy outcomes. Labor and environmental groups had little influence in the negotiation stage of the policy process. Thomas Donahue, Secretary–Treasurer of the AFL-CIO, explained to Congress that despite letters to the USTR emphasizing labor's position, their concerns were ignored (U.S. Congress, Senate, 1992, p. 215). Further, Mr. Donahue emphasized that the NAFTA negotiations depicted a "subversion of the advisory process and a crass and unprecedented demonstration of political manipulation" (U.S. Congress, Senate, 1992, p. 215). Representatives of environmental organizations consistently reported the same lack of influence over the negotiation process (Audley, 1997).

Reflecting the influence of business organizations within the Executive Branch, the negotiated policy included most of the provisions set forth by big business and few, if any, of the recommendations set forth by environmental or labor organizations. Following the negotiation of the trade policy by the USTR, the Presidents of Mexico, the United States, and Canada signed the NAFTA on December 17, 1992.

## Congressional Approval of NAFTA

After the NAFTA agreement was developed and completed within the Executive Branch, the policy process was shifted to Congress for final approval. As stipulated by the fast-track rules, Congress was able to approve or reject the NAFTA policy as it was negotiated in the Executive Branch; no amendments could be made. The fast track provided Congress with the final decision over trade policy. However, the organizational rules of the fast track resulted in a decision-making processes which Weber (1978) called "negative politics" (p. 1408). Owing to the influence of organizational structures such as the fast track, Weber (1978) predicted that Congressional bodies would be restricted to "negative politics" in which they "can support the complaints of the citizens against the administration only by rejecting appropriations and other legislation" (p. 1408). This is important because, under such a decision-making structure, Congressional input is excluded from "positive participation in the *direction* of political affairs" and the Executive Branch dominates the political process (Weber, 1978, p. 1408, emphasis in original). Thus, we now turn to an analysis of how the final stage of the NAFTA was affected by the fast-track organizational structure and how the political process relates to the concept negative politics.

When President Clinton took office in 1993, the NAFTA had already been completed and signed by the three countries as a foreign-policy agreement. However, Clinton could not be assured that Congress would approve the NAFTA. At this time, Congressional Democrats and some Republicans still voiced their opposition to the trade policy, most based on the fact that labor and environmental groups had been left out of the negotiation process. House Majority leader Richard Gephart explained in February 1993 that, as negotiated, the NAFTA provided no support for displaced workers, did not address the substandard environmental conditions in Mexico, and provided no provisions for building the needed infrastructure (U.S. Congress, House, 1993).

The Executive Branch and business responded quickly to Congressional opposition to the already negotiated NAFTA. First, business mobilized a new pro-NAFTA campaign. The Business Roundtable organized USA*NAFTA in order to spearhead business, media, and public support for the regional trade policy (see Dreiling, 2000, 2001). Further, in response to the concerns of Congressional Democrats, the Clinton administration set out to establish a set of side agreements. The aim of the side agreements was to overcome what Clinton expressed as "shortcomings in the agreement [that] are really a reflection of ... shortcomings of the Bush economic policy" (Congressional Quarterly, Inc., 1992, p. 156). As completed, the side agreements created the Commission for Labor Cooperation and the Commission for Environmental Cooperation, each with jurisdiction over labor and environmental disputes arising among the three countries. If the commission could not solve an environmental or labor dispute, it would be forwarded to an arbitration panel that could "recommend" trade sanctions (Congressional Quarterly, Inc., 1993, p. 173).

Labor and environmentalists responded to the side agreements with grave dissatisfaction. As AFL-CIO President Lane Kirkland lamented "[t]he side agreements would relegate worker rights and the environment to commissions with no real enforcement mechanisms, no power to impose trade sanctions and no effective remedies" (Congressional Quarterly, Inc., 1993, p. 173). Congressional Democrats reacted in a similar manner, with two of the party's top leaders – Whip David Bonior and Majority Leader Richard Gephart – dismissing the side agreements as inadequate and promising to vote against the NAFTA. While the Senate remained divided along party lines on the bill, vote projections showed that the NAFTA would pass. However, the House would be a close vote.

When Clinton sent the NAFTA implementing bill to Congress on November 3, 1993, its approval was not ensured. Under the fast-track rules, Congress had only two weeks before a final vote would be taken. Within these two weeks, President Clinton engaged in continual last-minute concessions and "deal making" with House members to ensure its passage. In order to assure Congressional approval of the NAFTA, President Clinton made a number of related and unrelated policy promises. However, because the NAFTA was already negotiated, none of the administration's concessions to Congress directly affected the NAFTA as a trade policy. Even so, Clinton was able to win enough support through unrelated promises and pork-barrel politics to ensure NAFTAs approval. For example, the administration gained support from Florida representatives by promising to prevent Mexico from exporting sugar to the U.S. (Congressional Quarterly, Inc., 1993, p. 178). Further support for the NAFTA was garnered from citrus and vegetable producing regions in turn for the administration's agreement to expedite procedures for the protection of U.S. producers from Mexican imports (Congressional Quarterly, Inc., 1993, pp. 178–179). Tom Lewis (R-Florida) remarked following the fruit and vegetable safeguards, that, in the end, "we got almost everything we asked for" (Congressional Quarterly, Inc., 1993, p. 179). On November 17, 1993, the House passed a resolution approving the NAFTA, and the Senate followed on November 20th (Congressional Quarterly, Inc., 1993).[5]

The final stage of NAFTAs formulation differs from the exclusionary politics of the negotiation stage. Labor and environmental groups were able to influence Congress on the NAFTA. However, Congressional, and therefore labor and environmental influence, over the final NAFTA policy was constrained by the decision-making structure established through the fast track. Because fast-track rules limited Congress' role to an out-and-out acceptance or rejection of a trade-policy negotiated within the Executive Branch, societal groups such as labor and environmentalists, which were excluded from the negotiations, had little, if any, mechanisms through which to influence trade policy.

In summary, by providing the Executive Branch with authority vis-à-vis Congress, the fast track insulated the formal negotiation process from labor and environmental groups. Consequently, the interests of labor and environmentalists were explicitly absent in the final NAFTA agreement. In contrast, business organizations used the advisory committees as a structure within which they could develop a trade policy benefiting both nationalist and internationalist business segments.

### The Outcomes of the NAFTA Policy Process

Does the organization of decision making within the state matter in terms of outcomes? In other words, did the fast-track exclusion of labor and environmental groups from the negotiation stage of the NAFTA affect the outcomes that the trade policy had on these groups? In the final stage of NAFTA, the excluded groups successfully worked through Congress in order to get last-minute concessions and side agreements on labor and environmental issues. However, what was the effectiveness of the side agreements relative to the more formalized benefits derived from business groups through the NAFTA negotiation stage?

By 1997, labor and environmental organizations could point to empirical evidence that the NAFTA side agreements had failed to deliver any appreciable protection to labor or the environment (U.S. Congress, House, 1997). The labor side agreements "did little more than create an apparatus for holding public meetings, which are often ignored by employers since the law itself provides no means to punish abuses" (Millman, 1997). By October 15, 1997, the Labor Cooperation panel, established by the NAFTA side agreements, had reviewed only six cases. Even though labor won all of these cases, a labor attorney explained that "not a single worker was ever reinstated, not a single employer was sanctioned, [and] no union was ever recognized" (Wall Street Journal, October 15, 1997, p. A19).

The environmental provisions of the NAFTA side agreements, which established the Commission on Environmental Compliance (CEC), also proved to have no real influence over environmental issues. By October 1997, there had been 11 environmental disputes filed. Only one of the disputes resulted in an actual investigation by the Commission, with the outcome remaining concealed to the public. CEC director, Greg Brock, asserted that the commission's objective was "to clarify the state of the facts, not to enforce compliance" (Wall Street Journal, October 15, 1997). As Richard Gephart, a key Democratic representative explained about the NAFTA:

> ... a lot of members on both sides of the aisle gave the administration the benefit of the doubt on a lot of issues: labor side agreements, environmental side agreements, infrastructure funds, training and education, jobs. And I think a lot of that was unfulfilled (Congressional Quarterly, Inc., 1997, p. 2668).

The same response concerning NAFTA is voiced by those business sectors excluded from the negotiation process but included along with labor and the environment in the side deals. While these business groups had been left out of the formal NAFTA negotiation process, the President promised that their interests would be upheld through the side deal programs. This was especially the case within the agricultural and textiles industries. Despite Executive Branch assurances of protection prior to the NAFTAs passage, these industries were hit hard by cheap imports from Mexico following the trade agreement's implementation. Thus, the National Farmer's Union, a professional organization representing mostly small farmers, spoke out about the damaging effects of NAFTA (Federal News Service, 1997).

Congressional representatives from Florida and other states with fruit and vegetable industries had similar views of the NAFTA (State News Service, 1997; The Tampa Tribune, 1997a, 1997b). Representative Porter Goss, a Republican from Florida, remarked that because the White House will not enforce the protective mechanisms put in place with the NAFTA, "[t]hey owe us an explanation why the next agreement they bring us will be any better" (State News Service, 1997). In sum, those groups excluded by the fast track from the NAFTA negotiation process all reported damaging effects from the trade policy's implementation. Despite the fact that they were able to influence Congress following the negotiation stage, because fast-track organizational procedures relegated Congressional input to "negative politics," those groups unable to influence the Executive Branch negotiations were pacified with the establishment of an ineffective, symbolic set of side agreements.

## SUMMARY AND CONCLUSIONS

In order to explain the recent shift in U.S. trade policy, we have shown the importance of analyzing organizational state structures as historical contingencies affecting state autonomy. Tracing the development of trade policy over the post-war period documents the structural constraints of economic crises framing the trade-policy debates. Increased foreign competition and declining terms of trade led to protectionist sentiments among some companies, especially automotive and electronics firms. The capitalist class became divided between nationalists and internationalists. By 1974, state managers enacted the organizational structure of fast track, specifically designed to protect the trade policy process from segmented business interests, who believed that the autonomy provided by this organizational structure would allow U.S. trade representatives to reduce both tariff and non-tariff barriers that threatened the GATT system. However, the U.S. economic downturn continued into the 1980s and, even as corporate profits began their return in the late 1980s and early 1990s, import competition ensued and became increasingly recognized by both corporations and the state as a major threat to U.S. capital accumulation.

As previous NAFTA research has shown (e.g., Dreiling, 2000, 2001) the unity and power of business organizations combined to produce a pro-business NAFTA policy. Alternatively, the inability of labor organizations to influence the NAFTA debate may reflect the general trend in the decline of labor union power in the United States during the last several decades. However, as shown above, the effectiveness of business and the related ineffectiveness of labor and environment was also a product of the organizational structures (i.e., fast track) defining the policy process and the resulting system of negative politics that this structure created. Not only did the fast track help create and maintain a unified business influence, it also helped exclude labor and environmental interests from the most important stages of the policy process.

Many social scientists have argued that the state attempted to move toward a greater degree of state autonomy in trade policy with the introduction and extension of the fast-track organizational structure (Destler, 1992). However, as Prechel (1990, p. 664) suggests, organizational structures also provide an opportunity for classes and class segments outside the state to influence state policy. Even though the fast-track structure provided the Executive branch a measurable degree of autonomy from Congress, it did not, as state autonomy theorists might suggest, separate the state from societal forces. In fact, the fast track provided the organizational mechanisms through which the capitalist class was able to influence the provisions of the NAFTA. Thus, the findings of this study give strong support to the historical-contingency model of the state. While the fast track shifted state policy to the bureaucratic office of the USTR with the apparent intention of making trade policy more autonomous from the demands of specific societal groups, this was not the final result. Moving trade policy formulation to the Executive Branch office of the USTR allowed for the increased influence of capitalists groups over the NAFTA.

For many years, social scientists have argued over the relative validity of a set of broadly defined and relatively ahistorical theoretical conceptions of the state–society relationship. The result was an impasse characterized by each set of scholars arguing that the state–society relationship was defined by those characteristics (e.g., state autonomy or class unity) emphasized by a given theory. The importance of a structural contingency model is in its capacity to demonstrate (1) that state autonomy and class unity (as well as other relevant theoretical conceptions explaining the state–society relationship) vary historically, and (2) that state structures create mechanism that provide business interests outside the state with opportunity to affect foreign policy while excluding other classes and interests groups. The focus on business involvement in the creation of fast track (Woods, 2003) and changes in this state structure moves beyond ahistorical arguments and explains how historical variation in state structures and class power affect the policy-formation process.

## ACKNOWLEDGMENT

We would like to thank John Alston, John Boies, Eduardo Bonilla-Silva, Harland Prechel, Steve Valocchi, and three anonymous reviewers for comments on previous versions of this paper.

## NOTES

1. See the appendix for a list of acronyms.
2. Orloff and Skocpol (1984) argue that state structures "may be sites of autonomous official action, not reducible to the demands or preferences of any social group" (p. 730).
3. Uruguay Round negotiations were launched in September 1986, but GATT-Uruguary Round legislation was not signed into law until December 1994.
4. In fact, as one reviewer argues, the fast track may also be beneficial to individual congressional members as it alleviates them from having to face the divisive views of business. They can blame the Executive Branch for the trade policy and even vote "No" on the final vote or at least complain about the final policy to win points with the losing business side.
5. The voting pattern for NAFTA is consistent with the argument that conservative congressional members supported NAFTA, while more liberal members opposed NAFTA. Congressional Quarterly, Inc. (1988, p. 3343) defines a conservative coalition voting alliance between Republicans and Southern Democrats as votes where a majority of Southern Democrats side with a majority of Republicans against a majority of Northern Democrats. This is exactly what happened in the House and the Senate on the NAFTA votes. In the House (House Roll Call Vote 575), Republicans voted in favor of NAFTA 132-43. Northern Democrats opposed NAFTA 49-124, but Southern Democrats supported NAFTA 53-32. In the Senate (Senate Roll Call Vote 395), Republicans supported NAFTA 34-10, as did Southern Democrats 9-5. However, Northern Democrats opposed NAFTA 18-23.

## REFERENCES

Akard, P. J. (1992). Corporate mobilization and political power: The transformation of U.S. economic policy in the 1970s. *American Sociological Review, 57*(5), 597–615.

Amenta, E., & Halfmann, D. (2000). Wage wars: Institutional politics, WPA wages, and the struggle for U.S. social policy. *American Sociological Review, 65*(4), 506–528.

Amenta, E., & Poulsen, J. D. (1996). Social politics in context: The institutional politics theory and social spending at the end of the new deal. *Social Forces, 75*(1), 33–61.

Audley, J. J. (1997). *Green politics and global trade: NAFTA and the future of environmental politics.* Washington, DC: Georgetown University Press.

Auerbach, S. (1991). Lobbyists gear up for battle: Farm, textile and labor groups oppose goals of Bush, big business. *Washington Post,* March 2, p. A8.

Barnet, R. J., & Cavanagh, J. (1994). *Global dreams: Imperial corporations and the new world order.* New York: Simon & Schuster.

Cameron, M. A., & Tomlin, B. W. (2000). *The making of NAFTA: How the deal was done.* Ithaca, NY: Cornell University Press.

Congressional Quarterly, Inc. (1988). Conservative coalition: Still alive, but barley. *Congressional Quarterly Weekly Report,* November 19, pp. 3343–3348.

Congressional Quarterly, Inc. (1991a). *Congressional quarterly almanac 1991.* Washington, DC: Congressional Quarterly, Inc.

Congressional Quarterly, Inc. (1991b). *Congressional quarterly weekly report, February 23.* Washington, DC: Congressional Quarterly, Inc.

Congressional Quarterly, Inc. (1992). *Congressional quarterly almanac 1992.* Washington, DC: Congressional Quarterly, Inc.

Congressional Quarterly, Inc. (1993). Trade policy. *Congress and the Nation, 1989–1992, 8,* 165–200.

Congressional Quarterly, Inc. (1997). Clinton sways few democrats as house sets fast track vote. *Congressional Quarterly Weekly Report,* November 1, pp. 2667–2668.

Destler, I. M. (1992). *American trade politics* (2nd ed.). Washington, DC: Institute for International Economics.

Domhoff, G. W. (1970). *The higher circles.* New York: Random House.

Domhoff, G. W. (1978). *The powers that be.* New York: Vintage Books.

Domhoff, G. W. (1990). *The power elite and the state: How policy is made in America.* New York: Aldine De Gruyter.

Dreiling, M. C. (2000). The class embeddedness of corporate political action: Leadership in defense of the NAFTA. *Social Problems, 47*(1), 21–48.

Dreiling, M. C. (2001). *Solidarity and contention: The politics of security and sustainability in the NAFTA conflict.* New York: Garland Press.

Eden, L., & Molot, M. A. (1996). Made in America? The U.S. auto industry, 1955–95. *The International Executive, 38*(4), 501–541.

Evans, P., Rueschemeyer, D., & Skocpol, T. (1985). *Bringing the state back in.* Cambridge, MA: Cambridge University Press.

Farnsworth, C. H. (1990). Winners and losers in trade talks. *New York Times,* November 29, p. D1.

Farren, J. M. (1991). Industry advisors: Their role in Brussels. *Business America,* January.

Federal News Service (1997). Prepared testimony of Richard Schlosser of the National Farmers Union. *Federal News Service,* September 23.

Goldstein, J. (1993). *Ideas, interests, and American trade policy.* Ithaca, NY: Cornell University Press.

Guthrie, D., & McQuarrie, M. (2005). Privitization and low-income housing in the United States since 1986. *Research in Political Sociology, 14,* 15–50.

202                        TIM WOODS AND THERESA MORRIS

Haggard, S. (1988). The institutional foundations of hegemony: Explaining the Reciprocal Trade
    Agreements Act of 1934. In: J. Ikenberry, D. A. Lake & M. Mastanduno (Eds), *The state
    and American foreign economic policy* (pp. 91–199). Ithaca, NY: Cornell University Press.
Harrison, B. (1994). *Lean and mean: The changing landscape of corporate power in the age of
    flexibility*. New York: Basic Books.
Harrison, B., & Bluestone, B. (1988). *The great U-turn: Corporate restructuring and the
    polarization of America*. New York: Basic Books.
Hartland-Thundberg, P. (1985). Case studies in structural adjustment: An interpretive sum-
    mary. In: C. Stirling & J. N. Yochelson (Eds), *Under pressure: U.S. industry and the
    challenges of structural adjustment* (pp. 17–30). Boulder: Westview Press.
Hicks, A., & Misra, J. (1993). Two perspectives on the welfare state: Political resources and the
    growth of welfare in affluent capitalist democracies, 1960–1982. *American Journal of
    Sociology, 99*(3), 668–710.
Ikenberry, G. J., Lake, D. A., & Mastanduno, M. (1988). *The state and American foreign
    economic policy*. Ithaca, NY: Cornell University Press.
Korten, D. C. (1995). *When corporations rule the world*. West Hartford, CT: Kumarian Press, Inc.
Krasner, S. D. (1978). *Defending the national interest*. Princeton, NJ: Princeton University Press.
Lake, D. (1988). The state and American trade strategy in the pre-hegemonic era. In:
    J. Ikenberry, D. Lake & M. Mastanduno (Eds), *The state and American foreign economic
    policy* (pp. 33–58). Ithaca, NY: Cornell University Press.
MacArthur, J. R. (2000). *The selling of free trade*. New York: Hill and Wang.
Maxfield, S., & Shapiro, A. (1998). Assessing the NAFTA negotiations: U.S.–Mexican debate and
    compromise on tariff and non-tariff issues. In: C. Wise (Ed.), *The post-NAFTA political
    economy* (pp. 82–118). University Park, PA: The Pennsylvania State University Press.
Mayer, F. W. (1998). *Interpreting NAFTA: The science and art of political analysis*. New York:
    Columbia University Press.
McKeown, T. J. (1999). The global economy, post-fordism, and trade policy in advanced capi-
    talist states. In: H. Kitschelt, P. Lange, G. Marks & J. D. Stephens (Eds), *Continuity and
    change in contemporary capitalism* (pp. 1–35). New York: Cambridge University Press.
Millman, J. (1997). NAFTAs do-gooder side deals disappoint. *Wall Street Journal*, October 15,
    p. A19.
Moore, G., Sobieraj, S., Whitt, A. J., Mayorova, O., & Beaulieu, D. (2002). Elite interlocks in
    three U.S. sectors: Nonprofit, corporate, and government. *Social Science Quarterly,
    83*(3), 726–744.
Orloff, A. S., & Skocpol, T. (1984). Why not equal protection? Explaining the politics of public
    social spending in Britain, 1900–1911, and the United States, 1880s–1920. *American
    Sociological Review, 49*(6), 726–750.
Petracca, M. P. (1994). Federal advisory committees, interest groups, and the administrative
    state. In: R. Himmelberg (Ed.), *Regulatory issues since 1964: The rise of the deregulation
    movement* (pp. 211–242). New York, NY: Garland Publishing, Inc.
Prechel, H. (1990). Steel and the state: Industry politics and business policy formation,
    1940–1989. *American Sociological Review, 55*(5), 648–668.
Prechel, H. (1991). Conflict and historical variation in steel capital-state relations: The emer-
    gence of state structures and a more prominent, less autonomous state. Reply to Gregory
    Hooks. *American Sociological Review, 56*, 693–698.
Prechel, H. (2000). *Big business and the state: Historical transitions and corporate transforma-
    tion, 1880s–1990s*. Albany, NY: SUNY Press.

Reich, R. B. (1991). *The work of nations.* New York: Vintage Books.

Skidmore, D., & Glasberg, D. S. (1996). State theory and corporate welfare: The crisis and bailout of the savings and loan industry from a contingency perspective. *Political Power and Social Theory, 10,* 149–191.

State News Service (1997). On the hill: Fast track back on track. *State News Service,* October 31.

Strauss, S. B. (1982). The industry consultations program: A major tool for formulating trade policy. *Business America,* May 31, 1.

The Tampa Tribune (1997a). Citrus growers fear Clinton proposal will result in squeeze. Business and Finance, *The Tampa Tribune,* October 26, p. 1.

The Tampa Tribune (1997b). Delegates unsure of 'fast track' plan. *The Tampa Tribune,* October 31, p. 6.

U.S. Congress, House (1991a). *President's request for extension of fast track trade agreement implementing authority.* Committee on Ways and Means, 102nd Congress, 1st Session. Washington, DC: Government Printing Office.

U.S. Congress, House (1991b). *Proposed negotiation of a Free Trade Agreement with Mexico.* Committee on Ways and Means, Subcommittee on Trade, 102nd Congress, 1st Session. Washington, DC: Government Printing Office.

U.S. Congress, House (1991c). *Fast track authority and the North American Free Trade Agreement.* Committee on Public Works and Transportation, Subcommittee on Economic Development, 102nd Congress, 1st Session. Washington DC: Government Printing Office.

U.S. Congress, House (1993). *The North American Free Trade Agreement: Environmental and labor agreements.* Committee on Foreign Affairs, 103rd Congress, 1st Session. Washington, DC: Government Printing Office.

U.S. Congress, House (1997). *Hearing on the President's comprehensive review of the NAFTA.* Committee on Ways and Means, Subcommittee on Trade. September 11, U.S. House of Representatives. web site: www.house.gov

U.S. Congress, Senate (1987). *Mastering the world economy, Part 2.* Committee on Finance, 100th Congress, 1st Session. Washington, DC: Government Printing Office.

U.S. Congress, Senate (1989). *Bilateral trade agreements.* Committee on Finance, Subcommittee on International Trade, 101st Congress, 1st Session. Washington, DC: Government Printing Office.

U.S. Congress, Senate (1992). *North American Free Trade Agreement.* Committee on Finance, 102nd Congress, 2nd Session. Washington, DC: Government Printing Office.

U.S. President (1992a). *The NAFTA: Report of the Advisory Committee for Trade Policy and Negotiations.* Washington, DC: Government Printing Office.

U.S. President (1992b). *The NAFTA: Report of the Industry Policy Advisory Committee.* Washington, DC: Government Printing Office.

U.S. President (1992c). *Report of the Industry Sector Advisory Committee for Trade in transportation, construction, and agriculture equipment of the NAFTA.* Washington, DC: Government Printing Office.

Useem, M. (1984). *The inner circle.* New York: Oxford University Press.

Weber, M. (1978). *Economy and society.* Berkeley: University of California Press.

Wolanin, T. R. (1975). *Presidential advisory commissions.* Madison, WI: The University of Wisconsin Press.

Woods, T. (2003). Capitalist class relations, the state, and new deal foreign trade policy. *Critical Sociology, 29*(3), 393–418.

# APPENDIX

*List of Acronyms*

| | |
|---|---|
| ACTPN | Advisory Committee for Trade Policy and Negotiations |
| AFL-CIO | American Federation of Labor-Congress of Industrial Organizations |
| CEC | Commission on Environmental Compliance |
| COC | Chamber of Commerce |
| EC | European Economic Community |
| EPA | Environmental Protection Agency |
| GATT | General Agreement on Tariffs and Trade |
| IPAC | Industry Policy Advisory Committee |
| ISAC | Industry Sector Advisory Committee |
| MFA | Multi-Fiber Arrangement |
| MTN | Multilateral Trade Negotiations |
| NAFTA | North American Free Trade Agreement |
| NAM | National Association of Manufacturers |
| NFTC | National Foreign Trade Council |
| NIC | Newly Industrializing Countries |
| RTA | Reciprocal Trade Agreements Act |
| TAA | Trade Adjustment Assistance |
| USTR | United States Trade Representative |

# CORPORATE POLITICAL ACTION AND GLOBAL TRADE REGIMES: FORTUNE 500 FIRMS IN THE U.S. TRADE POLICY FORMATION PROCESS [☆]

Derek Darves and Michael Dreiling

## ABSTRACT

*This paper examines corporate involvement in the formation of U.S. trade policies that structure the market and legal institutions of economic globalization. Testing theories concerning state–corporate relations, we examine the determinants of corporate appointment to 18 influential trade-consultation committees that serve as economic advisors to the Department of Commerce, the U.S. Trade Representative, and the President of the United States. Grouping firms at the two-digit industry code level, organizational, political, and network sources of participation are examined in three hierarchical non-linear models (HNLMs). Membership in*

[☆]The authors extend their sincere appreciation to several RPS reviewers for their helpful comments. A previous version of this paper was presented at the 36th annual Sunbelt Social Network Conference. Funding for this research was supplemented by the Williams Foundation Award at the University of Oregon.

Politics and Globalization
Research in Political Sociology, Volume 15, 205–239
ISSN: 0895-9935/doi:10.1016/S0895-9935(06)15007-X

*prominent policy groups, temporary trade policy alliances, board inter-
locks, PAC expenditures, and firm size all positively correlate with the
odds of firm participation in the advisory committees. Mean affiliation
was also found to differ significantly between different industries. Other
organizational indicators, such as foreign subsidiaries, failed to yield
significant partial correlations when the effects of size, product market,
network position, and PAC spending were controlled. The findings support class-based accounts of corporate political action and suggest a significant association between higher levels of firm embeddedness within
intercorporate networks and the likelihood to engage the state in building
global trade regimes.*

## INTRODUCTION

"Trade globally, prosper locally!" This was the slogan for the corporate
campaign to extend trade promotion authority (TPA) to the president in
1999.[1] Raising the banner to globalize trade, the group "America Leads on
Trade" (ALOT) was applying tools learned five years earlier in the conflict
over the North American Free Trade Agreement (NAFTA). Faced with
growing questions about globalization however, the "Battle in Seattle"
(November 29–December 1, 1999) abruptly stalled their efforts to promote
TPA for the president. The stage was already set for a wave of post-NAFTA
contention over free trade, and TPA was just one point of contention.
Despite these challenges, negotiations for new free trade agreements continued: plans to expand NAFTA to Central America and South America;
the bill to permanently normalize trade relations (PNTR) with China[2];
and the bilateral agreement with Doha. These initiatives, and most significantly the passage of China PNTR, concluded a decade of contentious
politics over international trade policy, highlighting the mounting controversy over trade politics in this recent phase of globalization.

In this paper we examine *corporate* participation in U.S. government advisory committees responsible for framing American trade policy, 1998 and
2003. Unique to our research, and the original dataset we developed, is an
analysis of factors that influence corporate involvement in non-elected posts
in the executive branch. By identifying the factors that drive corporate participation in U.S. trade policy, our research points to concrete means by
which organized business influence in trade politics may occur. While corporate involvement in the policy making committees of the Executive
Branch is not unusual, the broad, interindustry structure of these committees

hint at the active role played by some corporations in shaping the recent wave of regional and global trade institutions. We explore the factors that best explain their involvement in these committees.

Our data on *Fortune* and *Forbes* 500 companies (hereafter FF500) and our substantive attention to the political locations of corporate actors in deliberations over trade policy offer an unusual window for viewing the *interaction* between state and corporate actors in the construction of regional and global trade institutions. Using a range of firm-level and intercorporate network data, our primary aim is to examine whether corporate participation in these non-elected posts is driven by converging company rationalities, with individual firms pursuing their organizational interests, or influenced by broader, class-wide considerations forged in intercorporate political networks. Consequently, we examine "network" and "organizational" factors as we explain corporate participation in U.S. trade policy committees.[3] Our main question is whether a firm's network position or organizational attributes influence its odds of participation in 18 Department of Commerce (DOC) trade advisory committees.

# CORPORATE PARTICIPATION IN INDUSTRIAL SECTOR ADVISORY COMMITTEES

We explore corporate involvement in trade policy by modeling the determinants of firm participation in DOC Industrial Sector Advisory Committees (ISACs). These influential trade policy committees form part of the DOCs larger "Industry Consultation Program," and provide a unique institutional mechanism for transmitting the interests of various industries to state policy makers (Cohen, Blecker, & Whitney, 2003; Dreiling, 2001; see also Hillman, Keim, & Schuler, 2004). At the apex of these committees is the President's Advisory Committee of Trade Policy and Negotiations (ACTPN). Members in ACTPN are appointed by the president for two-year terms and "consider trade policy issues in the context of the overall national interest" (United States Trade Representative, 1994, p. 114). The second tier of the industry consultation program consists of 17 ISACs. The actual criteria that the state employs for admittance to an ISAC are unclear, although the DOC claims "the primary factor for consideration [of an application] is the company or association that a nominee will represent" (DOC, 2000). Additionally, product market undoubtedly plays an important role in selection, since each sub-committee focuses on a specific domain of trade policy, such as international finance or trade in services. Unsurprisingly, banks are heavily represented in the finance advisory committee, service firms in the service sector advisory committee, etc. Less clear, however, is what determines the participation of firms within the same industry.

The influence of these trade policy committees has expanded since their creation in 1974. Under the "fast track"[4] rules established by the Trade Act of 1974, the executive branch must submit pending trade legislation to the ISACs, which evaluate whether the pending trade legislation is "consistent" with U.S. producer interests. Because it is exceedingly rare for Congress to support trade legislation that is opposed by one or more of the various advisory committees, they possess a "de facto veto" over pending trade legislation (Cohen et al., 2003, p. 125). In addition to their evaluative function, ISACs provide direct input into active U.S. trade negotiations. It is common, for example, for ISAC members to communicate directly with U.S. officials during active trade negotiations to provide input on the language of a treatise or to make other requests.[5]

While information regarding the specific activities of ISACs is not disclosed, their organizational self-description explains that "The Department of Commerce, Office of the U.S. Trade Representative, and other agencies work side by side with business leaders [ISAC members] who serve as advisors to the Government" (DOC, 2000). Analysis of several speeches delivered during ISAC sessions indicates that the committees are highly committed to the expansion of international commerce through trade agreements such as NAFTA and CAFTA. For example, in a speech delivered to ISAC members, former Secretary of Commerce, William Daley, highlighted corporate leaders' potential influence on both public and legislative support for international trade:

Five years ago I was engaged full-time, along with many others, in convincing the country that the North American Free Trade Agreement would be good for America. The effort paid off: trade within the hemisphere is up 75 percent ... [but] we have a long way to go to convince people that globalization is good for the next century ... In the next century, if we want to open new markets – as I know you do – whether in China, Latin America, Europe, or Africa – the average American has to be for it. Globalization may play well in corporate boardrooms, but I really mean this: the rest of America has to hear your story, and buy into it. If the people are not behind us, we cannot expect Congress to go along with us on other trade initiatives – no matter who is the next President, or which party is in control of Congress. As President Clinton said ... he needs the ability to use trade talks to open markets for our companies and our workers. But we won't be able to get that fast-track negotiating authority, if the people are not behind him. So I hope we can count on you as we prepare for these WTO negotiations, as well as helping get the good word out about trade (Daley, 2000a).

During an earlier speech delivered to ISAC members on May 6, 1998, Secretary Daley also referenced the need for public support for free trade policies, claiming "We need to build a consensus in our country, and around the globe, that trade is good" (Daley, 2000b). These comments, together with other committee materials and interviews with ISAC staff suggest that the committees are proponents of neoliberal trade initiatives, such as NAFTA, and oppose tariff and non-tariff barriers to trade.

The construction of recent neoliberal trade initiatives – from NAFTA and CAFTA to PNTR with China – clearly involved both state and corporate actors. Because state agencies played an important role in shaping the U.S. trade agenda, and because corporate interests are active participants in these agencies, a theoretical approach that considers the inter-relationship of corporate political action and trade policy formation is needed. Such theory will aid our understanding of the relative roles of corporate and state actors in erecting trade regimes oriented to global and regional market governance. More immediately, an examination of the causes of corporate ISAC participation will contribute to longstanding debates concerning corporate political action and influence. By examining the factors that drive corporate participation in these committees, our research offers an opportunity to begin linking theories of corporate political action to a political theory of globalization, something we return to in the discussion.

## THEORIZING CORPORATE TRADE POLICY PARTICIPATION

Contemporary theories of trade policy and globalization have not developed a consistent model to explain corporate *collective* involvement with the U.S. government in creating recent international trade initiatives, such as the NAFTA. We begin to address this problem by probing two, broad theoretical frameworks to explain corporate political involvement in trade policy and participation in the ISACs in particular. The first theoretical perspective, which we term an organizational-interest perspective, typically emphasizes the influence of firm attributes and interests, such as foreign subsidiary operations or size, on corporate trade policy involvement (McKeown, 1984; Milner, 1988; see also Schattschneider, 1935). In this view, trade policy outcomes are a function of the ability of competing firms and sectors to organize and give their interests prominence in the policy process. Modeled on interest group theory of corporate political action, the state is viewed as a weak "intermediary" between competing economic and societal forces pursuing organizationally determined trade interests (Baldwin, 1986, p. 176; Milner, 1988; see also Ikenberry, Lake, & Mastanduno, 1988). Because firm "economic interests" are presumed to emerge from organizational characteristics, such as size or level of multinational investments, the role of extra-organizational networks is rarely considered in this literature. A second, contrasting body of literature stresses corporate political action as "class embedded," which posits a relatively cohesive, "inner circle" or "class segment" that is able and willing to act in concert with a responsive state apparatus to achieve wider class aims (Mizruchi, 1992, pp. 33–52; Burris, 1987, p. 732; Domhoff, 2005; Useem, 1984; Darves & Dreiling, 2002; Dreiling, 2001). We explore each of these perspectives below.

## Organizational-Interest Theories

An extensive body of literature investigating firm-level trade preferences has documented several postwar trends in corporate political efforts to promote trade relief or expansion (Destler, 1995; Milner & Yoffie, 1989; Bauer, Pool, & Dexter, 1963; Baldwin, 1989). In general, these studies stress the importance of a firm's position within product markets, and have found that firms that compete heavily with imported goods tend to favor protectionist trade policy, while multinational firms with several foreign subsidiaries or firms that benefit from exports, tend to support trade expansion. Accordingly, much of this research focuses on the organizational and market sources of firm trade preferences, while few analysts consider the role of prominent business lobbies and other interfirm political associations that shape a broader corporate consensus on trade (but see Woods, 2003 for a class segment approach to trade policy). Much of the trade policy literature conceptualizes firms as atomistic organizations motivated solely by the economic imperatives associated with their specific firm or industry (Baldwin, 1989; Destler, 1995; Krueger, 1995; Rogowski, 1989; see also Milner, 1988). A consequence of competing corporate interests on trade policy, it follows, is that state actors must create policy more or less independently of any larger business class segments. From this perspective, business political solidarity, when it occurs, is a function converging economic interests, not a class movement (Baldwin, 1989; Cohen et al., 2003; Vogel, 1989).

Within this framework, corporations – more or less independently – pursue a company- or industry-specific economic rationality by pressuring the political process, usually though the legislature. Trade dependent (and trade threatened) firms and industries enter the political arena in pursuit of *organizational* interests, not as an expression of the opportunities and constraints imposed by their network position within larger intercorporate networks. When the role of corporate collective action in trade policy outcomes is considered (if at all), this literature typically focuses on the aggregate economic inefficiencies imposed on the economy by rent-seeking corporate and industry lobbies, as with the tariff concessions secured by the sugar industry at the 1994 "Uruguay Round" of GATT negotiations.

A considerable body of literature builds on the seminal publication of Bauer et al. (1963), citing their study as evidence of business' perennial conflict over trade policy. Their empirical account defines a business lobby ripe with political "ineptness," "woefully ignorant" of the issues and often ineffective over trade policy, 1953–1962 (Bauer et al. 1963, p. 484). More contemporary studies have elaborated on the account of Bauer et al. (1963) to identify the ways in which state managers overcome business "ineptness" and conflict by formulating foreign economic policy agendas that advance both domestic and international political-economic hegemony or some "national interest" (Goldstein, 1993; see also Ikenberry, Lake, & Mastanduno, 1988). These accounts argue that the U.S.' economic position after WWII defined the advancement of an open trade policy agenda in line with the geopolitical and economic interests of the state. Liberal international relations theory and foreign-policy studies also adopt this perspective, although emphasizing the role of state managers as bearers of the "national interest" (Preeg, 1998). Thus, for state-centered theorists, the actual genesis of trade policy is explained as an outcome of state manager's visions – usually explained as a "national interest" or "system imperative" – for geopolitical and economic hegemony.

Often this literature stresses two important trade policy events in the 20th century. The first occurred when Congress granted significant autonomy in 1934 to the president in matters of international trade, arguing that this enabled the executive, unencumbered by "special interest" congressional politics, to devise foreign economic policy in the national interest (see Woods, 2003 for a discussion). The disastrous case of the 1930 Smoot-Hawley tariffs is usually referenced as an example of Congress' inability, pressured by competing industries and firms, to enact a rational trade program, and hence the reason for turning trade policy matters over to the more autonomous executive.[6] The second major trade initiative, the Trade Expansion Act of 1962, has again been viewed as a case where corporate political fragmentation undermined its potential role in the policy formation process.

For these models of trade policy formation, the executive branch's independence in negotiating trade agreements reflects state actors' broader autonomy to develop policy on behalf of an otherwise disengaged business sector or to advance the "national interest." The incorporation of trade-negotiating authority under the President, these theorists argue, circumvents business' conflicting economic interests, translating a plurality of contending economic and social interests into a unified national trade program. The result is a trade policy apparatus largely unhindered by protectionist, interest-group politics within the legislature. The implication is that trade policy interests begin from within the state, usually out of state managers' concerns for economic stability and growth, and then organized interests deliberate the superficial details of that policy in the legislature.

In so far as corporate policy activism is ostensibly limited to ad hoc firm and industry lobbies, state actors are left to meld a broader trade agenda from the competing voices over trade. While these state actors make occasional concessions to specific lobbies (as with the sugar industry), their actions, predominantly, are thought to represent more generalized economic, national, or social "interests" in the development of international trade agreements (Destler, 1995; Krueger, 1995). Structural imperatives for creating trade agreements arise from growth in international trade and corporate-foreign investment, which place twin demands on the state to facilitate international transactions and protect foreign capital expenditures (Fieleke, 1988). State actors, usually within the executive branch, presumably respond to these imperatives by promoting bi- and multilateral trade agreements, such as NAFTA and China PNTR. Interestingly, corporate actors, the engines of U.S. economic hegemony, remain politically silent in this picture, a perspective not easily reconciled with the obvious involvement of corporations in trade policy formation.

However, while the *economic* activities of multinational corporations are assumed to influence these processes, the actual *political* organization of these firms does not figure prominently in the trade policy literature (Cohen et al., 2003; Destler, 1995; Duina, 2006; Milner, 1988). What is typically absent in much of this literature is a larger consideration of the role of interfirm political solidarity in trade policy promotion. Business supportive organizations and the larger policy-planning network are seen as provincial, focusing on the issues of specific industries, not part of a larger, intersectoral network of trade policy advocacy. The notion of business political fragmentation on trade policy implies that trade institutions are largely organized by the pressure of competing corporate interests which are then fused by the initiative of state actors (Destler, 1995; Preeg, 1998) or impersonal market forces (Milner, 1988).[7] Interestingly, corporate actors, the engines of U.S. economic power, remain politically silent in this picture, a perspective not easily reconciled with the obvious involvement of corporations in trade policy formation.

While large firms, undoubtedly, possess varying trade policy preferences, the political cooperation of broad segments of business in support of recent trade initiatives, such as NAFTA, the WTO, and China PNTR, renders the assumption of business political fragmentation over trade policy somewhat suspect, if not highly problematic.[8] This is not to say that business is "unified" on all trade policy matters. However, despite continued conflict over trade policy, large U.S. firms have also displayed remarkable political cooperation in support of several major trade initiatives in recent years (Dreiling, 2000; Woodall et al., 2000). Recent research that is more attentive to intercorporate, class networks, such as Woods (2003) and Dreiling (2001), expose how class associations interact with organizational factors to shape the character and extent of corporate involvement in trade politics. Thus, a more appropriate question, perhaps, is not *whether* business is unified on trade, *but under what conditions* firms from a variety of sectors will enter the policy formation process (Mizruchi, 1992; Prechel, 1990).

## Class Embedded Theories

In contrast to the organizational interest perspectives presented above, theories that accentuate greater business unity, even temporally contingent unity, view business influence in state policy formation as a consequence of the political networks interconnecting prominent corporate leaders to government. Building on the work of Mills (1956), subsequent research on the relationship between corporations and the state identifies mechanisms linking corporate elite to decision-making sites within the state (Useem, 1984; Domhoff, 2005). The theoretical assumption is that business, or at least the largest corporations, form enduring political alliances and, hence, achieve lasting influence in government.

Within this framework, "network" and "class" are closely related concepts. The former refers to the interorganizational ties created by board of director interlocks, policy-planning organizations, and various social clubs (Useem, 1984; Domhoff, 2005). Together, these connections form part of a broader communication network that functions to link various segments of big business with strategically defined policy initiatives. By directing corporate resources toward a common political agenda, policy groups and other sites of business cooperation promote an expansive, *"class-wide"* business interest. It has been suggested that a form of class-consciousness among business elite – as in Marx's (1847/1978, p. 218) notion of a class "for itself" – may be a part of this phenomenon (Useem, 1984). Others have suggested a commonalty of material interests – i.e., where business is seen to form a class "in itself" – is sufficient to produce political cohesion, regardless of any broader concern for the business class (see Mizruchi, 1989, p. 404 for a discussion). However, and as Mizruchi (1992) notes, whether business cooperation arises through common worldviews or shared economic interests (or both) does not change the social consequences of interfirm political action. The intercorporate network thus connotes not only a complex of interfirm ties, but also a social formation with political consequences: a cooperative, business *class segment* that emerges from overlapping social networks and transcends the economic concerns of specific industries (Domhoff, 1990; Mills, 1956; Mizruchi, 1989; Useem, 1984; Zeitlin, 1974).

This perspective, which we classify as a theory of "class embeddedness," argues that corporate leaders, while competitive organizationally, form stable intercorporate networks to both state institutions and a wide range of non-state policy organizations, such as the Business Roundtable (RB). Corporate political action is conceptualized as a relational phenomenon, where unity stems not only from shared economic interests but also from the embeddedness of corporate actors in a wider structure of social class relationships and class segments (Allen, 1978; Clawson, Neustadtl, & Bearden, 1986; Domhoff, 1990, 2005; Dreiling, 2000; Mills, 1956; Mintz & Schwartz, 1985; Mizruchi & Swartz, 1987; Useem, 1984; Zeitlin, 1974). Within this framework, corporate political action takes on a unified character that "is socially constructed through negotiation among its leading representatives" (Mizruchi, 1992, p. 22).

Building from this larger theoretical framework, power structure and class-based accounts of trade policy formation emphasize the role of class segments in the policy formation process and their hegemony within the larger business class. Yet, following Prechel (1990), we are reluctant to suggest that business unity, and hence the capacity of class segments to control the state, is a uniform and absolute condition. Indeed, Prechel's (2000, p. 277) framework accounts for the contingent development of both state structures and class capacities in the rise of a "political capitalism." Here, the political coherence of any class segment is a historical contingency, shaped by political struggles and accumulation dynamics. These struggles are in turn given shape by "certain structural biases" derived from the form of the state (Jessop, 1990, p. 150). These "structural biases" in the state, such as the ISACs, we argue, emerge historically in political struggle; even as class segments vie for influence over trade policy agendas.[9] In fact, this line of argument resembles Domhoff's (1990) power structure explanation of changing trade politics in the 1930s. He offered a class-segment interpretation of trade policy conflicts between 1929 and 1934, one that specified the changing economic forces that contributed to changing class alignments in American business. There he argued that the legislative shift of the state signaled an usurpation of power by an "internationalist" wing of business in America, displacing the otherwise nationalist-oriented businesses who wielded political power on trade and tariff policy via the legislature and who were previously responsible for Smoot-Hawley tariffs in 1930 (see also Frieden, 1988; Woods, 2003). Subsequent changes in the state, which placed trade-negotiating authority in the hands of the executive, would shape corporate political struggles around trade policy in new directions, something we return to later.

Class-based accounts of corporate involvement in U.S. trade policy also identify the role of prominent policy-planning organizations in both shaping the trade policy agenda and in organizing business leaders via shared social networks. One way that policy-planning organizations shape trade policy and corporate political behavior is to influence the intellectual framing of state projects. Shoup and Minter's (1977) account of the rise of the postwar trading system, for example, emphasizes the role of prominent policy-planning organizations, such as the Council on Foreign Relations, in initiating and advancing a foreign economic policy agendas consonant with the interests of an internationalist segment of capital. Also, Dreiling (2001) points to evidence that the recent round of free trade agreements, from NAFTA to normalized trade relations with China, emerged from policy-planning organizations such as the BR and the Trilateral Commission.

The common assumption behind class-based perspectives is that some segments of the business community are unified – more or less under different historical circumstances – and that cooperation around trade policy emerges from participation in a wide range of corporate and upper-class networks. A class embedded milieu transcends the interests of any single organization or industry, letting broader, class-wide interests prevail in promoting the project of neoliberal globalization. A class embedded, business unity perspective thus expects that more networked firms – not necessarily the largest or most trade dependent – assume an active role in the creation and promotion of hemispheric and global free trade agreements.

## DATA AND HYPOTHESES

We integrate a variety of data sources to investigate hypotheses derived from the two general perspectives on corporate trade policy action outlined above. Our sample consists of publicly traded firms listed in the 1998 and 2003 *Fortune* 500 and/or *Forbes* 500 lists.[10] As both the *Forbes* and *Fortune* directories employ similar measures of firm size, most firms are listed in both directories. We drop privately held firms from the sample because most do not produce financial statements analogous to the 10k filings incumbent upon publicly traded companies.[11] Table 1 presents a summary of data sources, variable coding, and the hypothesized relationship between each explanatory factor and the dependent variable.

### *Dependent Variable*

Firm participation in one or more ISACs is employed as a proxy for involvement in the trade policy formation process. In 2003, 64 (13%) of FF500 corporations participated in one or more of these advisory committees. ISAC participation is Poisson distributed within the FF500 – most firms do not participate in the program, a smaller number belong to one committee, and a few are members of two or more committees.

### *Independent Variables and their Hypothesized Effects*

#### *Organizational-Interest Variables*
*Foreign Subsidiaries*: Firms with extensive interests or productive facilities benefit economically from lower tariffs on intrafirm transactions spanning national borders. A number of studies suggest that multinational firms are more likely to participate in some aspect of trade politics (Yarbrough & Yarbrough, 1992; Milner, 1988; Destler, 1995). We measure the scope of a firm's international operations as the number of its worldwide subsidiary operations in foreign countries. Because the count of subsidiary operations displays a strongly positive distributional skew in the FF500, the natural log is taken.

   **H1.** Firms with more foreign subsidiary operations are more likely to participate in an ISAC.

*Capital-Intensity of Operations*: Some analysts argue that high fixed-cost, capital-intensive industries generally demonstrate greater support for trade

***Table 1.*** Variables, Measures, and Hypotheses.

| Variable | Units and Coding | Source | Predicted Effect |
|---|---|---|---|
| ISAC participation | Count of total memberships in ACTPN and/or ISACs | U.S. Department of Commerce, 1998, 2003 | — |
| Size | Principle factor of sales, assets, and employees | 1998/2003 *Compustat Industrial Annual* | + |
| PAC contributions | Combined PAC expenditures in two preceding election cycles (for the 1998 firms, 1996 and 1998 election cycles; for the 2003 firms, the 2000, and 2002 election cycles) | U.S. Federal Elections Commission | + |
| Foreign subsidiaries | Log of the count of firm subsidiary operations in foreign countries | Uniworld Business Publications, *Directory of American Firms Operating in Foreign Countries* | + |
| Product market | Two-digit standard industrial classification (SIC) | 1998/2003 *Compustat Industrial Annual* | Variable[a] |
| Capital intensity | Log of the quotient of assets divided by number of employees | 1998/2003 *Compustat Industrial Annual* | + |
| Board interlocks | Log of the total number of firm direct board interlocks. Interlocks are calculated using the Freeman Degree Centrality score for a firm-by-firm matrix of board of director affiliations | Proxy statement, *Disclosure* (for 1998 firms), *IRRC* director database (for 2003 firms) | + |
| Policy network affiliation | Count of total membership ties to the Business Council, Conference Board, National Association of Manufacturers, Council of the America's, Trilateral Commission, and the United States Council for International Business | Public and requested membership rosters | + |
| Business roundtable participation | Dummy indicator of Business Roundtable membership | Publicly available membership roster | + |

*Table 1.* (*Continued*)

| Variable | Units and Coding | Source | Predicted Effect |
| --- | --- | --- | --- |
| Temporary trade policy alliances | Count of participation in temporary trade policy alliances (for 1998 firms, membership in America Leads on Trade and/or USA Engage, for 2003 firms, membership in the Business Coalition for U.S.-Central America Trade and/or the U.S. Trade Coalition) | Public membership rosters | + |
| Year control | Dummy variable for observation year (1998 = 0, 2003 = 1) | — | — |

[a]Product market is modeled as a level-2 grouping variable such that firms within each two-digit SIC code are assigned a unique mean rate of ISAC participation (intercept).

liberalization, since open markets (potentially) increase aggregate demand for their products (Gill, 1990, p. 97; Piore & Sabel, 1984). Firms and sectors capable of mass-quantity production will tend to favor open investment and trade with potentially large consumer markets, such as China. We measure capital-intensity as the log of the ratio of firm assets to total number of employees.

**H2.** Capital-intensive firms are more likely to participate in an ISAC.

*Firm Sector*: Prior research demonstrates that a firm's trade preferences are closely tied to its product market (Bauer et al., 1972; Milner & Yoffie, 1989). Because each ISAC addresses different aspects of international commerce (e.g., intellectual property rights), motivation to participate in a given committee will be shaped by the primary industrial activity of a firm. Thus, we expect mean ISAC participation to vary significantly between industries. In particular, firms and sectors (measured as two-digit standard industrial classification (SIC) categories) more dependent on international sales will have a greater likelihood to participate in U.S. trade politics.

**H3.** Firms that operate in tradable good sectors are more likely to participate in an ISAC.

*Size*: Company size is also associated with higher levels of trade policy activism in the literature. The first and most general reason for this association is that large firms possess greater resources to devote to the political process and, hence, are expected to be more politically active. Bauer et al. (1972, p. 228), for example, found that larger companies devoted greater resources (such as executive time, money, or various public relations efforts) to trade policy advocacy than smaller firms.

A second reason why large firms may be more politically active is that they stand to gain a larger distributive proportion of any favorable trade policy outcome (Olson, 1965; Mizruchi, 1992). While smaller firms require associations and other collective mechanisms to achieve political influence, for the largest and most resourceful firms, the very pursuit of corporate interests often produces a social consequence. As a result, political activism may yield a sufficient economic return even without the assistance of other firms.

Third, Useem (1984) argues that executives representing the largest firms are more politically active because they require a "scan" of the business community that transcends a single product market (most often, because their firms simultaneously operate in several distinct industries). Large firms are thus more likely to establish a host of ties to other firms, policy makers, and advocacy groups in order to "scan" the economic, social, and regulatory conditions facing big business.

Firm size was estimated using data on sales, assets, and employees. The relationship of each of these factors to the size of a company varies by sector. In the insurance industry, for example, many of the largest firms have low sales (compared to other *Fortune* companies), but assets significantly greater than the sample mean. In other sectors, such as retail, total number of employees may instead provide a better estimate of size. Thus, because each of these measures assumes variable importance in different sectors, we used principle factor analysis to extract a single factor solution for size. This approach yields a singe, composite score for each company that estimates size using all three pieces of information (i.e., sales, assets, and employees). Several other operationalizations for size found in the literature, such as overall sales rank, summing sales and assets, or entering each measure as a separate variable, were also analyzed. Because the factor analytic solution generally produced the best model fit it was chosen over other operationalizations.

**H4.** Large firms are more likely to participate in an ISAC.

*Political Action Committee Expenditures*: Prior research consistently finds that corporate PAC spending is influenced by both ideological factors

(Clawson & Neustadtl, 1989, p. 751) and pragmatic regulatory considerations (Sorauf, 1991, p. 221). While a range of other factors influence corporate PAC spending, e.g., geographic location or industry regulatory environment (see Burris, 1987, 1992a for a review), overwhelmingly, the evidence suggests that corporate PAC donations are most often aimed at ensuring future access to legislators and/or special favors (Sorauf, 1991; Boies, 1989). While the PAC expenditures of large U.S. firms typically favor Republican candidates, they are to a much greater extent biased toward incumbent candidates, who overwhelmingly defeat challengers in U.S. House and Senate elections. For example, in 1996 and 1998 election cycles, FF500 PAC contributions favored Republican over Democratic candidates by a ratio of ~2.5:1, but incumbents over challengers ~12:1.[12] Similarly, Sorauf (1991) found that partisan and ideological affiliation weakly predicted corporate PAC spending, and concluded that most corporations form PACs to gain access to "the places of power in the legislature" (Sorauf, 1991, p. 220).

Drawing from Sorauf's model of corporate PAC donations, we hypothesize that firms that donate large sums to the election cycle do so to gain access to governmental officials and committees. Since our dependent measure (ISAC participation) is a proxy for influence over government trade policy, we expect that PAC spending will act as an intervening variable, such that firms with greater total PAC expenditures will be more likely to be members of a governmental advisory committee(s).

**H5.** Firms with larger PAC contributions are more likely to participate in an ISAC.

### Network Variables

*Board Interlocks*: Useem (1984) posits that directors who sit on two or more corporate boards (the "inner circle") are more likely to engage in both interfirm alliances and consultation to the state. The unique perspective of directors who occupy two or more boards allows them to apprehend issues of broader concern to the business community. In this way, board interlocks promote the formation of a "class-wide" rationality among broad segments of business. Inasmuch as trade liberalization promotes the aggregate welfare of the corporate community – with variable economic risks or benefits associated with any single industry – firms more embedded in the board interlock network should be more active in the creation and promotion of free trade agreements.

**H6.** Firms with more board interlocks are more likely to participate in an ISAC.

In addition to board interlocks, several researchers note the unique and central role of the BR in coordinating the political activities of large corporations (Burris, 1987; Dreiling, 2000; Mizruchi, 1992). The restriction of BR membership to CEOs of the largest U.S. corporations renders the organization qualitatively different in its political influence than other business interest groups. As a site of political coordination for a range of policy issues (including those pertaining to international trade), its members are more politically active than comparable non-member firms. Thus, it is expected that:

**H7.** Firms in the Business Roundtable are more active in trade policy formation and advocacy.

*Policy Network Affiliation:* In addition to the BR, a host of related policy organizations assume a crucial role in the ongoing coordination of corporate political activity. The most important such organizations in the area of trade policy include the Business Council, Conference Board, Emergency Committee on Trade, National Association of Manufacturers, Council of the America's, Trilateral Commission, and United States Council for International Business.[13] The two defining features of these organizations are (1) the tremendous economic resources of their members and (2) their similar mission to inform policy makers of the political objectives of big business. Prior research suggests that firm affiliation with these organizations – collectively referred to as the "policy network" – is positively correlated with a range of political behavior, from campaign spending to participation in temporary issue alliances (Boies, 1989; Burris, 1992b; Dreiling, 2000; Domhoff, 2005; Useem, 1984). As mechanisms for political cooperation, policy groups are instrumental to the promotion of "class-wide" business policy agendas that transcend sectoral interests (Domhoff, 2005; Mizruchi, 1992). This rationality generates a greater propensity to participate in political activities beneficial to the aggregate welfare of the corporate community (Useem, 1984). While corporate policy group memberships are only a proxy for this network embeddedness (and do not measure actual communication per se), it is not difficult to imagine how executive contact within these groups (and through board of director interlocks, etc.) may yield similar political behavior at the organizational level. Burris (2005, p. 273), for example, argues that micro-level communication of corporate directors through various formal channels facilitates information exchange, persuasion, deference, and conformity with group norms. While Burris studied the similarity of executive political behavior, it is plausible that these communication processes would also influence the political behavior of the companies these executives represent (Useem, 1984). Thus, firms more embedded in the policy network should also be more active in the creation and promotion of free trade agreements within the state.

**H8.** Firms with more numerous ties to the corporate policy-planning network are more likely to participate in an ISAC.

*Temporary Trade Policy Alliances*: In recent years the BR and other prominent business groups have directed member resources into temporary trade policy alliances promoting specific policy outcomes, such as the NAFTA or normalized trade relations with China. USA*NAFTA, ALOT and USA-Engage are recent examples of such alliances. Despite their transitory character, these alliances often prove quite effective because the major business groups provide resources and a ready-made organizational structure (Dreiling, 2001; see also Hillman et al., 2004). Since prior research demonstrates a positive association between leadership in issue-specific political alliances and participation in state policy planning (Useem, 1984; Dreiling, 2001), it is predicted that participation in these alliances increases the odds of ISAC participation.

**H9.** Firms that participate in legislative lobby groups are more likely to participate in an ISAC.

# RESULTS

Table 2 presents the zero-order correlations between all variables. All of the independent variables are positively correlated with the dependent variable and none of the correlations exceeds 0.6. Table 3 presents a cross-tabulation of ISAC participation by one-digit SIC code (see appendix for a detailed list of SIC codes). As predicted by Hypothesis 3, mean ISAC affiliation varies significantly across one-digit product market groupings. Firms in tradable goods sectors (one-digit SICs 1, 2, and 3) have the highest levels of ISAC participation (22%, 30%, and 37%, respectively), while the participation rate in other sectors does not exceed 10%. This finding suggests, consistent with our hypotheses, that firms in tradable goods sectors are more likely to enter into the trade policy formation process. Equation 1 in Table 4, which is equivalent to a one-way ANOVA with random effects, models the unconditional variance in ISAC participation across two-digit

***Table 2.*** Correlations for all Variables ($N = 966$).

|  | 1 | 2 | 3 | 4 | 5 | 6 | 7 | 8 |
|---|---|---|---|---|---|---|---|---|
| 1. ISAC total | | | | | | | | |
| 2. Capital intensity | −0.0357 | | | | | | | |
| 3. Subsidiaries | 0.2948 | −0.1030 | | | | | | |
| 4. Size | 0.3262 | 0.1554 | 0.2684 | | | | | |
| 5. PAC expenditures | 0.2636 | 0.1633 | 0.1774 | 0.5106 | | | | |
| 6. Interlocks | 0.2833 | 0.0039 | 0.3732 | 0.4976 | 0.2966 | | | |
| 7. Policy network | 0.4882 | 0.0717 | 0.4708 | 0.5207 | 0.3832 | 0.4420 | | |
| 8. Bus. roundtable | 0.3916 | 0.0034 | 0.3718 | 0.3877 | 0.3320 | 0.3989 | 0.5512 | |
| 9. Temp. T.P. alliances | 0.4905 | −0.0339 | 0.4362 | 0.3565 | 0.2719 | 0.3529 | 0.5602 | 0.4631 |

***Table 3.*** ISAC Participation by One-Digit Primary SIC[a].

| ISAC Participant | One-Digit SIC Code | | | | | | | | |
|---|---|---|---|---|---|---|---|---|---|
|  | 1 | 2 | 3 | 4 | 5 | 6 | 7 | 8 | Total |
| No | 28 | 127 | 124 | 126 | 151 | 169 | 46 | 18 | 789 |
| (Col. %) | 77.78 | 69.40 | 62.31 | 90.00 | 96.18 | 92.86 | 90.20 | 100.00 | 81.68 |
| Yes | 8 | 56 | 75 | 14 | 6 | 13 | 5 | 0 | 177 |
| (Col. %) | 22.22 | 30.60 | 37.69 | 10.00 | 3.82 | 7.14 | 9.80 | 0.00 | 18.32 |
| Total | 36 | 183 | 199 | 140 | 157 | 182 | 51 | 18 | 966 |
|  | 100.00 | 100.00 | 100.00 | 100.00 | 100.00 | 100.00 | 100.00 | 100.00 | 100.00 |

*Note:* Pearson $X^2 = 118.91$, $Pr = 0.000$.
[a]See appendix for detailed SIC codes.

sector groupings. In other words, this equation estimates the amount of variance in ISAC participation that is within and between sectors before the effect of other variables is controlled. Using the within- and between-sector variance estimates from the ANOVA, the intraclass correlation coefficient (ICC) can be computed. The ICC estimates the percentage of variance accounted for by firm sector. The ICC is given by (Raudenbush & Bryk, 2002, p. 71):

$$\hat{\rho} = \frac{\hat{\tau}_{00}}{(\hat{\tau}_{00} + \hat{\sigma}^2)} = \frac{0.9937}{(0.9937 + 0.6477)} = 0.605$$

This finding indicates that approximately 61% (0.605) of the unconditional variance in ISAC participation is between sectors. The remaining variance

***Table 4.*** 1998/2003 Estimated Effects of Organizational and Network Variables on the *Number* of ISACs (Unstandardized Regression Coefficients with SEs in Parentheses).

| Fixed Effect | Eq. 1 | Eq. 2 | Eq. 3 |
|---|---|---|---|
| Constant | −1.8754** | −2.5652** | −2.8884** |
| | (0.1780) | (0.4651) | (0.4981) |
| Year = 2003 | — | −0.5651** | −0.4602** |
| | | (0.1187) | (0.1175) |
| *Organizational variables* | | | |
| Capital intensity | — | 0.05742 | 0.03821 |
| | | (0.0729) | (0.075) |
| Foreign subsidiaries | — | 0.1271* | −0.03822 |
| | | (0.057) | (0.054) |
| Firm size | — | 0.4037** | 0.1448* |
| | | (0.059) | (0.067) |
| PAC expenditures | — | 0.0029** | 0.00187* |
| | | (0.0008) | (0.0008) |
| *Network variables* | | | |
| Board interlocks | — | — | 0.1811* |
| | | | (0.089) |
| Policy network affiliations | — | — | 0.1785** |
| | | | (0.046) |
| Bus. roundtable | — | — | 0.3056* |
| | | | (0.155) |
| Temporary trade policy alliances | | | 0.3970** |
| | | | (0.082) |
| Random Effect | Variance (df) | Variance (df) | Variance (df) |
| Sector mean $\mu_{0j}$ | 0.9937** (57) | 10.1413** (57) | 0.8521** (57) |
| Level-1 effect, $r_{ij}$ | 0.6477** | 0.5664** | 0.5290** |
| Compound symmetry parameter | 0.2700** | 0.1090** | 0.0750* |

**$p<0.01$.
*$p<0.05$.

($\sim$39%) is unique to firms within the same two-digit sector. Clearly, these findings indicate that the effects of sector must be controlled in our model of ISAC participation. One way to control for the effect of sector is to include dummy variables for each two-digit sector grouping.[14] This approach is typically referred to as a "fixed effects model." However, given that there are 57 two-digit SIC groupings represent in the 1998/2003 FF500, this approach, while unbiased, would yield inefficient estimates (Kennedy, 2003).

Thus, we use hierarchical non-linear models, which more efficiently model inter-sectoral variability by allowing the intercept to vary randomly across two-digit product markets. In other words, this approach models each firm's odds of participation as a function of both its individual characteristics (e.g., size, board interlocks, etc.) and the average level of participation among firms operating in the same industry. Specifically, the odds of ISAC participation for the *j*th sector are a function of both the grand mean across all sectors and the unique increment to the intercept associated with sector *j* (Raudenbush & Bryk, 2002).[15]

As our dependent variable (ISAC participation) is an ordered count we use a Poisson sampling model (Long, 1997).[16] Additionally, because approximately two-thirds of the sample firms appear during both sample years, it is possible that the errors are temporally dependent (i.e., display serial autocorrelation). Because there are only two panels of data and the populations differ in each panel, standard corrections for serial correlation, such as the first-order autocorrelation coefficient (AR1), are not indicated (Ostrom, 1978). Thus, we correct for temporal dependency in two ways. First, we add a dummy variable for one of the observational years.[17] This is an important statistical precaution because systematic variation unique to a single time period may yield biased standard error *and* slope estimates if left unmodeled (Green, Kim, & Yoon, 2001). Second, we use SAS's compound symmetry residual transformation to correct for error dependency among firms with two observations in the combined dataset. This procedure corrects for autocorrelation created by firms with two observations in the sample (i.e., firms that were listed in the FF500 directories in both 1998 and 2003).

The general form of our equation is:

*Level 1 Model*

$$\ln(\lambda_{ij}) = \beta_{0j} + \beta_{1j} \, (Subsidiares) + \beta_{2j} \, (Cap.Inten.) + \beta_{3j} \, (Size)$$
$$+ \beta_{4j} \, (PAC) + \beta_{5j} \, (Brd.Interlocks) + \beta_{6j} \, (Pol.Network)$$
$$+ \beta_{7j} \, (Temp.Pol.Alliances) + r_{ij}$$

*Level 2 Model*

$$\beta_{0j} = \gamma_{00} + u_{0j}$$
$$\beta_{1j} = \gamma_{10}, \ \beta_{2j} = \gamma_{20}, \ \beta_{3j} = \gamma_{30} \cdots \beta_{7j} = \gamma_{70}$$

*Combined Model*

$$\ln(\lambda_{ij}) = \beta_{0j} + \beta_{1j} \, (Subsidiares) + \beta_{2j} \, (Cap.Inten.) + \beta_{3j} \, (Size)$$
$$+ \beta_{4j} \, (PAC) + \beta_{5j} \, (Brd.Interlocks) + \beta_{6j} \, (Pol.Network)$$
$$+ \beta_{7j} \, (Temp.Pol.Alliances) + u_{0j} + r_{ij}$$

Eq. 2 (Table 4) presents the results of a baseline "organizational" model of ISAC participation. Four key findings emerge from Eq. 2. First, foreign subsidiaries are significant in the predicted direction. Multinational firms, which stand to benefit the most economically from reduced international transaction costs, are more likely to advise government officials on foreign trade policy. The significance of this relationship is not entirely surprising given the strategic importance of recent trade liberalization programs for multinational corporations. Second, firm size is strongly associated with participation in trade policy formation. As both business unity and interest group theories would predict, large firms are more likely to engage the state due to their greater capacity to mobilize resources for political purposes. Third, the PAC expenditures variable yields a significant, positive coefficient. Consistent with expectations, this finding suggests that political expenditures increase the odds of firm political activism even when controlling for the effects of firm size. Fourth, and finally, the dummy variable for firm year is significant and negative, indicating that the mean rate of ISAC affiliation decreased in 2003. This finding is unsurprising considering that the unconditional rate of FF500 ISAC affiliation decreased from 23% to 13% between 1998 and 2003.[18]

In Eq. 3,[19] the four network variables are introduced to the model. Their inclusion nullifies the statistical significance of the foreign subsidiaries variable, although size, PAC spending, and the variance component estimate of two-digit sector grouping remain statistically significant. Consistent with a business unity perspective, BR membership, policy network affiliation, board interlocks, and membership in temporary trade policy alliances significantly increase the odds of ISAC participation. BR membership, for example, increases the expected count of ISAC participation by 36%.[20] Similarly, membership in a prominent policy organization increases the expected count by 20%, while membership in two organizations increases the expected count by 43%. These findings largely confirm our main hypothesis that embedded firms are more likely to participate in trade policy, even when the influence of sector and size is controlled.

Thus, three factors seem critical to ISAC participation. First, the largest firms in certain sectors, especially those influenced by, or dependent upon, trade (e.g., SICs 28 and 36, chemical and electronic manufacturers, respectively), are more likely to serve as state advisors. Second, *political action* through PAC expenditures is positively correlated with the odds of ISAC participation. Finally, network position within board interlock, policy group, and temporary alliance networks – associative mechanisms that link together a larger, business class segment – significantly influence the odds of participation. These results are particularly important because the network determination of corporate involvement in the policy process is both theoretically and empirically underappreciated in the literature on trade policy. The type of analysis conducted here, and the significance of the "class embedded" network variables, calls for a more robust, social class interpretation of corporate involvement in trade policy. In sum, our results reveal that trade advisory participation is predictably patterned by firm sector and size, while political and network influences predominate within any given sector.

# DISCUSSION: FACILITATIVE STATE STRUCTURES AND CLASS NETWORKS

Analysts have long been aware of the need to study the effects of "situational constraints," i.e., structural embeddedness (Granovetter, 1985). However, the application of a structural approach within a rigorously specified empirical model has often proved elusive (Emirbayer, 1997). In this study, we have attempted to measure corporate policy action as a contingent function of *both* organizational attributes and network position. Confirming our hypotheses, organizational attributes significantly predicted corporate political behavior. The reasons for this are not difficult to ascertain. Large, multinational firms in trade-dependent product markets typically benefit from lower transaction costs on intrafirm exchange: they have an organizational interest in free trade. Interpreting the effects of the network parameters, however, is somewhat less direct and warrants additional consideration. We have argued that proxies for network embeddedness, such as policy group affiliation, capture processes of class coalescence that produce a variable capacity to articulate the broader interests of business. With respect to trade policy in particular, class networks spanning between state and para-state institutions channel the resources of well-connected corporations toward strategically defined policy initiatives.

We shall consider two alternative interpretations. First, it is possible that our proxies for network participation do not measure a relational phenomenon per se, but the general effects of firm size on policy activism. In this regard, a number of studies indicate that firm size is strongly correlated with common indicators of inner circle status (e.g., the BR), because the heads of the largest firms have historically been most active in these organizations (Mizruchi & Koenig, 1991, p. 308; Useem, 1984). To the extent that the network parameters actually capture the effects of size, a model of business political fragmentation becomes more plausible: large firms are more politically active not because of the structural constraints imposed by network position, but because their organizational capacity to produce political change is so great that independent political action produces an adequate economic return. From this perspective, interfirm networks do not exert an independent influence on political activism, but follow as an ancillary consequence of the individual pursuit of favorable policy outcomes by the largest companies. While our data cannot disconfirm this hypothesis conclusively, we would not have expected the network variables to achieve statistical significance after controlling for the effects of size and political spending (Eq. 3) were participation primarily driven by firm size. This is especially evident given that other studies of firm political behavior, albeit using different dependent variables, have found that policy network affiliation via the BR is not statistically significant at conventional levels when size (and other organizational measures) is controlled (Mizruchi & Koenig, 1991, p. 307). With respect to the current study, while ISAC participation is not evenly distributed across the distribution of firm size, there are a significant number of ISAC participants at all levels of the distribution. While almost 50% of FF500 ISAC participants have a size ranking in the 76th percentile or higher, an additional 40% are distributed in the 26th–75th percentiles. Thus, while larger firms are considerably more likely to participate in an ISAC, there are a significant number of participants at all levels of firm size. This suggests, together with the significant partial correlations of the network and political spending variables, that raw organizational capacity and sales rank are not the only determinants of ISAC participation.

A second alternative interpretation would view the network measures as proximate to the social processes they are intended to capture but distant in their importance to actual policy outcomes. From this perspective, China PNTR, for example, was ratified because it was in the state's interest to do so, irrespective of preceding political actions by business elite. This strictly state-centered view of trade policy has an obvious limitation, however: both NAFTA and China PNTR, for example, did not initially have sufficient House and Senate votes to pass (Dreiling, 2000; Woodall et al., 2000). While, as discussed above, the DOC and its associated trade advisory committees strongly support global trade expansion, federal law requires that the House and Senate ratify bilateral and multilateral trade agreements. Class segments assert their presence in the policy formation process precisely because the motivation for elected officials to support trade initiatives is not static, and subject to reversal when influenced by competing constituencies – something often recognized by pluralists.

Corporate promotion of trade policy thus centers on *both* the executive and legislative branches of government. In the legislature, corporations advance trade initiatives such as NAFTA and China PNTR through temporary trade policy alliances, which, in turn, are formed by the more enduring policy organizations, such as the BR. Indeed, these are their stated objectives. Within the executive branch, a deeper form of corporate influence is evident.[21] Under the banner of industry consultation programs, state actors work in concert with strategic business allies to form the policy objectives and broader trade program ultimately advanced by the DOC and the president. The competing dynamics within the executive and legislative branches result in contradictory abilities to promote trade policy. On one hand, the executive branch, essentially captured by industry interests in *this* policy domain, offers preordained support for trade expansion initiatives. On the other, trade policy outcomes in the legislature are more contested, given the greater number of actors competing for influence in Congress.

Together, these competing dynamics combine within a state policy milieu that is best described as a "weak" autonomy (Prechel, 1990). In the executive branch, what Dreiling (2000) refers to as "facilitative state structures" – structures that enable corporate involvement in policy formation – interact with organized class segments to create and promote hemispheric and global trade regimes, often despite broad opposition in the public sphere. Facilitative state structures promote business unity for political purposes. Prechel (2000) further clarifies the contingent, historical nature of these state structures. He argues that "[r]ather than providing a basis for state autonomy, once established, state structures provide capitalists with a legitimate political-legal apparatus within which to pursue their interests politically" (p. 274). Because these ISACs, like other state advisory committees, provide a forum for corporate executives to interact with members of other corporations, trade associations and various Cabinet-level officials under the President, they are likely to result in a cooperative orientation to trade policy, as stated explicitly in their documents. Yet, these very structures were created by state actors in response to changing political economic environments in the 1970s. Thus, these facilitative state structures imbue the state with the capacity to create common policy goals by bringing together business representatives, or other groups, from diverse backgrounds and, in the process, expand business support and establish the perception of legitimacy.

However, business unity is not simply a function of state coordination. Equally (or more) important are the associative mechanisms of corporate class networks that channel business elite toward sites of influence within the executive branch (as policy advisors) and the legislature (via transitory political alliances). This cooperation also emerges from common participation in a host of closely associated policy groups and industry alliances. With respect to the major policy groups, for example, 80% of 2003 FF500 firms involved in the ISACs also belonged to a major policy organization, such as the BR, the U.S. Council for International Business, or the Emergency Committee on American Trade. In contrast, among the 2003 FF500 firms that were *not* involved in an ISAC, only 20% belong to these outside policy organizations. Likewise, and with respect to temporary trade policy alliances that lobby the legislature, 50% of 2003 FF500 ISAC participants were members of the National Business Coalition for U.S.-Central American Trade or U.S. Trade, which lobbied extensively for Congressional passage of CAFTA and the FTAA. Corporations already connected outside the state are more likely to engage state structures for political aims.

Political theories that stress the capacity for business unity would predict these relationships and emphasize the important function of the policy network and associated lobbying alliances in coordinating corporate policy activism within state institutions (Useem, 1984; Domhoff, 2005). Building on this perspective, we argue that the elaborate web of DOC trade advisory committees, together with policy organizations and transitory political alliances, provide a range of associative mechanisms through which an organized business class segment exerts influence over trade policy formation. In this way, extant networks among corporations and across industries serve as a source of political leverage. Together, class structure and state organization meet, making it possible for these structures to provide, as Prechel (1990, p. 664) observed, "class segments with the mechanisms to exercise control over the state."

# CONCLUSION

Analysts have long recognized the potential for concentrations of economic and political power within the large corporation to impede democratic processes (Dahl, 1961; Schattschneider, 1935; Vogel, 1989). However, most

models of corporate political behavior in trade policy have been inattentive
to the structure of intercorporate organization, viewing trade policy as a
product of autonomous state actors or the result of competing, ad hoc
business interests. Given our results, such an interpretation is insufficient.
Instead, corporate appointments to non-elected posts throughout the U.S.
trade policy apparatus reveal a more engaged corporate presence than prevailing theories predict. Corporate involvement in these committees, and
indeed the politics of trade and globalization more generally thus raise critical questions about the character of the political forces shaping global and
regional economic priorities. A more cogent theory, we argue, is attentive to
firm position within the array of overlapping networks created by policy
groups, board interlocks, and temporary trade policy alliances. At the center
of these various communication networks, prominent business associations
such as the BR create a stable institutional framework for the expression of
broader class interests. Class segments seek to influence the political system
because the state will not, in all circumstances, produce business-favorable
legislation (Vogel, 1989). In this way, corporate policy activism is best conceptualized as a relational phenomenon: while less connected corporate actors perceive their interests in terms of short run, organizational interests,
more connected actors perceive the corporate "interest" in broader terms,
channeling firm resources toward strategic alliances promoting class-wide
interests, and production for profit more generally.

The observations presented here suggest the need for a more dynamic
theory of trade policy formation, one that accounts for the close coupling of
state and class actors. Prechel's (1990) organizational state environment
perspective provides the kind of theoretical synthesis needed for grasping
the contingent alignment of organized class segments and the state's trade
policy apparatus. The project of neoliberal trade expansion in the western
hemisphere, and across regional economies, cannot be reduced to autonomous actions on the part of state actors, as much of the trade policy literature suggests. Instead, firms populate the state structures responsible for
making U.S. trade policy. These state structures are important, of course –
but not because they maintain state autonomy. Mediated by important
policy-planning organizations, such as the BR, the Emergency Committee
on American Trade, and the U.S. Council for International Business, large
corporations in the U.S. create links to these extant state structures, thereby
forging a stable basis for coupling class and state actors. In this way, state
advisory committees and the enduring policy groups create an interorganizational system capable of advancing the interests of MNCs and the larger
political project behind neoliberal globalization.

Trade policy initiatives during the 1990s emerged from the active and deliberate participation of state and corporate actors, fueling a heightened politicization of global markets. These politics, imbued with strands of class, environmentalism, and nationalism, did not simply react to "anonymous" forces of globalization. Rather, the politics of trade policy – with included active participation by state and non-state actors – drove neoliberal globalization to new heights. As Sassen (1996) posits, it is not enough to argue that the "state is in decline," buried by the seemingly inevitable advance of liberalized global markets. Instead, Sassen (*ibid*) argues that both corporations and state agents are actively engaged in constructing global and regional market regimes. From this perspective it would be a mistake to assume that state agents are autonomous agents; indeed, state actors may also be corporate actors, representing firms, and the policy objectives of class segments, inside state advisory committees. Economic globalization, then, is not simply an additive phenomenon, that is, a spillover effect of international transactions made on the "margin." Far from inevitable, it takes shape through processes driven by differentiating market factors such as technology, wages, land, and capital, but also by political factors that are conditioned by the coordinated political activities of broad segments of business and supportive state agencies. In this way, the role of private agents in constructing the new global trade apparatus is both a political and an economic affair. Market frameworks – the legal, the political, the normative, and the organizational – are thus social, and indeed, political endeavors. In this regard, demands by global justice activists to democratize trade institutions reflect an understanding that markets and trade institutions, indeed the legal, organizational and political dimensions of "globalization" can be constructed and modified – with sufficient political power. As we theorize transformations in trade globalization, let us not lose sight of the political role played by class embedded corporations and historically structured state agencies.

# NOTES

1. Trade promotion authority, once called "fast track," enables the president to submit international trade agreements to the legislature for a yes–no, simple majority vote. Unencumbered by the complex issues likely to be raised in the Legislature, trade negotiations and trade policy take the shape of actors' interests in the Executive branch. Like in the NAFTA conflict, recent efforts to grant this authority to the president were challenged by labor, environmental groups, and human rights groups,

questioning the legitimacy of trade policy unbound from societal regulation. After three years of conflict, Congress granted President Bush Trade Promotion Authority in August 2002.

2. In the span of a little over one year, a sweeping pan-corporate alliance spent over $113 million to pass the legislation, making it the most expensive policy campaign in U.S. history (Woodall, Wallach, Roach, & Burnham, 2000).

3. Network factors refer to firm ties to other companies (via board interlocks) and outside policy groups (such as the BR). "Organizational" factors, in contrast, refer to corporate characteristics that might influence the trade policy preferences of individual firms, such as size and number of foreign subsidiaries.

4. Fast track allows the executive branch to submit a recently concluded trade negotiation to Congress for an up-or-down vote, without the possibility for the inclusion of amendments.

5. Information obtained in a 10/4/2005 interview with Angela Cazada, a DOC official who oversees the trade policy committees.

6. The Reciprocal Trade Agreement Act (RTAA) (1934) transferred trade-negotiating authority to the President (and advisors within the State Department), thereby bypassing provincially motivated conflicts. Subsequent amendments to the RTAA have consolidated this authority under the Office of the U.S. Trade Representative and through the legislative vehicle previously known as "fast track" (it is now referred to as trade-promotion authority). See note 1. TPA enables trade agreements to be treated as foreign treaties and thereby avoid more strict legislative criteria.

7. As with the trend toward greater firm multinationality (see Milner, 1988).

8. See Dreiling (2000) for a discussion of the corporate mobilization in support of NAFTA, and Darves and Dreiling (2002) for a discussion of the legislation to permanently normalize trade relations with China.

9. We recognize that differences between "instrumentalist" theories of class unity and structuralist theories of class segments, or "power blocs" (Poulantzas, 1968/1973) have significant and unique arguments concerning business political influence in the state. We, however, adopt a perspective following Mizruchi (1992) that it is the conditions under which business unity are forged that is most accessible empirically. We are not theorizing – or empirically testing – whether corporate collective action reflects a class exercising control over the state or a contingently aligned class segment. Such an argument is beyond the empirical scope of this paper. Rather, we are interested in the question whether common involvement in the trade policy committees is a coincidental convergence of firms pursuing their company-specific goals (organizational interests) or are involved in the state in part because of common participation in class-embedded networks. Our approach thus examines the class-embedded networks that, theoretically, would contribute to business unity; in this instance, within the state's trade-policy apparatus.

10. In other words, our sample consists of firms in *one or both* lists in each panel (i.e., 1998 and 2003).

11. After dropping privately held firms and firms our $N$ is 484 for the 1998 sample and 482 for the 2003 sample. We recognize that some firms within our sample are subsidiaries of other firms in the FF500. Thus, we also estimated our model including a dummy variable measuring whether a firm is a whole or partial subsidiary of another FF500 firm. Firm subsidiary status is potentially significant because firms

related through ownership may not, in the strictest formulation, be statistically independent cases. However, because our sample is limited to large, publicly traded companies, only a small number of firms were not the ultimate parent ($N = 13$ in the combined 1998/2003 dataset). Of these 13 firms, only two were subsidiaries of another FF500 firm (*Directory of Corporate Affiliations*, 1998/2003). Because the substantive interpretation of the model estimates did not change when a dummy variable was included for the two subsidiary firms, the results presented here omit this variable.

12. FF500 PAC contribution data were obtained from 1996 to 1998 FEC PAC summary files.

13. See Dreiling (2001) for a detailed discussion of the political activities of each of these organizations.

14. Specifically, one sector is not represented by a dummy variable to avoid a perfect linearity (i.e., the "dummy variable trap").

15. We also estimated a fixed-effects model of ISAC participation using dummy variables for each two-digit sector grouping. The main substantive difference between the HNLM and fixed-effects model is that board interlocks and PAC expenditures fall below statistical significance in the saturated equation (Eq. 3). Additionally, the $p$-values for board interlocks and BR membership move slightly above 0.05 but are still significant if a one-tailed test is accepted. While both models support similar substantive conclusions, we utilize HNLM because it provides a more statistically *efficient* model of the effect of firm sector.

16. Poisson regression, which assumes that the conditional mean is equal to the conditional variance, was too restrictive to be employed in our models (Long, 1997). Thus, we estimated our models using SASs GLIMMIX macro, which corrects for over-dispersion in multilevel count models. Our models were estimated using the canonical log link function.

17. Specifically, this dummy variable for observation year shifts any *unique* residual time dependency into the **X** vector.

18. We also estimated the models separately for each panel (i.e., 1998 and 2003). Because coefficient confidence intervals for the significant predictors of ISAC participation overlap in the uncombined models, the observed drop in total participation may simply indicate an absolute decline in mean participation more than a significant change in the predicted direction of key explanatory variables.

19. As per the suggestion of one reviewer, we also estimated Eq. 3 using several measures of capital dependence and profitability (again, using *Compustat* data). Because we found no significant relationship between capital dependence or profitability and ISAC participation (nor a significant improvement in model fit), we omit them from the results presented here. In addition, although we have no theoretical reason to suspect that firms in certain regions would be more likely to participate in an ISAC, we also estimated Eq. 3 with regional dummy controls, using census region codes for firm headquarters (Northeast, South, Midwest, and West, with West as the reference category). Since we found no significant regional effect, and because their inclusion did not significantly improve model fit, we omit them here for parsimony.

20. The coefficient transformation to estimate the percent change in the expected count of a Poisson model is given by Long (1997): [(exb b) − 1]100.

21. See also Center for Responsive Politics (2005) for an example of the DOC agricultural advisory committee's involvement in drafting U.S. tariff rates on sugar.

# REFERENCES

Allen, M. P. (1978). Economic interest groups and the corporate elite structure. *Social Science Quarterly, 58*, 597–615.

Baldwin, R. E. (1989). *Trade policy in a changing world.* Chicago: University of Chicago Press.

Bauer, R. A., Pool, I. S., & Dexter, A. L. (1963). *American business and public policy.* Chicago: Aldine-Atherton.

Boies, J. (1989). Money, business, and the state: Material interests, Fortune 500 corporations, and the size of political action committees. *American Sociological Review, 54*, 821–833.

Burris, V. (1987). The political partisanship of big business. *American Sociological Review, 52*, 732–744.

Burris, V. (1992a). PACs, interlocks, and regional differences in corporate conservatism. *American Journal of Sociology, 97*, 1451–1456.

Burris, V. (1992b). Elite policy-planning networks in the United States. *Research in Politics and Society, 4*, 111–134.

Burris, V. (2005). Interlocking directorates and political cohesion among corporate elites. *American Journal of Sociology, 111*, 249–283.

Center for Responsive Politics. (2005). The politics of sugar: NAFTA, GATT, and sugar. Available electronically at: http://www.opensecrets.org/pubs/cashingin_sugar/sugar06.html

Clawson, D., & Neustadtl, A. (1989). Interlocks, PACs, and corporate conservatism. *American Journal of Sociology, 94*, 749–773.

Clawson, D., Neustadtl, A., & Bearden, J. (1986). The logic of business unity: Corporate contributions in the 1980 election. *American Sociological Review, 51*, 797–811.

Cohen, S. D., Blecker, R. A., & Whitney, P. D. (2003). *Fundamentals of U.S. foreign trade policy: Economics, politics, laws, and issues.* Boulder, CO: Westview Press.

Dahl, R. A. (1961). *Who governs?* New Haven: Yale University Press.

Daley, W. M. (2000a). *Remarks by Secretary of Commerce William M. Daley to Industrial Sector Advisory Committees opening Plenary Session.* Washington, DC: Department of Commerce Press Releases.

Daley, W. M. (2000b). *Remarks by U.S. Secretary of Commerce William M. Daley – Industry Sector and Industry Function Committees.* Washington, DC: Department of Commerce Press Releases.

Darves, D., & Dreiling, M. (2002). Corporate political networks and trade policy formation. *Humanity and Society, 26*(1), 5–27.

Destler, I. M. (1995). *American trade politics.* Washington, DC: Institute for International Economics.

DOC. (2000). *Industry consultation program mission and history.* Washington, DC: http://www.ita.doc.gov/td/icp/home.html

Domhoff, W. G. (1990). *The power elite and the state: How policy is made in America.* New York: Aldine De Gruyter.

Domhoff, W. G. (2005). *Who rules America? Power and politics and social change.* New York: McGraw-Hill.

Dreiling, M. (2000). The class embeddedness of corporate political action: Leadership in defense of the NAFTA. *Social Problems, 47*, 21–48.

Dreiling, M. (2001). *Solidarity and contention: The politics of class and sustainability in the NAFTA conflict.* New York: Garland Publishing.

Duina, F. (2006). *The social construction of free trade: The European Union, NAFTA, and MERCOSUR.* Princeton: Princeton University Press.

Emirbayer, M. (1997). Manifesto for a relational sociology. *American Journal of Sociology, 103,* 281–317.

Fieleke, N. (1988). Economic interdependence between nations: Reason for policy coordination? *New England Economic Review,* May/June.

Frieden, J. (1988). Sectoral conflict and U.S. foreign economic policy, 1914–1940. In: I. G. John, D. A. Lake & M. Mastanduno (Eds), *The state and American foreign economic policy.* Ithaca: Cornell University Press.

Goldstein, J. (1993). *Ideas, interests, and American trade policy.* Ithaca: Cornell University Press.

Granovetter, M. S. (1985). Economic action and social structure: The problem of embeddedness. *American Journal of Sociology, 91,* 481–510.

Green, D. P., Kim, S. Y., & Yoon, D. H. (2001). Dirty pool. *International Organization, 55,* 441–468.

Hillman, A. J., Keim, G. D., & Schuler, D. (2004). Corporate political activity: A review and research agenda. *Journal of Management, 30,* 837–857.

Ikenberry, J. G., Lake, D. A., & Mastanduno, M. (1988). Approaches to explaining American Foreign Economic Policy. *International Organization, 42,* 1–14.

Jessop, B. (1990). *State theory: Putting capitalist states in their place.* Cambridge: Polity Press.

Kennedy, P. (2003). *A guide to econometrics.* Cambridge: The MIT Press.

Krueger, A. O. (1995). *American trade policy: A tragedy in the making.* Washington, DC: The American Enterprise Institute Press.

Long, S., & Long, J. S. (1997). *Regression models for categorical and limited dependent variables.* Thousand Oaks: Sage Publications.

Marx, K. (1847/1978). The poverty of philosophy, the coming upheaval. In: C. T. Robert (Ed.), *The Marx-Engels reader* (2nd ed.). New York: W.W. Norton & Company.

McKeown, T. J. (1984). Firms and tariff regime change: Explaining the demand for protection. *World Politics, 36,* 215–233.

Mills, C. W. (1956). *The power elite.* New York: Oxford University Press.

Milner, H. V. (1988). *Resisting protectionism: Global industries and the politics of international trade.* Princeton: Princeton University Press.

Milner, H. V., & Yoffie, D. B. (1989). Between free trade and protectionism: Strategic trade policy and a theory of corporate trade demands. *International Organization, 43,* 239–272.

Mintz, B., & Schwartz, M. (1985). *The power structure of American business.* Chicago: University of Chicago Press.

Mizruchi, M. S. (1989). Similarity of political behavior among large American corporations. *American Journal of Sociology, 95,* 401–424.

Mizruchi, M. S. (1992). *The structure of corporate political action: Interfirm relations and their consequences.* Cambridge: Harvard University Press.

Mizruchi, M. S., & Swartz, M. (Eds). (1987). The structural analysis of business: An emerging field. *Intercorporate relations: The structural analysis of business.* New York: Cambridge University Press.

Mizruchi, M., & Koenig, T. (1991). Size, concentration, and corporate networks: Determinants of business collective action. *Social Science Quarterly, 72,* 299–313.

Olson, M. (1965). *The logic of collective action.* Cambridge, MA: Harvard University Press.

Ostrom, C. W., Jr. (1978). *Time series analysis: Regression techniques.* Thousand Oaks: Sage Publications.

Piore, M. J., & Sabel, C. F. (1984). *The second industrial divide: Possibilities for prosperity.* New York: Basic Books.

Poulantzas, N. A. (1968/1973). In: T. O'Hagan (Trans.), *Political power and social classes.* London, NLB: Sheed and Ward.

Prechel, H. (1990). Steel and the state: Industry politics and business policy formation, 1940–1989. *American Sociological Review, 55,* 648–668.

Prechel, H. (2000). *Big business and the state: Historical transitions and corporate transformations, 1880s–1990s.* Albany: State University of New York Press.

Preeg, E. H. (1998). *From here to free trade: Essays in post-Uruguay round trade strategy.* Chicago: University of Chicago.

Raudenbush, S., & Bryk, A. (2002). *Hierarchical linear models: Applications and data analysis methods* (2nd ed.). Thousand Oaks: Sage Publications.

Rogowski, R. (1989). *Commerce and coalitions: How trade affects domestic political alignments.* Princeton: Princeton University Press.

Sassen, S. (1996). *Losing control?: Sovereignty in an age of globalization.* New York: Columbia University Press.

Schattschneider, E. E. (1935). *Politics, pressures, and the tariff.* New York: Prentice Hall.

Shoup, L., & Minter, W. (1977). *Imperial brain trust.* New York: Monthly Review.

Sorauf, F. J. (1991). PACs and parties in American politics. In: A. J. Cigler & B. A. Loomis (Eds), *Interest group politics.* Washington, DC: Congressional Quarterly Press.

United States Trade Representative. (1994). 1994 trade policy agenda and 1993 annual report. Government Printing Services, Washington, DC.

Uniworld Business Publications. (1999/2005). In: *Directory of American firms operating in foreign countries* (9th, 10th, 11th, 12th, 13th ed.). New York: Uniworld Business Publications, Inc.

Useem, M. (1984). *The inner circle: Large corporations and the rise of business political activity in the U.S. and U.K..* New York: Oxford University Press.

Vogel, D. (1989). *Fluctuating fortunes: The political power of business in America.* New York: Basic Books.

Woodall, P., Wallach, L., Roach, J., & Burnham, K. (2000). *Purchasing power: The corporate-White House alliance to pass the China trade bill over the will of the American people.* Washington, DC: Public Citizen.

Woods, T. (2003). Capitalist class relations, the state, and new deal foreign trade policy. *Critical Sociology, 29,* 393–418.

Yarbrough, B. V., & Yarbrough, R. M. (1992). *Cooperation and governance in international trade: The strategic organizational approach.* Princeton: Princeton University Press.

Zeitlin, M. (1974). Corporate ownership and control: The large corporation and the capitalist class. *American Journal of Sociology, 79,* 1073–1119.

# APPENDIX. SIC CODES

01 Agricultural production crops
02 Agricultural production livestock and animal specialties
07 Agricultural services

08 Forestry
10 Metal mining
12 Coal mining
13 Oil and gas extraction
14 Mining and quarrying of nonmetallic minerals, except fuels
15 Building construction general contractors and operative
16 Heavy construction other than building construction
17 Construction special trade contractors
20 Food and kindred products
21 Tobacco products
22 Textile mill products
23 Apparel and other finished products made from fabrics
24 Lumber and wood products, except furniture
25 Furniture and fixtures
26 Paper and allied products
27 Printing, publishing, and allied industries
28 Chemicals and allied products
29 Petroleum refining and related industries
30 Rubber and miscellaneous plastics products
31 Leather and leather products
32 Stone, clay, glass, and concrete products
33 Primary metal industries
34 Fabricated metal products, except machinery and transportation
35 Industrial and commercial machinery and computer equipment
36 Electronic and other electrical equipment and components
37 Transportation equipment
38 Measuring, analyzing, and controlling instruments
39 Miscellaneous manufacturing industries
40 Railroad transportation
41 Local and suburban transit and interurban highway passenger
42 Motor freight transportation and warehousing
43 United States postal service
44 Water transportation
45 Transportation by air
46 Pipelines, except natural gas
47 Transportation services
48 Communications
49 Electric, gas, and sanitary services
50 Wholesale trade-durable goods
51 Wholesale trade-non-durable goods

52 Building materials, hardware, garden supply, and mobile homes
53 General merchandise stores
54 Food stores
55 Automotive dealers and gasoline service stations
56 Apparel and accessory stores
57 Home furniture, furnishings, and equipment stores
58 Eating and drinking places
59 Miscellaneous retail
60 Depository institutions
61 Non-depository credit institutions
62 Security and commodity brokers, dealers, exchanges
63 Insurance carriers
64 Insurance agents, brokers, and service
65 Real estate
67 Holding and other investment offices
70 Hotels, rooming houses, camps, and other lodging places
72 Personal services
73 Business services
75 Automotive repair, services, and parking
76 Miscellaneous repair services
78 Motion pictures
79 Amusement and recreation services
80 Health services
81 Legal services
82 Educational services
83 Social services
84 Museums, art galleries, and botanical and zoological gardens
86 Membership organizations
87 Engineering, accounting, research, management
88 Private households
89 Services, not elsewhere classified
91 Executive, legislative, and general government, except finance
92 Justice, public order, and safety
93 Public finance, taxation, and monetary policy
94 Administration of human resource programs
95 Administration of environmental quality and housing programs
96 Administration of economic programs
97 National security and international affairs
99 Non-classifiable establishments

# PART IV:
# THE REALIZATION CRISIS AND GLOBALIZATION

# GLOBALIZATION, THE CRISIS OF REALIZATION AND NEW FORMS OF CONSUMPTION

Alessandro Bonanno and Robert J. Antonio

## ABSTRACT

*At the outset of this essay we stress that the Fordist interventionist state was key in preventing the crisis of realization theorized by Marx. Later, Fordist state-centered interventionist strategies were viewed as "costly rigidities" and attacked by promoters of Globalization. We further argue that, under globalization, those mechanisms set up to control unwanted consequences of capitalism have been severely weakened and/or removed. In a situation in which social polarization characterized world development, Marx's "crisis of realization" assumes renewed importance. The difficulties that transnational corporations encounter in their effort to realize capital, we conclude, allow for the possibility of democratization of global social relations fueled by new forms of consumption.*

## INTRODUCTION

Countering Marx's view of the consequences of "large-scale capitalism" (Antonio, 2002), Talcott Parsons (1971) stressed that one of the strongest

Politics and Globalization
Research in Political Sociology, Volume 15, 243–267
Copyright © 2007 by Elsevier Ltd.
All rights of reproduction in any form reserved
ISSN: 0895-9935/doi:10.1016/S0895-9935(06)15008-1

indications of the inadequacy of Marxist theory was Marx's failed prediction of the end of capitalism. For Parsons (1971), and likeminded social theorists, not only did the collapse of capitalism never materialize, but post World War II United States – the world's leading capitalist society – was positioned to continue its social and economic growth. It was also destined to eradicate the problems that Marx highlighted as the reasons for the contradictory and unsustainable nature of capitalism. For Marx, it was the exploitative nature of market-based social relations that would generate the end of capitalism. Attacking Adam Smith's and David Ricardo's claims that the capitalist market tends to automatically reach equilibrium, Marx contended that the working of the free market created overproduction and class polarization that prevented the achievement of any form of stability. Hence, capitalism entailed recurrent crises that could not be avoided: the capitalist market could not control the consequences of its functioning.

Marx further elaborated that the capitalist class's appropriation of labor surplus value created an insurmountable gap between production (supply) and consumption (demand). Workers' wages, Marx documented, are only a fraction of workers' production and equal only to the cost of reproduction of labor. This signifies that workers' consumption can equal only a fraction of the commodities produced (Marx, 1981, p. 359). This gap between production and consumption would hamper the "realization of capital," or the transformation of commodities into capital and the further transformation of this capital into new commodities. This condition would ultimately produce a crisis of capital accumulation and the collapse of the entire system (Marx, 1978).[1]

The issue of Marx's "erred" prediction of the imminent end of capitalism continued after Marx's death. Not only was this debate fueled by those who opposed Marx's theory,[2] but involved the participation of a significant number of Marxists (see Sweezy, 1942). A crucial point of contention was the "assumed" ability of the free market to automatically achieve equilibrium between production and consumption. While pro laissez-faire arguments maintained a constant and – often powerful – presence in academic and political debates, the contention that the free functioning of the market could lead to a crisis of realization occupied the attention of a diverse group of thinkers.

In the Marxian camp, early twentieth century analyses maintained that capital realization was an "impossibility." Often associated with the intellectual and political activities of the Second Communist International, these analyses saw the growth of capitalism as characterized by the development of an automatic gap between the commodities produced and the ability of the market to absorb them. According to this economic deterministic view, the realization crisis proposed by Marx was not only accurate, but it would have materialized without any further political and/or socio-economic action (Howard & King, 1989).

Countering this view and proposing an alternative leftist political strategy,[3] Antonio Gramsci (1971) spoke of the development of a much more sophisticated form of capitalism that he named "Fordism" or "Americanism".[4] Through state intervention consisting of a combination of economic, institutional, and cultural measures, Fordism not only avoided the realization crisis, but transformed production and consumption to mass production and mass consumption.

Gramsci's point of the relevance of state intervention was also stressed outside the Marxian camp. Albeit in significantly different terms, the industrialist Henry Ford ([1926]2004) and the economist John Keynes (1936) agreed on the inability of the market to match production and consumption and promoted the introduction of mechanisms that could address this issue. For both of them, state intervention in the economy, the consequent increases in wages, and popular participation in consumption patterns represented key elements for the continued expansion of capitalism.

The history of capitalism in the second half of the twentieth century demonstrated the power of the Fordist project and its ability to address the systemic gap between production and consumption highlighted by Marx. While contradictions at various levels remained and new ones developed, Fordism fueled the post World War II Pax Americana and the era's exponential socio-economic growth. Additionally, it generated new levels of inclusion for subordinated classes along with much more advanced forms of social control and culturally based domination (Harvey, 1989; Marcuse, 1964).

This essay continues with a brief discussion of key aspects of the Fordist project. Our position rests on analyses that distinguish globalization from internationalization. More specifically, we follow those analyses that distinguish the process of internationalization of capitalism – that culminated with the post-World War II Pax Americana – from the subsequent regime of capital accumulation that we term globalization. We stress the importance that state intervention in the economy and society has in order to avoid the crippling contradictions discussed by Marx in his crisis of realization. We point out that globalization emerged – among other things – as a response to the socio-economic rigidities of Fordism and its "costly" state intervention centered strategies. In the central sections of the paper, we argue that because globalization greatly reduced state intervention in the social and economic spheres, those mechanisms set up to address the gap between production and consumption have been severely weakened and/or removed. In a situation in which social polarization characterized world development, the conditions for the "crisis of realization" predicted by Marx are reintroduced. In this context, the difficulties that transnational corporations encounter in their effort to realize their capital, we conclude, allow for the possibility of democratization of global social relations fueled by new forms of consumption. While this may be interpreted as an "optimistic' reading of the importance of consumption, the essence of our concluding remarks is that the current situation is quite problematic and cannot be sustained for the long run.

# FORDISM AND THE RESPONSE TO THE MARKET INSTABILITY OF LAISSEZ FAIRE CAPITALISM

## State Intervention in the Economy and Society: Gramsci, Ford, and Keynes

In the early 1930s, Antonio Gramsci (1971) proposed a theorization of the new form of capitalism that had emerged in the United States and later was to expand to Europe and the rest of the world. Fordism, Gramsci argued, represented one of the most significant attempts to address capitalism's inability to match production and consumption. Following Marx's analysis of the contradictions of capitalism, Gramsci was well aware of capitalism's lack of direct connection between production and consumption. Production under capitalism is not directed toward the objective of consumption, but it expands independently from it (Marx, 1981, pp. 377–379). Simultaneously, Gramsci stressed the changed conditions of capitalism in the new century. Gramsci's concept of Fordism built on Marx's analysis of the transition from small-scale capitalism to a complex, increasingly global capitalism that employs science/technology as its leading productive force, mechanizes production, deskills workers, and generates large firms, an intervening and controlling state, and big unions. He stressed the sweeping rationalization of production, the central role of finance capital, and the linkages between "petty bourgeois savers" (i.e., middle-class stockholders) and financial elites. However, his core concept of hegemony also emphasized the increasingly significant role of mass culture, mass media, mass consumption, and above all the enlarged state (e.g., expanded regulation, planning, intervention, and propaganda). His discussion of "Americanism and Fordism," a titled section of his *Prison Notebooks*, articulated his view that the capitalist economy is embedded in broader, historically specific socio-cultural regimes, each with distinct structures and processes, dominant and subordinate strata, hegemonic and counter-hegemonic blocs, and patterns of struggle.[5]

The term *Fordism* signifies the importance that Gramsci attributed to the assembly-line production, managerial hierarchy, technical control, and the overall vision of the importance of matching production and consumption introduced by automobile magnate Henry Ford (see Aglietta, 1979). According to Ford's industrial philosophy (Ford, [1926]2004), successful mass production required strict labor discipline, careful industrial planning, and sophisticated admistrative structures. It also required the creation of a sustained mass consumption that could be achieved by expanding the consumption capabilities of the working masses. While Ford instituted industrial mass production, he deemed mass consumption the key aspect of economic growth. He realized that if he paid his factory workers a real living wage and produced more cars in less time for less money, everyone would buy them. This "wage motive" as Ford called it, underscored the importance of the idea that "workers must be also consumers" (Keller, 1993, p. 20). He established a system of increased wages ($5 daily) to match what Gramsci (1971) identified as mass production's "monotonous, degrading, and life draining work process." Sharply moving away from the dominant industrial philosophy of the time that stressed that the most efficient manner to maximize profits was to produce for the rich, Ford believed "that the guys who made the cars ought to be able to afford one themselves" (Iacocca, 1988, p. 45). This posture, however, was not limited to corporate strategies, but entailed state intervention through the creation of a variety of public policies, institutions, and governance mechanisms intended to mitigate the failures of the free market (Ford, [1926]2004).

The idea of the establishment of an interventionist state that could manage production and consumption levels was also debated in formal scientific circles. In this regard, central was the contribution of John Keynes (1936).[6] In the 1930s, Keynes theorized the possibility of using government fiscal and monetary policy to counter recessions and control economic booms. His prescription for controlling unwanted consequences of capitalism – primarily unemployment and recessions and the gap between supply and demand – involved the presence of a state that would stimulate the economy by creating new investments through "deficit spending." The years following World War II were characterized by the wide acceptance and use of Keynesian economic theory. His ideas became, first, the backbone of the 1944 Bretton Woods agreement that codified the post-war "Pax Americana," and, subsequently, the cornerstone of the economic policies of the US and its allies world wide.

## HIGH FORDISM AND STATE INTERVENTION

The extraordinary convergence of ideas on the importance of the intervention of the state in the economy and society was embodied in the triumph of post-war Fordist Capitalism or "High Fordism" (Antonio & Bonanno, 1996). While most major capitalist societies were forced to rebuild after the war, US manufacturing firms dominated their huge home market and much of the world market in the 1950s and 1960s. Despite major growth of the service sector, manufacturing still drove the US postwar expansion. Explosive growth of federally subsidized suburbs (single family homes and highway systems) and of the standard middle-class consumer package (e.g., autos and home appliances) forged a new mass consumer society. Employing breakthroughs in mainframe computer and other information processing technologies, managers of the primary sector's vertically integrated corporate firms increasingly rationalized, centralized, and automated their operations. The dramatic expansion of higher education facilitated a new wave of managerial professionalization, increased the upper middle-class ranks of highly trained technical, financial, and legal specialists, and expanded basic research for the military and corporate sectors. Innovations and growth of mass media and mass entertainment, especially TV, and expansion of the retail sector (e.g., shopping centers and chain stores) revolutionized marketing. The private sector's much enhanced methods of advertising and marketing and the state's Keynesian managing of aggregate demand fostered High Fordism's unparalleled ability to balance production and consumption and to maintain low unemployment, steady accumulation, and high rates of profit.

During the postwar "capital-labor accord," union membership peaked, but unions generally cooperated with management, trading aspirations for stakeholder rights in capital and shared control of the labor process for higher wages and benefits and stable employment. There was increased affluence, social security, and educational opportunity, especially for white males, and much upgraded standards of living for unionized blue-collar workers, the middle-class, and above. Policy intellectuals and the press proclaimed the United States to be a new type of ultramodern, middle-class democracy that escaped classical capitalist crises and class conflicts and effectively ended debates over basic ideology (Hodgson, 1978, pp. 67–98).

Many critics and advocates alike held that High Fordism worked so well for the enlarged and politically decisive middle-class that alternatives were hard to imagine. However, sharp class, racial, and gender inequalities remained entrenched. Criticizing American intellectuals' acquiescence to injustice and regimentation, radical sociologist and social critic C. Wright

Mills warned that a "postmodern" world of "Cheerful Robots" was arising. Following Gramsci's early recognition of the oppressive nature of Fordism inclusive actions, Herbert Marcuse, the leading theoretician of the 1960s "New Left," asserted that the United States was a "society without opposition." He held that its structure of "total administration" and technical coordination retained "stupefying" and "exhausting" types of work, but integrated the working-class into the system by effectively and widely delivering entertainment and consumer goods that "indoctrinate and manipulate" and destroy critical sensibilities and the desire for liberation. Mass consumption and social control were delivered through consumerism. Contesting these views, the era's leading sociological theorist, Talcott Parsons, contended that the American "working-class" approximated "the leisure class," while "upper occupational groups" were among the hardest "'working' groups in human history" (Mills, 1961, pp. 165–176; Marcuse, 1964; Parsons, 1971, pp. 86–87, 112–114, 129, 140–143).

The social philosopher Jürgen Habermas (1975) stressed the historical limits encountered by the Fordist state to control unwanted consequences of capitalism. The transformation of the market into an oligopolistic system mandated increased state intervention. Increased state intervention, therefore, emerged as a tool to control economic fluctuations, regulate the economic cycle and, as stressed by Gramsci and Keynes, maintain full employment and growth. In essence, the emergence of this social state (the Fordist welfare state) limited the "social and material costs resulting from private production" (p. 35). Simultaneously, state intervention raised expectations about social equality and greater participation in decision-making processes. However, and in spite of state regulation, economic downturns continued to disproportionally affect the lower and middle classes exposing the false equivalence between claims about the just and equal nature of market exchanges and their unequal and exploitative historical dimensions. The ability of the state to sustain its expanded intervention in the economy and society clashed with the continued decline of the rate of profit and the private appropriation of surplus value. In this context, the Fordist attempt to reconcile corporate control of capital accumulation with enhanced lower classes participation in the working of society lost legitimacy.

## THE CRISIS OF HIGH FORDISM

By the late 1960s, race riots and campus disturbances, increased inflation, slower economic growth, and socio-political fragmentation had begun to erode High Fordist consensus. Numerous crises during the 1970s (racial tensions, oil shortages, recession, Watergate, the Vietnam War, increased taxation, and stagflation) increased socio-political fragmentation. Also, American manufacturers faced stiff challenges from European and Asian competitors in the US home market, profit squeezes, and diminished corporate profits. The rise of anti-Western movements (e.g., Islamic fundamentalism), worldwide challenges to Western modernization models, and new political alignments (e.g., OPEC) threatened US dominance in international politics and economics. By the mid-1970s, Western Europe also faced slower economic growth, increasing threats of terrorism, growing tensions over immigration, political fragmentation, and other problems. Critics declared that the High Fordist state experienced not only a crisis of legitimation but also a fiscal crisis. The state could not fulfill its promises of social well-being, integration, and equality, on the one hand, and, it was increasingly unable to provide the resources to maintain social benefits and economic growth, on the other (O'Connor, 1973; Habermas, 1975).

In this climate, the US corporate right mobilized politically and culturally against the social side of Keynesianism; well-funded conservative foundations and think-tanks initiated an effective ideological counteroffensive against regulation, income and wealth redistribution, and taxation (Akard, 1992; Prechel, 1994, 1990). Rising "neoconservatives" revived free-market economics and fused it with cultural conservatism. They charged that Lyndon Johnson's vision of a "Great Society" empowered a "New Class" of welfare state bureaucrats and policy intelligentsia, backed by an "adversary culture" of young radicals, who imposed egalitarian agendas that overreached realistic possibilities for reform, overloaded the state, rewarded free-riders, and undermined authority, civic morality, and labor discipline. By the end of the decade, a number of politically diverse thinkers stressed an "end of consensus," "the decline of American morale," "the erosion of American power," or "the end of the American Century" (Hodgson, 1978).

The election of Ronald Reagan in 1980 marked the political ascension of neoconservative forces that blamed High Fordist strategies for American economic and socio-cultural decline and framed a project of "American renewal" that instituted "neoliberal" economic policies and, with less success, a right-wing cultural agenda (Brohman, 1996). The US left, with libertarian support, resisted the cultural changes, but mounted little opposition to the neoliberal economic tide. Even postwar liberalism's timid version of "equal opportunity" disappeared from the vocabulary of both political parties. Envisioned a little more than a decade before as the chief motor of postwar growth, High Fordist strategies were now seen as crippling "rigidities" – nefarious inefficiencies and the prime causes of American socio-economic decline.

In an influential work of this period, Daniel Bell ([1976]1996) held that capitalist work and productive organization were historically undergirded by Puritan morality and character structure and that this nonmarket culture constrained the desires unleashed by capitalist acquisition. In his view, however, bourgeois culture's workaday values and habits were being ravaged by the hedonistic popular culture that had emerged in the postwar era. Bell argued that the late nineteenth and early twentieth centuries' avant garde fashioned an "aesthetic" modernism contradicting Protestant "asceticism." He contended that the reconstructed "postmodern" version of avant garde aestheticism, revived by the 1960s counterculture revolt against bourgeois culture and then commercialized by the mass media and entertainment industry, universalized artistic alienation and shock, exhausted modernism's creative impulses, and neutralized values of work, saving, prudence, rationality, and responsibility. In this view, popular culture had evaporated the Puritan views of sexuality and work that Gramsci had argued were central in regulating the American working-class in the early days of Fordism. By contrast to the support that Gramsci claimed that American culture provided Fordist production, Bell asserted that a radical "disjunction of realms" had emerged (Bell, 1996, pp. 3–171). His cultural critique resonated with the neoconservative pleas to revive authority, religion, and Puritan austerity and work habits.

By the end of the 1980s the results of this anti-Fordist campaign were clearly visible (Antonio & Bonanno, 1996). Not only the US and many of its closed allies had embraced neoliberal economic policies, but the world industrial apparatus and labor market had undergone significant transformations that created a set of overall conditions qualitatively different than those experienced during High Fordism. Often grouped under the umbrella concept of globalization, they affected the socio-economic and cultural sphere alike.

## GLOBALIZATION

Globalization entailed a number of strategies to revive capital accumulation, stimulate production, and overcome a stagnant consumer demand. Most significantly among them were those designed to free capitalism from the assumed "rigidities" engendered by state intervention. "No big government" became the cry of those who supported globalization and envisioned a much more free-market oriented global economy and society. The strongest attack was against Fordist "regulated capitalism" (Harvey, 1989; Robinson, 2004). Its result can be captured by the dramatic increase in the "flexibility" of capital (McMichael, 2002; Robinson, 2004; Sassen, 2000; Sklair, 2001). Capital is now free to colonize and commodify practically every sphere shattering the relatively fixed social and temporal-spatial boundaries and generating decentralized production and global consumption. Under globalization, production is to a much greater extent – but not exclusively – decomposed into sub-units and sub-production processes, carried out by globally dispersed firms with highly divergent forms of labor, managerial, and financial organizations that may even follow traditional and local business practices and customs. More importantly, it is the ability of global companies to select strategies that fit their interests with an unprecedented – although not total – freedom. This freedom is the primary result of neoliberal policies, reduced forms of regulation, favorable economic incentives and an overall cultural climate that welcomes corporate mobility and autonomy. Public enterprises have been privatized and increasingly the availability of vital services has become associated with the capacity to pay and/or overall profitability. Nation-states and their regional counterparts – once the motor forces of regulation and control of undesirable consequences of capitalism – have actively contributed to the elimination of rules and regulations that hampered the free mobility of capital (deregulation). They effectively engineered the opening of their economies and the creation of conditions amenable to corporate interests but were often adverse to labor, communities, and environmental well-being (reregulation) (Robinson, 2004; Sassen, 2000).

Through global sourcing (Heffernan, 2000; McMichael, 2002) transnational corporations have been able to search for the most convenient factors of production across the globe. Often associated with less expensive labor and natural resources, global sourcing allows the search for better business, political, and social climates that would place corporations at a competitive advantage over other competitors. This free mobility and global extension of capital renders permeable a great number of spatial-temporal, political, and social "borders" that once regulated capital, creating new vulnerabilities for the well-being and identities of individuals and national, regional, and local communities. Despite the importance of local specific resources and groups, the free mobility of capital qualitatively altered established social, political, and economic relations.

In this context, the spatial-temporal unity of the polity and the economy that characterized the earlier phases of capitalist development has been fractured. In previous phases of capitalism – from the early competitive one to

Fordism – the growth of economic relations was centered on the existence of nation-states whose polities (the state) coordinated and mediated activities of economic actors. Since its inception, capitalism mandated a political system that coordinated and assisted capital accumulation while controlling opposition and legitimating capitalist social relations (Arrighi, 1998; Habermas, 2002; Offe, 1985). Under these historical circumstances, a spatial and temporal unity between the economy and the polity was maintained whereby the state was able to coordinate and mediate activities of economic actors who operated within its territory and – as indicated above in the case of Fordism – acted to address negative consequences of the expansion of capitalism.

Under globalization, these conditions have been altered. The nation-state's capacity to mediate between the market and society has been weakened, and the state is also increasingly unable to control the flow of economic resources according to the rules established through democratic processes (Habermas, 2002; Harvey, 1989). This situation should not be interpreted simply to signify that the state has been generally weakened and will disappear. It shows, conversely, that globalization has reduced the nation-state's control over its economic and non-economic environments when these forms of control clash with corporate interests and those of the groups that support them (Sklair, 2001). Simultaneously, to support capital accumulation, many nation-states have increased their control over a number of domestic spheres, including surveillance and social control, while deliberately acting to open up their economies and societies to global flows (McMichael, 2002; Sassen, 2000). While some interpreted these facets of globalization as necessary conditions for social and economic growth (Friedman, 2000), others associated them with the shrinking of the social state and the expansion of the pro-capitalist state (McMichael, 2002).

While this flexibility of globalization certainly signifies a sharp move away from the Fordist regulate capitalism, it is not "disorganized" (Lash & Urry, 1987; Offe, 1985). "Flexible" structures serve financial rationalization, concentrating resources, by-passing obstacles, locating more efficient forms of production, hedging against possible economic shifts, and taking advantage of new financial and tax instruments. Decentralized production goes hand in hand with more highly centralized control of finance, research, and information. Globalization "economic development" and free trade policies utilize the state itself to enhance capital mobility, erode its own local, regional, and national regulatory instruments, and reduce labor's bargaining power and influence[7] (Sassen, 1998).

Globalization advocates viewed Fordism as a regime that eventually generated a stagnant demand for industrial and consumer goods. Globalization, therefore, has been heralded as the way to revive demand world wide (Friedman, 2000). While it is a fact that wealth and consumption have increased for the upper class, it is equally clear that economic inequality has grown sharply since the end of Fordism (Mishel, Bernstein, & Schmitt, 2004). In many parts of the world, the middle and lower classes have experienced declining purchasing power and wages. In the United States, most wage earners had either stagnating or falling wages and family income also stagnated, even though the numbers of hours worked and corporate profit increased substantially. The last years of the old century and the initial ones of the new millennium have been characterized by the unprecedented situation in which corporate profitability and labor productivity increased but actual wage levels declined (Mishel et al., 2004). Regardless of increases in the federal minimum wage, its purchasing power has eroded by $2.00 per hour since 1968. By contrast, the richest one percent of families has good reasons to concur with "best ever" assessment of the so-called new economy; their net worth increased on average from about a million dollars to about 11 million dollars between 1989 and 2003. The rest of the upper 20 percent also made substantial gains, and have good reasons for their exuberant optimism. However, the nearly one-third (33 percent) of American families that had a net worth of $12,000 or less in 2003 had reason to disagree. The United States has the highest level of economic inequality, the least upward mobility for low-wage workers, and the highest poverty rates of the leading economies (Mishel et al., 2004). Additionally, from the 1980 to 2002 the adjusted-for-inflation incomes of the richest 5 percent of US families rose by an average of $80,488 per year. During the same time, the adjusted-for-inflation incomes on the mid 20 percent and lower 20 percent of American families rose by an average of $225 and $70 per year respectively (Economic Policy Institute, 2006). These are the fruits of "the longest peacetime expansion without a recession in the nation's history" (Schwartz, Leyden, & Hyatt, 1999, p. 47).

Economic inequality between the rich and poor nations is even more extreme than the sharp divides in American society. Data for the United Nations (United Nations, 2002) indicates that the gap between the rich and poor is widening. It is maintained that economic globalization is fueling a "dangerous" polarization between a small group of super rich and a large segment of impoverished members of the globe's population. According to the data, from 1995 to 2001 alone, the 200 wealthiest people of the world doubled their fortunes to more than one trillion dollars while the number of those surviving with only one dollar a day has remained constant at 1.3 billion. In the early 1970s, the wealthiest fifth of the world's population was 30 times richer that the poorest fifth. By 1990 this ratio grew to 60 to 1, and at the end of the twentieth century it stands at 74 to 1 (United Nations, 2002, see also Robinson, 2004).

## MARKET CAPITALISM AND THE CONTROL OF UNWANTED CONSEQUENCES OF CAPITALISM

If the analysis of globalization presented above is correct, the picture that emerges is one in which state regulation and control of capitalism has been radically altered from its Fordist past. The Fordist mechanisms that were set in place to create the "organized capitalism" (Offe, 1996; Lash & Urry, 1994) of most of the twentieth century, have been replaced by a set of new rules of organization that view in the ideology and practices of the "free market" the basic condition for the reproduction of capitalism.

As documented above, it is important to stress that the return to"free market" capitalism does not automatically involve the end of the intervention of the state nor does it indicate the emergence of a "disorganized capitalism" exclusively based on a truly "free market" system. It signals, instead, that the state has moved away from those interventions in the social and economic spheres that promoted relatively stable salaries and wages for middle- and lower-class workers and enhanced consumption. Globalization, in other words, signifies the abandoning of postures aimed at maintaining mass consumption through the organized enhancement of the socio-economic conditions of subordinate classes.

The alternative proposed by globalization involves the strengthening of the power of transnational corporations (TNCs) through mechanisms, such as global sourcing. In populist-sounding pronouncements about competitive individualism, globalization advocates hold that elimination of special protections and programs for the subordinated classes (labor, racial, and ethnic minorities) makes for a more just society (Friedman, 1982, pp. 108–118). Most importantly and strongly departing from classical free market advocates' calls for compassion and care for the disenfranchised, globalization supporters write off Fordist efforts to reduce class disparities and the growing numbers of people who lack resources for the nurturance of selves capable of competing for middle-class roles in the private economy and exercising their citizenship rights. For globalization advocates, Fordist attempts to control unwanted consequences of capitalism are the truly "unwanted" aspects of capitalism.

The rosy picture presented by globalization advocates brushes aside the classical objection that the market's free functioning creates – rather than addresses – inequality and instability. This has been not only one of the key points of the Marxian inspired critiques of capitalist, but also a position that inspired advocates of Fordist measures, such as Keynes and Henry Ford, to argue for state intervention. The point is that – in spite of claims about the effectiveness of the free market – classical limits to the accumulation of capital are reproposed under globalization. This is particularly the case in regard to the assumed equality between production and consumption as the elimination of the Fordist measures to match increased production with an increased consumption have been drastically transformed. In essence, the restructuring of state intervention and the end of Fordism have affected the process of *realization of capital*. In this context, Marx's critique of capitalist realization assumes renewed importance and contemporary relevance.

## The Reproposition of Marx's Critique

According to Marx, the realization of capital is one of the primary aspects of the overall process of capital accumulation. For economic growth and equilibrium to occur, money capital must be transformed into commodities, which in turn must be transformed back into money. In volumes I and II of *Capital,* Marx distinguished between circulation and realization of capital. The first one refers to the scope of growth of capital. That is, through circulation, time- and place-bound production escapes its original condition and acquires new forms and meanings. This is a situation which cannot be omitted as commodities "cannot acquire universal social validity ... except by being converted into money." (Marx, 1977, p. 201). Additionally, "the ceaseless augmentation of value ... is achieved by the more acute capitalist by means of throwing his money again and again into circulation" (Marx, 1977, pp. 254–255). Realization refers to the fact that production (commodities) must be transformed into the money form (i.e., it must be sold, that is realized into the money form) for the process of capitalist accumulation to continue smoothly (Marx, 1978, pp. 465–585). For Marx, the primary contradiction of realization rests on the fact that capitalist production mandates the creation of surplus value. Surplus value refers to the quantity of value created by workers through labor, which is expropriated by the capitalist class. Because the quantity of value produced (more or less the equivalent of the commodity price) is always greater than the amount of value (wages) received by workers, the latter cannot consume what they produce. Therefore there will be a situation in which commodity produced could not be transformed into their money form and reintroduced into the process of circulation of capital (Marx, 2000[1910], pp. 107–113). This situation generates crises. For Marx, the re-equilibrium of the system can only occur through the "destruction" of value, that is, economic crises that impoverish the working masses and increase the gap between the dominant and subordinate classes. In the long run, these crises could not be controlled and the system equilibrium will not be restored.[8]

The processes of circulation and realization of capital mandate the lack of obstacles to the transformation of money into commodities and back into money. Yet, as has been recognized by both classical and contemporary theories,[9] the manner in which commodities are transformed into money is historically determined, that is, it depends on the availability of socio-economic conditions which allow the equilibrium between production and consumption to be achieved. This situation signifies that the ability of firms to realize their production depends on the conditions, which characterize the markets through which their commodities are exchanged.

### Marx's Critique of Realization under Globalization

Under globalization, these conditions involve the achievement of equilibrium between corporations' global production and the existence of stable communities of consumers, which can effectively contribute to the process of capital realization. As illustrated above, the problem with the current historical conditions rests on the fact that the establishment of this equilibrium is problematized by at least two fundamental consequences of globalization. The first consists of the growth of the socioeconomic inequality at the world level. As pointed out earlier, this class polarization increasingly marginalizes significant segments of the world population and excludes them from the type of consumption patterns needed to sustain current levels of global production. The second consequence of globalization refers to the dismantling of Fordist inclusionary measures that increased consumption of the lower and middle classes and provided – albeit partial – control of key unwanted consequences of capitalism (e.g., Gray, 1998; Hammond, 1998; Robinson, 2004; United Nations, 2002). While Fordism addressed the gap between production and consumption through the fostering of mass consumption, state intervention, and social inclusion, under globalization the same gap is addressed through social polarization and exclusion. From this point of view, it appears that Marx's argument about the crisis of realization assumes a much greater relevance than during the Fordist era. In essence, the elimination of Fordist measures reproposes the danger of recurrent economic instability and the lack of instruments to control its social consequences.

## The Crisis of Realization and New Forms of Consumption

The renewed importance of the crisis of realization reminds us of the unstable character of this global capitalism. Paradoxically, however, this renewed importance associated with new patterns of consumption generates the opportunity to open up new possibilities for the democratization of global social relations. This situation refers to the growth of "new social movement inspired consumption." Pertinent literature (e.g., Bauman, 1998; Beck, Giddens, & Lash, 1994; Giddens, 2000, 1994) stresses the role that *new social movements* have played in the process of resisting undemocratic aspects of globalization. Great emphasis has been placed on the contributions that movements, such as the feminist movement, the gay and lesbian movement, and, to a greater extent, the environmental movement provided to the establishment of democratic spaces. Because of these movements' emphasis on individual emancipation, quality of life, and identity, they created a fresh version of radical democracy, which decisively broke with traditional interest groups-based politics and political organizations.

The environmental movement, for example, has been heralded as the force which could bring about new, more equitable and sustainable social arrangements and could be the catalyst for the aggregation of emancipatory forces (e.g., Beck, 1992, 1995; Buttel, 1994; Dreiling, 1997). This movement's challenges to traditional projects of socio-economic development, modernization theories, modern science and technology, sclerotic political strategies coupled with support for local groups, local knowledge, diversity, and identity contributed to the development of novel sensitivities which now permeate contemporary society and culture. Indeed, new social movements' emphasis on culture as the primary site of emancipatory struggles revived and reinvigorated – but also transformed – critical themes which in the past the historical left was never able to elevate to shared societal visions.

To be sure, the environmental movement – like other new social movements – is far from being a unified entity. Its fragmentation and plurality of theoretical outlooks have been widely documented (e.g., Benton, 1996; Merchant, 1997; Mingione, 1993; Shabecoff, 1993). Additionally, splits within the movement have translated into overt opposition and conflict in political debates and practices. Moreover, critics question this movement's ability to effectively direct anti-establishment struggles as they view it as a new form of traditional politics, which divides progressive forces and neglects to address socio-economic inequality. The phrase "sandals turned into suits" captures the charge that environmentalism has become a new bureaucratically organized elite of "pseudo-leftist professionals" (Piccone, 1995).

Regardless of the debate about the emancipatory power of the environmental movement and its capacity to propose new forms of radical democracy, its impact on the culture and practices of today's society is significant (Beck, 1997; Giddens, 2000; Gray, 1998; Harvey, 2000). Core items of the environmental agenda – e.g., protection of natural resources, sustainability, and ecological equilibrium – are fundamental elements of contemporary discourses and represent new sensitivities which are now constitutive components of today's culture. As Beck (1995, p. 6) states, the environmental movement's "topics and issues have become established: all political groups have inscribed them on their banners." While pro-environmental claims vary, and it would be erroneous to equate them with substantive behaviors, they are commonly adopted across socio-economic and political spectra. Additionally, as Lash and Urry (1994, p. 297) pointed out, even phenomena which historically taxed the environment, like the expansion of consumerism, have been captured by this movement and contributed to the development of enhanced levels of consciousness about the centrality of ecological issues.

More importantly, struggles for the creation of alternative forms of production and consumption not only denounce and contrast TNCs' actions, but propose strategies which transcend the accumulation-based rationality of mass production. The point is that because of this widespread consciousness existing in today's society, there is a favorable climate for calls, which demand the opening of democratic spaces.

Consumption patterns based on new social movement-centered sensitivities represent important forces in countering the behavior of TNCs. Because of the large economic power associated with these types of consumers, TNCs have been forced to be attentive to their demands. In an arguably extreme rendering of this situation, Bauman (1992, 2002) maintains that consumption-substituted labor as the primary social site where identity and behaviors are formed. Standing at the opposite extreme, Fredric Jameson (1994) questions the emancipatory scope of consumption. He points to TNCs' hegemonic powers and their ability to transform new and augmented consumption into novel markets, which expand sales and corporate power.

Kim Humphery (1998) describes food consumption as a potential arena for the empowerment of individuals, the development of cultural alternatives, and political resistance. Moreover, he insists on denouncing the misguided view that consumers are simply instruments of corporate power. Consumers, instead, are viewed as active actors who – while remaining subjects to the clout of corporate guided consumerism – are the producers of usage and meanings, which transcend the intentions of producers. In other words, it is erroneous, in his view, to reduce consumers to passive recipients of corporate messages and objectives. They form a group which has historically empowered itself in contemporary society. Similarly, Tim Lang (1999) stresses the emerging power of the "food movement" which despite setbacks "... has been successful in questioning the New Right logic of laissez-faire and deregulating" (Lang, 1999, p. 175; see also Gabriel & Lang, 1995; Miller, 1995).

Addressing the same issue, Lash and Urry (1994, pp. 296–298) indicate that contemporary social arrangements translate into expanded consumerism as individuals augmented their ability to consume. This expanded consumption, however, entails a departure from early established, quantity-based models. Today's consumers, they continue, tend to stress quality rather than quantity of consumption. Consumers, in other words, are much more thoughtful about the content and values of their consumption and these are processes often inspired by the quality of the environment (air, water, scenery) which precedes, accompanies, and follows consumption. We have reached a form of "reflexive consumption" (Lash & Urry, 1994). This "reflexivity" about the conditions of consumption becomes an emancipatory process, they continue, which remains a condition for the creation of free spaces in society. Their notion of aesthetics captures the emergence of consumption patterns centered on meanings established through a critique of conventional postures. Departing from postures which do not problematize consumption, our point is that the convergence of new social movement-based sensitivities and consumption offers an historical possibility for the democratization of social relations.

This "new social movement-centered consumption" and "reflexive consumption" empowers consumers and pushes them toward cultural subversion and political resistance. They mandate consumers' behaviors that pay particular attention to the forms of production and products' social contents (e.g., Lang, 1999; Lash & Urry, 1994; Miller, 1995). This type of consumption questions key features of global corporate production (e.g., it stands against sweatshop-based manufacturing; the use of child labor; the exploitation of women in maquiladora plants; the abuse of human and environmental resources; the destruction of cultural enclaves, etc.) and the quality of products (e.g., it supports healthier, environmentally sound, and multicultural products). More importantly, this type of consumption expresses a critique of corporate quantity-based mass production and its substantive neglect for quality production. The existence of new social movements-centered consumption signifies that individuals and groups who share this posture have the opportunity to establish enhanced forms of democracy by intervening in the realization process. Because TNCs need to "realize," emancipated consumers can demand that TNCs modify their actions to generate qualitatively advanced products and more ethically and socially acceptable forms of production. They could use this corporate weakness to control TNCs' activities and demand accountability in a context in which other forms of control (i.e., the nation-state) experience a crisis.

These possibilities of establishing democratic spaces are contextualized in a situation in which TNCs remain endowed with significant powers including that of shaping consumption. Indeed it is possible that consumers could not escape what Jameson termed the "logic of capitalist production." Additionally, the actual exploitation of TNCs' weaknesses depends on the strength of anti-corporate movements that seldom appear to be unified and armed with coherent visions that decisively break with patterns of global capital accumulation. Yet, globalization's contradictions remain. TNCs expansion has been based on the breaking of Fordist social arrangements, the transnationalization of social relations, and augmented exploitation fueled by global sourcing for less costly resources and capital friendly socio-political conditions. While production and consumption increased to the benefit of the upper and middle classes, socio-economic polarization and inequality have significantly grown both within and between the world North and South. More importantly, they are now largely viewed more as physiological rather than pathological forms of development. These conditions dramatically repropose the question of the "ability" of global capitalism to automatically match production and consumption levels, avoid disruptive crises, and control opposition and resistance.

However, the conditions, problems, and possibilities, which we have been discussing, are embedded in a still emergent larger context. Thomas L. Friedman's reference to a supposedly irreversible "Golden Straightjacket," which has been forged by relentless deregulation, privatization, securitization and has reduced political decisions to "Pepsi and Coke," celebrates the end of US High Fordism and its Keynesian social state and its inevitable global expansion. Joseph Stiglitz (2003) and other critics of Friedman suggest and fear the same US-led trend – the triumph and consolidation of worldwide US-led neoliberal regime or the "globalization system." The stripped-down state now is reduced increasingly to a mechanism to facilitate and subsidize global capitalist development, which is influenced especially by the machinations and veto-votes of finance capital. This regime is not sustainable and is subject to severe systemic crisis tendencies. Most importantly, about three billion people have been added to the global capitalist economy during the last 25 years. Friedman contends that this includes about a billion and a half new workers and, at least, one-hundred and fifty million new skilled workers. Moreover, he and many other thinkers have argued that automation, outsourcing, and portability of jobs will continue. One of Freidman's corporate informants asserted that we have to trust economic theory and the fact that job creation will rise to meet needs of the millions of new workers. However, in China about eight-hundred million people remain in rural areas, where monetarization and overall capitalist development has destroyed the traditional peasant economy. Even China's meteoric expansion and its state-guided approach cannot possibly absorb the newly proletarianized masses. In the global economy, millions of workers face unemployment, underemployment, or marginalization in the informal economy. In the US, where official unemployment is low, the minimum wage is set below any reasonable standard of subsistence and many millions of people belong to the working poor. Again, the point is that the current situation, in many parts of the world, approximates the scenario that Marx portrayed. How will the global economy produce sufficient jobs to employ a new global labor force and maintain sufficient demand to fuel the new global division of labor and productive system? Currently, US hyper-consumption, subsidized by exceptionally high levels of state and personal debt, has prevented a crisis of global overcapacity. Moreover, if, as Friedman says, the "Lexus trumps the olive tree" (i.e., the globe follows the American model and is able to substantially increase its consumption) and employment growth is consequently, greatly accelerated, how can the demand for oil and resources be met in a fashion that would not choke the economic expansion or generate a global environmental crisis? These are questions that do not find immediate answers in the current historical conditions and some critics have argued that the onset of this crisis has already begun (e.g., a new era of permanent high gas prices, global warming, world-wide water problems, etc.).

Two pressing issues are especially pertinent to the points we have made throughout the paper. First, the state remains a vital factor in fostering and subsidizing global capitalist development and neoliberal policy formation, but, in its current stripped down form it cannot mediate the type of crisis tendencies we suggest directly above. Such planning and policy would contradict the imperative of maximizing return on invested finance capital and the main interests of the so-called Electronic Herd (which includes many millions of American's who are relying on their 401Ks and mutual funds for retirement, education, and other priorities as well as the top 1% who have enormous influence on the financial markets and on the political parties). However, returning to the postwar model of the Keynesian policies, in the US, is deeply problematic and, perhaps, even impossible, in the new global system and given the weight of the debt. The High Fordist state was also forged in an era of postwar reconstruction and the long-wave of capitalist expansion, but before today's type of demand and pressure for global resources and nascent environmental crisis.

The second point is that coping with the current crisis tendencies demands a break with the High Fordist consumption, especially as it has been practiced in the United States. The neoliberal regime was designed to maintain and increase consumption by squeezing hard the lower quartiles of American workers, cutting their entitlements and expanding a transnational working class, which often has suffered by miserable authoritarian conditions and low pay and benefits. Perpetuating the current form of high consumption and spreading it globally seems to be limited by environmental and resource imperatives. It is possible that Weber's scenario comes true; that the inexorable rule of the economic growth imperative holds until the "last ton of fossilized coal is burned"! The inability of the US to face the most basic issues related to the petroleum-centered and energy-intensive economy suggests that this nightmare could become reality. Our earlier point about consumption as a point of contradiction and political action does not deny the need to also organize with regard to work and to production. However, a change in consumption patterns and perhaps a radical transformation of them may be necessary for any meaningful political change and may indeed be imposed by the scope of the environmental crisis itself. Genuine democratic reconstruction requires a radical rethinking of environmental priorities and of the very idea of a "consumer society." Thus, the agenda and conditions we discuss in this essay dictate both a going back to Marx and, at the same time, a transcendence and reconstruction of his work.

## NOTES

1. Marx was very well aware that, in spite of these crippling crises, counteracting factors would allow capital accumulation to continue in the immediate future (Marx, 2000[1910], pp. 427–469). For Marx, the tendency of the rate of profit to fall was historically countered by a variety of factors that included the more intense exportation of labor, the reduction of wages, the existence of unemployed labor, and the expansion of foreign markets (Marx, 1981, pp. 339–348).

2. The most well-known early attack to Marx's economic theory came from the Austrian economic theorist Eugen von Böhm-Bawerk. In 1896, Böhm-Bawerk published an influential neoclassical critique of Marx's theory of value that would influence the work of a number of Marxian economists for decades to come. See Sweezy (1966).

3. Gramsci proposed a strategy for the emancipation of subordinate classes that contemplated a prolonged participation in the bourgeois political system (as opposed to overturning it through an overt revolution) and intervention in the cultural sphere.

4. Gramsci used the terms Fordism and Americanism as alternatives for capitalism, a word that the Italy's Fascist censorship would have not allowed. Indeed, Gramsci wrote his analysis of Fordism while jailed for his opposition to Mussolini's totalitarian regime.

5. Gramsci held that the Fordist labor process relied centrally on Taylorist rationalization, which simplified necessary operations, eliminated others, and radically routinized, deskilled, and intensified labor. For Gramsci, Fordist elites were aware of the physically and psychologically demanding nature of the new labor process that conventional methods of labor regulation – which relied on simple force – could not control. Contending that the emergent strategy was to regulate workers also by consent, Gramsci held that Fordist's improved wages and fringe benefits provided more stable employment and expanded the state's role in protecting workers' well-being, while augmenting a culturally based and much more sophisticated form of subordination of the working masses (Gramsci, 1971, pp. 310–313). This subordination entailed the expansion of consumption and the mobilization of the seductive power that the satisfaction of material needs entails. Consumerism – as this process was later named (Marcuse, 1964) – distracted the masses away from critiques of the dominant regime and provided the conditions for its legitimation. For Gramsci, the contradictory nature of Fordism was represented by this more insidious and repressive form of exploitation accompanied by the creation of a social state that actually enhanced the living conditions of the subordinated masses.

6. Keynes' theory was opposed by Friedrich von Hayek (1960, 1972) whose defense of the "spontaneous order" constitutes the theoretical grounds upon which neoliberal anti-Fordist positions developed in second part of the twentieth century. Hayek argues that a harmonious, evolving order arises from the interaction of a heterogeneous group of self-seeking agents with a limited knowledge of market information. Their knowledge of the market is limited because they may be very well informed about some segments of the market, but they have an approximate knowledge of the many other aspects of the market itself. Because of this situation, this order could not be designed by state intervention but spontaneously evolved from the complex network of interactions among these agents. State planning, therefore, is a source of economic and social instability.

7. To be sure, these changes should not be interpreted as the results of the emergence of a fully globalized system where the local territorial dimension is irrelevant (Hirst & Thompson, 1996). On the contrary, globalization is a system which allows transnational capital to be mobile, relatively free of state control and regulations, and to take advantage of qualitatively new instruments which are employed to avoid perceived rigidities in the economy and society. Indeed, local consumption and labor markets are viewed as resources that can be included in or excluded from global circuits in accordance with corporations' needs. Simultaneously, localities are viewed

as social relations that are capable of opposing as well as favoring corporate strategies. Globalization is not a globalized system; it is a system of global mobility and global actions, which operates in reaction to conditions which manifest themselves in local and regional enclaves. More specifically, globalization is a project to revive capital accumulation and thereby counter many of the successes of democratic social movements that limited the ability of corporations to maintain profitable business operations.

   8. As indicated at the outset of this essay, Marx recognized the existence of factors which delay the realization crisis. One of these factors is the expansion of consumption fueled by financial strategies (credit) and cultural models (today's consumerism) (see also, Marcuse, 1964; O'Connor, 1988; Sweezy, 1942). Yet, Marx strongly emphasized that, ultimately, capitalism cannot solve the problem of realization due to its exploitative nature.

   9. Marx describes this condition in these terms: "The division of labor converts the product of labor into a commodity, and thereby makes necessary its conversion into money. At the same time, it makes it a matter of chance whether this transubstantiation succeeds or not" (Marx, 1977, p. 203). Keynes speaks of the inadequacy of models, which contemplate the automatic translation of the production of commodities into money. He, therefore, highlights the danger of underconsumption as the socially grounded phenomenon in which production cannot be sold, i.e. transformed into money.

# REFERENCES

Aglietta, M. (1979). *A theory of capitalist regulation: The U.S. experience*. London: New Left Books.

Akard, P. J. (1992). Corporate mobilization and political power: The transformation of US economic policy in the 1970s. *American Sociological Review, 57*, 597–615.

Antonio, R. J. (2002). *Marx and modernity*. Malden, MA: Blackwell.

Antonio, R. J., & Bonanno, A. (1996). Post-Fordism in the United States: The poverty of market-centered democracy. *Current Perspectives in Social Theory, 16*, 3–32.

Arrighi, G. (1998). Globalization and the rise of East Asia: Lessons from the past, prospects for the future. *International Sociology, 13*(1), 59–77.

Bauman, Z. (1992). *Intimations of postmodernity*. London: Routledge.

Bauman, Z. (1998). *Globalization: The human consequences*. New York: Columbia University Press.

Bauman, Z. (2002). *Society under siege*. Malden, MA: Polity Press.

Beck, U. (1992). *Risk society: Towards a new modernity*. London: Sage.

Beck, U. (1995). *Ecological enlightenment*. Atlantic Highlands, NJ: Humanities Press.

Beck, U. (1997). In: Mark Ritter (Trans.), *The reinvention of politics: Rethinking modernity in the global social order*. Cambridge, UK: Polity Press.

Beck, U., Giddens, A., & Lash, S. (1994). *Reflexive modernization: Politics, tradition and aesthetics in the modern social order*. Stanford, CA: Stanford University Press.

Bell, D. ([1976]1996). *The cultural contradictions of capitalism*. New York: Basic Books. Twentieth anniversary edition.

Benton, T. (1996). *The greening of Marxism*. New York: The Guilford Press.

Brohman, J. (1996). *Popular development: Rethinking the theory and practice of development.* Oxford, UK: Blackwell.

Buttel, F. H. (1994). Agricultural change, rural society, and the state in late twenty century: Some theoretical observations. In: D. Symes & A. J. Jansen (Eds), *Agricultural restructuring and rural change in Europe* (pp. 13–31). Wageningen: The WAU Press.

Dreiling, M. (1997). Remapping North America environmentalism: Contending visions and divergent practices in the fight over NAFTA. *Capitalism, Nature, Socialism, 8*(4), 65–98.

Economic Policy Institute. (2006). *Income trends in The United States.* Washington, DC: Economic Policy Institute.

Ford, H. ([1926]2004). *Today and tomorrow, corporate leadership.* Dearborn, MI: Production Press.

Friedman, M. (1982). *Capitalism and freedom.* Chicago: The University of Chicago Press.

Friedman, T. L. (2000). *The lexus and the olive tree.* New York: Anchor Books. Revised edition.

Gabriel, Y., & Lang, T. (1995). *The unmanageable consumer.* London: Sage.

Giddens, A. (1994). *Beyond left and right.* Stanford: Stanford University Press.

Giddens, A. (2000). *Runaway world: How globalization is reshaping our lives.* New York: Routledge.

Gramsci, A. (1971). In: Quintin Hoare and Geoffrey Nowell Smith (Eds and Trans.), *Selections from the prison notebooks.* New York: International Publishers.

Gray, J. (1998). *False dawn: The delusions of global capitalism.* New York: The New Press.

Habermas, J. (1975). In: Thomas McCarthy (Trans.), *Legitimation crisis.* Beacon Press: Boston.

Habermas, J. (2002). The European nation-state and the pressures of globalization. In: P. Greiff & C. Cronin (Eds), *Global justice and trasnational politics* (pp. 217–234). Cambridge, MA: MIT Press.

Hammond, A. (1998). *Which world? Scenarios for the 21st century: Global destinies, regional choices.* Washington, DC: Island Press.

Harvey, D. (1989). *The condition of postmodernity: An enquiry into the origins of cultural change.* Oxford, UK: Blackwell.

Harvey, D. (2000). *Spaces of hope.* Berkeley: University of California Press.

Hayek, F. (1960). *The constitution of liberty.* Chicago: Henry Regnery and Company.

Hayek, F. (1972). *A tiger by the tail. Compiled by Sudha Shenoy.* London: Institute for Economic Affairs.

Heffernan, W. D. (2000). Concentration of ownership and control in agriculture. In: F. Magdoff, J. B. Foster & F. H. Buttel (Eds), *Hungry for profit: The agribusiness threat to farmers, food and the environment* (pp. 61–75). New York: Monthly Review Press.

Hirst, P., & Thompson, G. (1996). *Globalization in question.* Cambridge: Polity Press.

Hodgson, G. (1978). *America in our time.* New York: Vintage Books.

Howard, M. C., & King, J. E. (1989). *A history of Marxian economics.* Princeton, NJ: Princeton University Press.

Humphery, K. (1998). *Shelf life. Supermarket and the changing cultures of consumption.* Cambridge: Cambridge University Press.

Iacocca, L. (1988). *Talking straight.* New York: Bantam.

Jameson, F. (1994). *Postmodernism or the cultural logic of late capitalism.* Durham: Duke University Press.

Keller, E. (1993). *Mr. Ford – What have you done? Henry Ford's views on economics.* Quibin, MO: Keaton Keller.

Keynes, J. M. (1936). *The general theory of employment interest and money.* New York: Prometheus Books.

Lang, T. (1999). The complexity of globalization: The UK as a case study of tensions within the food system and the challenge to food policy. *Agriculture and Human Values, 16*(2), 169–185.

Lash, S., & Urry, J. (1987). *The end of organized capitalism.* Cambridge, UK: Polity Press.

Lash, S., & Urry, J. (1994). *Economies of signs & space.* London: Sage.

Marcuse, H. (1964). *One dimensional man: Studies in the ideology of advanced industrial society.* Boston: Beacon Press.

Marx, K. (1977). *Capital volume I.* New York: Vintage Books.

Marx, K. (1978). *Capital volume II.* London: Penguin Books.

Marx, K. (1981). *Capital volume III.* New York: Vintage Books.

Marx, K. (2000[1910]). *Theories of surplus value.* New York: Prometheus Books.

McMichael, P. (2002). *Development and social change* (3rd ed.). Thousand Oaks, CA: Pine Forge Press.

Merchant, C. (1997). *Ecology.* Atlantic Highlands, NJ: Humanities Press.

Miller, D. (Ed.) (1995). *Acknowledging consumption.* London: Routledge.

Mills, C. W. (1961). *The sociological imagination.* New York: Grove Press.

Mingione, E. (1993). Marxism, ecology, and political movements. *Capitalism, Nature, Socialism, 4*(2), 85–92.

Mishel, L., Bernstein, J., & Schmitt, J. (2004). *The state of working America: 2003–04.* Ithaca, NY: ILR Press.

O'Connor, J. (1973). *The fiscal crisis of the state.* New York: St. Martins Press.

O'Connor, J. (1988). Capitalism, nature, socialism: A theoretical introduction. *Capital, Nature Socialism, 1*(1), 11–38.

Offe, C. (1985). *Disorganized capitalism.* Cambridge, MA: MIT Press.

Offe, C. (1996). *Modernity and the state: East, west.* Cambridge, MA: MIT Press.

Parsons, T. (1971). *The system of modern societies.* Englewood Cliffs, NJ: Prentice-Hall.

Piccone, P. (1995). Postmodern populism. *Telos, 103,* 45–86.

Prechel, H. (1990). Steel and the state: Industry politics and business policy formation, 1940–1989. *American Sociological Review, 55,* 648–668.

Prechel, H. (1994). Economic crisis and the centralization of control over the managerial process: Corporate restructuring and neo-Fordist decision-making. *American Sociological Review, 59,* 723–745.

Robinson, W. (2004). *A theory of global capitalism: Production, class, and state in a transnational world.* Baltimore: John Hopkins University Press.

Sassen, S. (1998). *Globalization and its discontents.* New York: The New Press.

Sassen, S. (2000). Regulating immigration in a global age: A new policy landscape. *The Annals of the American Academy of Political and Social Science, 570,* 65–77.

Schwartz, P., Leyden, P., & Hyatt, J. (1999). *The long boom: A vision for the coming age of prosperity.* Reading, MA: Perseus Books.

Shabecoff, P. (1993). *A fierce green fire. The American environmental movement.* New York: Hill and Wang.

Sklair, L. (2001). *The transnational capitalist class.* Oxford, UK: Blackwell.

Stiglitz, J. E. (2003). *The roaring nineties: A new history of the world's most prosperous decade.* London, NY: W. W. Norton & Company.

Sweezy, P. (1942). *The theory of capitalist development.* New York: Oxford University Press.

Sweezy, P. (Ed.) (1966). *Karl Marx and the close of his system.* New York: Kelley.

United Nations. (2002). *Annual human development report.* New York: The United Nations.

# ABOUT THE AUTHORS

**Paul D. Almeida** is assistant professor of sociology at Texas A&M University. His research focuses on the dynamics of social movement mobilization in lesser-developed countries. His articles on social movements have appeared in the *American Journal of Sociology*, *Latin American Perspectives*, *Mobilization*, *Realidad* (El Salvador), *Research in Social Movements, Conflicts and Change, and Social Problems*. He is currently completing a book manuscript on waves of popular unrest in El Salvador between 1925 and 2005 and an edited collection (with Hank Johnston) entitled, *Latin American Social Movements: Globalization, Democratization, and Transnational Networks* (Rowman and Littlefield 2006).

**Robert J. Antonio** is a professor of sociology at the University of Kansas. He offers courses and writes on social theory, globalization/economic sociology, and American culture, institutions, and politics. He has edited *Marx & Modernity* (Blackwell 2003), and has collaborated with Professor Bonanno on the topic of globalization for more than a decade. Their "Periodizing Globalization: From Cold War Modernization to the Bush Doctrine" recently appeared in *Current Perspectives in Social Theory* (2006).

**Alessandro Bonanno** is a professor and chair of the sociology Department at Sam Houston State University. In recent years, Dr. Bonanno has researched the implications that globalization has for social relations and institutions. In particular and employing the agro-food sector as an empirical area of concentration, he investigated the impact that globalization has on the state, democracy and the emancipatory options of subordinate groups. Dr. Bonanno has written 11 books and more than 90 referred publications which appeared in English and other major languages. His upcoming book, *Stories of Globalization*, will appear in 2006. Dr. Bonanno is the current President (2004–2208) of the International Rural Sociological Association.

**Derek Darves** recently completed his PhD at the University of Oregon. His doctoral research examined corporate involvement in U.S. trade policy formation through Congressional testimony and advisory committee participation. Together with Michael Dreiling, he has, for the last five years, been engaged in a larger project on U.S. trade policy formation and corporate political activism. One of his previous publication in the journal *Humanity and Society* explores the role of corporate policy networks, PAC contributions and levels of participation in trade policy groups.

**Diane E. Davis** is professor of political sociology in the Department of Urban Studies and Planning at MIT, as well as associate dean of the School of Architecture and Planning. She is the author of *Urban Leviathan: Mexico City in the Twentieth Century* (Temple University Press, 1994; Spanish translation 1999) and *Discipline and Development: Middle Classes and Prosperity in East Asia and Latin America* (Cambridge University Press, 2004), and co-editor of *Violence, Coercion, and Rights in the Americas* (Sage Publications, 2004) and *Irregular Armed Forces and Their Role in Politics and State Formation* (Cambridge University Press, 2003). In addition to her writings on the history and politics of urbanization, Davis has published articles on local governance, leftist mayors, urban social movements, development, and democratic transition in Latin America. Her current research, supported by the Carnegie Corporation of New York and the John D. and Catherine T. MacArthur Foundation, examines the evolution of policing in twentieth century Mexico, and the rise of private security and rule of law in Mexico City.

**Michael Dreiling** is an associate professor of sociology at the University of Oregon. In 2001, his research on the political conflicts over the NAFTA was published as a book titled *Solidarity and Contention: The Politics of Class and Sustainability in the NAFTA Conflict*. Since 1997, he has published eight research articles on political conflicts over trade policy and globalization. He is currently engaged in a collaborative project with Derek Darves examining "corporations and the making of U.S. trade policy." At the University of Oregon, he teaches courses on nonviolence, work and labor, social movements and revolutions, and American society.

**Dana R. Fisher** is an assistant professor in the Department of sociology at Columbia University. Her research interests focus on the role of non-state actors in decision-making processes at multiple scales. Current projects include the study of large-scale protest events, local civic networks engaging in urban stewardship, and the formation of international scientific communities. Her new book, *Activism, Inc.*, is being published by Stanford University Press in September 2006.

**Leslie C. Gates** is an assistant professor of sociology at State University of New York, Binghamton. As a Fulbright scholar in Venezuela, Gates is currently examining the diverging politics of market-oriented reforms in Mexico and Venezuela. Her prior research on the gendered social effects of market-oriented reforms in Mexico and the historical role of labor movements in gendering social policy in El Salvador has been published in *Social Politics* and the *Bulletin of Latin American Research*.

**Theresa Morris** is associate professor of sociology at Trinity College in Hartford, Connecticut. Her research focuses broadly on the dialectic relationship between the political economy and organizations. She has published articles in *Sociological Forum, Sociological Inquiry,* and *The Sociological Quarterly.*

**David A. Smith** is a professor of sociology and a faculty member of Center for the Study of Democracy at the University of California, Irvine. His research interests include globalization and inequality, world city networks and global commodity chains and development. He has published many articles in these areas; his recent co-edited books include *Labor Versus Empire: Race, Gender and Migration and Nature, Raw Materials and Political Economy.* He is the former editor of *Social Problems* and current co-editor of *Contemporary Sociology.*

**Tim Woods** is assistant professor of sociology and psychology at Manchester Community College in Manchester, Connecticut. His research focuses on the development of U.S. trade policy from the New Deal through the present. He has published articles in *Critical Sociology* and *Social Science Quarterly.*

# SET UP A CONTINUATION ORDER TODAY!

Did you know that you can set up a continuation order on all Elsevier-JAI series and have each new volume sent directly to you upon publication? For details on how to set up a **continuation order**, contact your nearest regional sales office listed below.

To view related series in Sociology, please visit:

## www.elsevier.com/sociology

## 30% Discount for Authors on All Books!

A 30% discount is available to Elsevier book and journal contributors on all books *(except multi-volume reference works)*.

To claim your discount, full payment is required with your order, which must be sent directly to the publisher at the nearest regional sales office above.